CIVIL RIGHTS IN NEW YORK CITY

CIVIL RIGHTS IN NEW YORK CITY
FROM WORLD WAR II TO THE GIULIANI ERA

Edited by
CLARENCE TAYLOR

FORDHAM UNIVERSITY PRESS ■ *New York 2011*

Chapter 2 is from *Ella Baker and the Black Freedom Movement: A Radical Democratic Vision* by Barbara Ransby. Copyright © 2003 by the University of North Carolina Press. Used by permission of the publisher.

Chapter 9 is reprinted by permission from *David Dinkins and New York City Politics: Race, Images, and the Media* by Wilbur C. Rich, the State University of New York Press © 2007, State University of New York. All rights reserved.

Fordham University Press has no responsibility for the persistence or accuracy of URLs for external or third-party Internet websites referred to in this publication and does not guarantee that any content on such websites is, or will remain, accurate or appropriate.

Fordham University Press also publishes its books in a variety of electronic formats. Some content that appears in print may not be available in electronic books.

Library of Congress Cataloging-in-Publication Data

Civil rights in New York City : from World War II to the Giuliani era / edited by Clarence
    Taylor.—1st ed.
       p.   cm.
    Includes bibliographical references and index.
    ISBN 978-0-8232-3289-5 (cloth : alk. paper)
    ISBN 978-0-8232-3291-8 (ebook : alk. paper)
    1. Civil rights—New York (State)—New York.   2. New York (N.Y.)—Race
relations.
    I. Taylor, Clarence.
    JC599.U52C35   2010
    323.09747′109045—dc22

                                                                            2009054039

Printed in the United States of America
First paperback printing 2013
ISBN 978-0-8232-5554-2 (pbk. : alk. paper)

For my son, Jason;
my daughter-in-law, Tara;
and my grandchildren,
Amanda, Nevaeh, Jayden,
and Alana

Contents

Acknowledgments

I wish to thank Martha Biondi, Jerald Podair, Daniel Perstein, Brian Purnell, Peter Eisenstadt, Wilbur Rich, Johanna Fernandez, and Barbara Ransby for their contributions to this volume. Their generosity made this book possible. But more important than helping to produce a book, their scholarship is helping to rewrite the history of civil rights and urban history. I owe a special thanks to Jeanne Theoharis and Peter Levy, two leading scholars in the field of Northern civil rights, who were kind enough to read the manuscript and provide extremely valuable suggestions.

I am very grateful to Myra Chase for her careful reading of the entire manuscript and for providing very helpful recommendations. I am indebted to Jonathan Birnbaum for his thorough reading and helpful suggestions on several chapters. I am also indebted to Johanna Fernandez for her help with Chapter 4 and the photographs for this work. My colleague and friend Arthur Lewin was kind enough to read chapters and make useful recommendations.

I wish to thank Fredric Nachbaur, Helen Tartar, and Eric Newman of Fordham University Press for their support and helping to shape the manuscript into a book.

I appreciate the support I have received from my good friends Douglas Egerton, Bob Kelly, Sarah Ramsey, and Carol Berkin.

Last, but not least, I wish to thank my wife, Marsha, for her support, patience, and love.

CIVIL RIGHTS IN NEW YORK CITY

Introduction: Civil Rights in New York City

CLARENCE TAYLOR

Since the 1960s, most U.S. history has been written as if the civil rights movement were primarily or entirely a southern history. Of course, this is incorrect. The fight for civil rights has always been a national struggle, although the historian Thomas Sugrue writes: "Most northern communities did not erect signs to mark separate black and white facilities. . . . Northern blacks lived as second-class citizens, unencumbered by the most blatant of southern-style Jim Crow laws but still trapped in an economic, political, and legal regime that seldom recognized them as equals." Northern activists mounted campaigns to confront racial discrimination. "Throughout the twentieth century, black and white activists (and occasionally Latino and Asian allies, who were a minuscule segment of the region's population until recently) rose to challenge racial inequality in the North."[1] For many years now historians have been attempting to correct this view. My own contribution to this effort has focused on the struggle in New York City, through a history of the black churches in Brooklyn, a biography of one of the most prominent religious leaders in New York City, and a forthcoming history of the teachers' union. I also coedited a survey history of the civil rights movement that emphasizes the national—both northern and southern—character of this ongoing struggle. One of the first chapters in that book discusses the fight for school integration in Boston in 1787.[2]

Of course, no one has been alone in this work. There is a new generation of scholarship rewriting our understanding of this history.[3] *Civil*

1

Rights in New York City represents one of the first compilations surveying this effort. The chapters in this volume focus on this northern history from a New York perspective.

Brian Purnell points out that the focus on the South in civil rights scholarship prevents us from grasping the significant role that the civil rights movement in Brooklyn as well as other places in New York City played in persuading the political elites and even ordinary New Yorkers that racial discrimination was a reality in the Big Apple. In their challenge to the southern paradigm, scholars not only have questioned the 1954 starting date of the civil rights movement but have argued that voting rights, public accommodation, and integration were not the only goals of civil rights campaigns. Jeanne F. Theoharis, for instance, has argued that the northern wing of the movement embraced black economic empowerment and a fairer distribution of governmental services and resources. Campaigns outside the South, she argues, did not limit their approach to nonviolent protest but adopted self-defense, and some campaigns were influenced by Black Nationalism. Theoharis and other scholars of northern civil rights struggles also challenge the portrayal of the Black Power movement in the late 1960s as a force that derailed the "triumphant" struggle for civil rights. Periodization is also an important question in this literature. Some contend that the objective that would later be identified with the black freedom struggle of the late 1960s was evident in the late 1940s and 1950s. Not only have northern civil right studies been more geographically inclusive; they have also moved beyond the white-black dichotomy so pervasive in studies on the South and have turned to the plight and agency of other people of color, especially Latinos and Asians.

There are at least four important components noted by scholars studying northern civil rights. The first component was a secular left that included members of the American Communist Party. Communists, especially during the Popular Front years, pushed a far-reaching civil rights agenda. However, Communists were not the only leftists fighting for racial justice. Other members of the secular left included anti-Communist democratic socialists and social democrats. A good example is Bayard Rustin, who was the main organizer of the February 3, 1964, New York City School Boycott and who would later support the United Federation of Teachers in its battle against a black and Latino school board in Ocean Hill–Brownsville in 1968. Some historians have also noted the pivotal role of labor in civil rights campaigns outside the South.

A second component was liberalism. The Cold War was, in part, a war of propaganda between the capitalist and Communist nations. One of the strongest weapons in the propaganda war was the Soviet Union's charge that the United States violated the rights of millions of African Americans. This accusation challenged the United States' claim that it was the paragon of democracy. Concerned that the Soviet Union's accusation might have hurt its chances of winning the hearts and minds of nations in Asia, Africa, and Latin America, U.S. liberals embraced a civil rights agenda. President Harry Truman created a Committee on Civil Rights in December 1946. The purpose of the committee was to investigate the condition of civil rights in the United States and to make recommendations to protect those whose civil rights were being violated. The committee's report was titled "To Secure These Rights: The Report of the President's Committee on Civil Rights." Its recommendations included the creation of a permanent commission on civil rights, equal opportunity in education, and a civil rights division of the Justice Department; protection against lynching; and the creation of a federal fair employment practices commission. By the early 1960s American liberalism had become the dominant political ideology in the United States. The administration of President Lyndon B. Johnson was responsible for the passage of two of the most important pieces of civil rights legislation of the twentieth century: the 1964 Civil Rights Act and the 1965 Voting Rights Act.[4] New York City's liberal government outlawed discrimination in housing and employment. It also provided public housing to the working class and poor.

Another important component of the northern civil rights movement was the religious community. Various religious communities, including ministers of different denominations and non-ministerial lay people, were at the fore, organizing and carrying out demonstrations. It was not just in the South but in many places outside that region that black churches became the center force of civil rights campaigns. Nightly meetings in churches became revivals where people heard eloquent speeches and sermons, sang freedom songs, gave testimony, and helped finance the movements. Moreover, many from the black religious communities joined and rose to leadership in the local chapters of civil rights and grassroots organizations. Two examples are Ella Baker and Milton Galamison.

A fourth component of northern civil rights campaigns was those who advocated Black Nationalism. Those goals attributed to Black Nationalists did not first appear in the late 1960s but were evident in earlier civil rights campaigns such as the "Don't Buy Where You Can't Work" crusades in Chicago, Washington, D.C., and New York during the Depression years. Historian Peter Levy notes that black activists involved in a civil rights struggle led by Gloria Richardson in the early 1960s in Cambridge, Maryland, were willing—as Black Nationalists often advocated—to defend themselves and not turn the other cheek. Those activists had ties with Black Nationalists, including Malcolm X, and even decided not to integrate lunch counters in the city. In some cases the line dividing those advocating civil rights and those in favor of Black Nationalist objectives was blurred. A good example is Malcolm X's decision to publicly support the second citywide boycott of New York public schools in March 1964. Although he never moved away from Black Nationalism, he opposed school segregation and said he considered himself "aligned with everyone who will take some action to end this criminal situation in the schools."[5] Undeniably, New York City was one of the most important centers of civil rights activities. Long before the Montgomery Bus Boycott, the Reverend Adam Clayton Powell Jr. helped launch the Harlem Bus Boycott of 1941.

Civil Rights in New York City is unique because it is the only anthology that focuses on the civil rights movement in New York City from such a variety of perspectives. The highly acclaimed *Freedom North*, edited by Jeanne F. Theoharis and Komozi Woodard, examines a number of northern black freedom campaigns. The book has received a number of glowing reviews and has been cited by numerous scholars, indicating the interest in northern civil rights. However, there is little attention paid to New York in the work, and only one chapter on New York City, home to the largest black population in the United States. Moreover, no other northern city had the number of civil rights campaigns that New York did. In fact, some of the largest civil rights demonstrations took place in New York City, and these campaigns had a direct impact on national politics.

Civil Rights in New York City consists of ten chapters covering various aspects of the struggle in New York, from the role of labor to the struggle at the City University of New York. The first chapter takes a look at the New York City Teachers Union from 1942 to 1945, and how it connected civil rights to the war effort. The union had been fighting for racial equality since 1935, when the Communist Rank and File Caucus gained control of it. The union fought to eliminate racist textbooks from the public schools, promoted "Negro History Week," and put pressure on the Board of Education to hire black and Latino teachers. Some scholars have argued that the TU was nothing more than a Communist Party front following the dictates of Moscow. As proof, they point to the World War II period, when, they allege, the union abandoned its struggle for civil rights in favor of Moscow's push for collective security. However, I argue that instead of moving away from the fight for racial equality, the union placed that struggle in the context of World War II, arguing that racism and racist attacks were undermining America's capability to defeat the Axis powers.[6] According to the TU, fighting racism was every American's patriotic duty, and a necessity in the war effort.

Chapter 2 turns the reader's attention to Ella Baker's years in New York City working with the NAACP and the city's grassroots movement to force the city to integrate its public school system. Many scholars note Baker's efforts with the Southern Christian Leadership Conference and her pivotal role in the formation of the Student Nonviolent Coordinating Committee. However, few have examined her role in the freedom campaign in New York. Barbara Ransby points out that Baker was one of the most vocal grassroots leaders in the city, attempting to help develop leadership skills in ordinary men and women. This chapter explores Baker's involvement in the New York City branch of the NAACP and in the grassroots organization Parents in Action, challenging school segregation and police brutality. Ransby contends that Baker's involvement with grassroots movements and leaders at times challenged the cautious "go slow" politics of the national leaders of the NAACP. Her objective in New York, as it would later be in the southern civil rights struggle, was to increase the involvement of people on the ground level.

Many national civil rights organizations and their local chapters were active in New York City. Brian Purnell highlights one of the most active chapters, the Brooklyn branch of the Congress of Racial Equality, and its effort to address racial disparities in city services. A strong social contract provided city workers with high wages, benefits, and the right to collectively bargain as well as provided affordable housing and health care services for the working class and poor. New York developed a reputation as a bastion of liberalism. Its antidiscriminatory policies, however limited, helped the city acquire a similar reputation for racial liberalism. However, the Brooklyn chapter of the Congress of Racial Equality (CORE) questioned the reality of that reputation. Purnell examines the 1962 direct action campaign by Brooklyn CORE, a racially integrated membership organization, to force the city to provide better sanitation services to Bedford-Stuyvesant, Brooklyn's largest black community. It was Brooklyn CORE that exposed the city's racially discriminatory policy on garbage removal and the intransigence of city officials to seriously address those discriminatory practices and policies. Purnell details this community-wide campaign involving Brooklyn CORE activists and residents of Bedford-Stuyvesant and examines the campaign's larger impact on structural inequality in New York City.

Although scholars now argue that integration was not the major objective of northern civil rights campaigns and prefer to describe the struggle as a fight for "desegregation," Peter Eisenstadt maintains that integration was a pivotal objective of battles in New York City. In the fourth chapter, he examines the fight for racial equality in housing, investigating the attempt in the 1960s to integrate the largest middle-class housing cooperative in New York, Rochdale Village in South Jamaica. Eisenstadt notes that the housing integration effort in the city's third-largest black community brought together a coalition of leftists, liberal Democrats, moderate Republicans, pragmatic government officials, and business executives. He details how powerful city figures such as Robert Moses, New York City's commissioner of parks, and Abraham Kazan, president of the United Housing Foundation, helped create Rochdale, and he points out the crucial role played by residents of the housing cooperative in maintaining a racially harmonious community. Unlike some recent scholars of northern civil rights who questioned the view that Black Power derailed the civil rights movement, Eisenstadt distinguishes these two social protest movements by contending that the rise of Black Power sentiment in the late 1960s and 1970s undermined the experiment at Rochdale.

One of the most explosive civil rights issues in New York in the 1950s and early 1960s was school integration. A number of scholars have blamed militant civil rights activists for the failure of school integration. However, these scholars ignore the fact that white parents organized a grassroots campaign opposing any effort to integrate schools. Moreover, important segments of the liberal community of New York also publicly opposed school integration. While a great deal of attention has been paid to southern white resistance to school integration in the 1950s and 1960s, little has been said of the fierce campaign in New York City. Chapter 5 explores New York City's school integration battle of the 1950s and 1960s and the well-organized campaign to defeat a small effort at integration by the Board of Education.

The sixth chapter, "The Dead End of Despair: Bayard Rustin, the 1968 New York School Crisis, and the Struggle for Racial Justice" by Dan Perlstein, turns our attention to the labor movement in New York City in the late 1960s by exploring one of the leading figures of the civil rights movement, Bayard Rustin, and his alliance with the moderately liberal United Federation of Teachers against black activists in the late 1960s. Perlstein takes on recent scholarship that contends that Rustin was consistent throughout his years as a leading civil rights strategist and theoretician. Perlstein depicts a Rustin who became quite pessimistic about the American people's willingness to accept racial equality and increasingly felt that they were willing to accommodate the system. By the late 1960s, the once left-wing organizer of the 1963 March on Washington was siding with the United Federation of Teachers against more militant community activists and black trade unionists, who insisted that community control of schools was a necessary goal for gaining racial equality. Unfortunately, the strike led to tragic results, dashing all hopes of an alliance between labor and New York's black and Latino communities, and helping shift city politics to the right.

Johanna Fernandez's "The Young Lords and the Social and Structural Roots of Late Sixties Urban Radicalism" looks at the post-migration experience of Puerto Ricans, African Americans, Chicanos, and Mexicans in New York, and the impact of deindustrialization on these new arrivals. At the same time that these new groups were arriving in New York, Chicago, and other northern cities, there was a rapid shift in these cities from highly industrial-based economies that provided workers with living wages to service-oriented economies that offered newcomers mostly low-paying jobs or permanent unemployment. The Young Lords Party, which originated as a Chicago youth gang, was formed in response to the changing economic landscape, police brutality, and racism faced by young Puerto Ricans, African Americans, and others. Fernandez contends that the YLP was also shaped by the social protest movements of the 1960s, in particular, the Black Panther Party. Contrary to social science literature that blamed the conditions of people of color on cultural deficits, the YLP placed the blame on structural inequalities caused by exploitative capitalism and a racist system that targeted people of color. Members of YLP were not reformists but revolutionary nationalists who recognized their African roots and called for Puerto Rican Independence from United States imperialist rule. They identified with the national liberation movements in Africa, Latin America, and Asia and concluded that revolutionary, not reformist, methods were needed to address the plight of the urban poor.

While a great deal attention has been paid to the struggle to end racial disparities in elementary and secondary education, little has been written on the fight for racial equality in public higher education during the

1960s. In Chapter 8, Martha Biondi examines how black students at Brooklyn College and other branches of the City University of New York in 1969 led civil rights campaigns that helped redefine CUNY's mission and relationship with black and Latino communities in the city. The students fought to end the attempt by colleges to marginalize them and insisted that these institutions help remedy the impact of segregation and unequal education. The students' civil rights protest helped usher in open admissions, which resulted in larger numbers of blacks and Latinos gaining seats in the public colleges of New York, and eventually the expansion of the black middle class.

David Dinkins, the first black mayor of New York City, took office in 1990 when New York was undergoing a dramatic demographic shift. Between 1980 and 1989, 854,000 immigrants made New York City their home, spreading out to the five boroughs. The black population had the largest increase with 381,175, many of whom came from the Caribbean and almost half of whom moved to Brooklyn. This 17 percent increase brought the black population to 2,102,512. The number of Hispanics in the city grew by 281,797 to 1,783,511. The Asian population more than doubled, growing from 281,218 to over 500,000 and making up 7 percent of the city's population. More than half of the Asians lived in Queens and Brooklyn. One of the fastest-growing Asian groups in the city was Korean Americans. Throughout the 1990s, Koreans flocked to New York and became the third-largest Asian group in the city. By 2000 close to 91,000 Koreans resided in New York, over 63,000 of them living in Queens, 12,459 in Manhattan, and 7,392 in Brooklyn. This large influx of immigrants ensured that race could not be seen simply as black and white.[7]

After a series of racial incidents in the 1980s, David Dinkins came to office declaring that his administration would heal the racial divide in New York. However, two major incidents undermine Dinkins's image as a racial healer. The first involved the boycott of the Red Apple, a Korean business, by residents of a predominantly black neighborhood in Brooklyn after a young Haitian woman alleged that the owner of the store assaulted her. The second occurred in the predominantly black and Jewish neighborhood of Crown Heights when a Hassidic driver accidentally hit two black children, killing one of them. In response, a crowd of black youths killed a rabbinic scholar, leading to several days of racial unrest. Political scientist Wilbur C. Rich contends that Dinkins failed to communicate to the public the actions he took to settle the disputes. The media framed Dinkins as weak and incompetent. More importantly, the

Red Apple and Crown Heights affairs demonstrate the complexities of race in New York and the limits of electoral politics. The coalition that brought Dinkins to office overestimated his reach in white ethic communities. Moreover, before these incidents there was little outreach to the new immigrant communities.

The media portrayal of Dinkins as a weak mayor who allowed black militants to run rampant throughout the city helped deny him a second term and led to the election of Rudolph Giuliani in 1993. In the last chapter, Jerald Podair focuses on the impact that Giuliani's policies had on New York's black residents. In particular, Podair looks at the "Broken Window" policies, workfare, and privatization of public services—all reflecting the mayor's vision of creating "one standard" for all New Yorkers. Podair argues that Giuliani programs reflected the vision of white ethnic groups who saw spending on social services to assist African Americans as anathema to equality. They argued that government should adopt "race-neutral" polices only, extending the same legal protections to all. But Giuliani's goal of establishing one standard for all New Yorkers conflicted with the goals of civil rights forces and others who had a more substantive definition of equality. They argued that equality of outcome, including access to employment, fair housing, an end to racial discrimination, and the "reallocation and equalization of resources in the City," was the true meaning of equality. According to Podair, Giuliani's one-standard policy, his inflammatory racial rhetoric, and his public backing of the police in high-profile killings of blacks failed to provide a definition of equality that could unite New Yorkers, leaving the city racially divided.

This book demonstrates that the struggle for civil rights in New York City has a long history and has been fought in a number of venues by numerous groups and individuals with a variety of political perspectives. Those political perspectives helped individuals and groups shape their approaches and objectives, from collaborating with elites to adopting revolutionary tactics. Several campaigns for racial justice covered in this work had an impact on both the city and the nation. *Civil Rights in New York City* provides a sample of the rich historical record of the fight for racial justice in the city, making it essential that scholars of civil rights pay greater attention to New York.

1

To Be a Good American: The New York City Teachers Union and Race during the Second World War

CLARENCE TAYLOR

In 1942, May Quinn, a civics teacher at Public School 227 in Brooklyn, read an anti-Semitic leaflet titled "The First Americans" in her class. The publication listed the names of "brave Americans" during wartime. Absent from the list of those who served honorably during wartime were Jewish Americans, which was particularly unusual in a city with a notable Jewish population. The leaflet also contained the names of Americans who performed dishonorable acts, and all the names that Quinn read to her class from the leaflet that day were Jewish. Quinn also praised Hitler and Mussolini. She called Jews a "dull race," and Italians "greasy," and she praised the cause of racial segregation.[1]

The New York City Teachers Union (TU) highlighted the Quinn affair in its weekly publication, *New York Teacher News*, by placing the episode into a wartime context. In one issue of the paper it was reported that Quinn's fourteen accusers blamed her for inciting racial tension, creating disunity, and undermining the war effort. The fourteen teachers also charged their colleague with spreading "defeatist propaganda and anti-Semitic slanders in the classroom." *New York Teacher News* pointed to the fact that she was defended by the *Educational Signpost*, the organ of the profascist American Education Association. Milo McDonald, the principal of Bushwick High School, who was associated with the rabid

10

anti-Semitic priest Father John Coughlin, headed this group. *New York Teacher News* also pointed out that McDonald even wrote for the *National Republic*, a publication edited by Walter S. Steele, a man who, the United States secretary of the Interior, Harold Ickes, claimed, belonged to a "Fascist ring in America." Thus, Quinn was in close contact with those whom the union labeled "seditious forces" and implied were pro-Nazi fifth columnists conspiring with the enemies abroad.[2]

The Quinn incident was not simply portrayed by the union as proof of a bigoted school employee who should be fired for her outlandish acts. The incident was also described as a flagrant act of disloyalty during wartime. Quinn was depicted as an adversary of the American people, someone who had committed treasonous acts. Thus, her crime was more than an act of racial bigotry or the upholding of white supremacy; her transgression threatened the very existence of the United States during a time of crisis. To be sure, May Quinn was characterized by the TU as un-American. The TU saw bigotry itself as un-American.

The New York Teachers Union was organized in 1916 by a group of teachers who believed that the interests of teachers could be best served by collective action. The year that it was organized, the TU received a charter from the American Federation of Teachers, becoming Local 5 and the first teachers' union in New York City. In its early years, social democrats, socialists, Communists, and liberals made up the TU. However, in the early 1930s teachers who were members of the Communist Party organized the Rank and File Caucus and attempted to win control of the union. In 1935, after failing to convince the American Federation of Teachers to oust the Communists from the TU, the social democratic leadership of the union and 700 members split from Local 5 and formed a rival union, the Teachers Guild. Despite the schism and the fact that there were several other teachers' organizations operating in New York, the TU remained the largest teachers' union in the city. By 1940 the union had 6,034 members. Its closest rival, the Guild, had half that number.[3]

From 1936 through World War II, the union, in large part, shared the politics of the political and social movement known as the Popular Front. This movement, which began in 1935, was made up of a coalition of the Communist Party, the Socialist Party, independent socialists and leftists, the Congress of Industrial Organizations and other labor groups, anti-fascist groups, social democrats, and progressives who advocated New Deal programs to create a more egalitarian America. The movement championed several causes, including labor's right to organize, industrial democracy, support of the loyalist government in Spain, an independent

Ethiopia, aiding refugees fleeing Hitler's Germany, and protesting lynching and other forms of racial terror.[4] The TU had diligently championed the black freedom struggle since 1935, when the Communist-led Rank and File Caucus of the union gained control of the TU. Indeed, during the Popular Front years, Communists in the TU continued its crusade to save the lives of the young men sentenced to death in Scottsboro, Alabama. In particular the union promoted black history and culture, and it argued that this history disproved the claim that African Americans were a detriment to the nation and had contributed little to America. The union's approach was a means not only to prove that blacks were not inferior but to show that racial discrimination hurt the country because such discrimination deprived Americans of knowledge of the rich heritage of blacks and the great contribution they made to the country. However, the union challenged many forms of racial discrimination, including anti-Semitism.

Leonard Dinnerstein notes that World War II led to a "rising tide of anti-Semitism" in the United States. The popularity of Father Charles Coughlin, who blamed Jewish bankers for the economic ills of the United States, and the publication of his magazine, *Social Justice,* which was used to lash out at Jews, was an indication of the growing anti-Semitism in the country. The Teachers Union, the membership of which was predominantly Jewish, was fully aware of the heightened anti-Semitism in the United States and therefore took action. Ruth Jacknow Markowitz contends that "anti-Semitism caused many Jewish teachers to become sensitive to the invidious effects of bigotry of all kinds." The explicit racist ideology of Nazi Germany and its racist genocidal actions made the issue of race a prominent subject of discussion during World War II. Of the 6,034 members of the TU, well over 5,000 were Jewish.[5] The war provided TU members who led its antiracist campaign an opportunity to intensify its efforts. Nazism also gave the union's antiracist campaign an opening to point to the ongoing racial discriminatory polices and practices in the United States and particularly in the New York City school system.[6]

During the war the union continued all its prewar efforts. The Harlem Committee remained active and the union even helped form the Bedford-Stuyvesant-Williamsburg Council, a group made up of TU members and parents from the two Brooklyn neighborhoods. The organization pushed for the replacement of day-to-day substitute teachers with those who held regular licenses, full days of instruction for children, and an end to "discriminatory zoning." But the war changed the context of these antiracist struggles. Racism and bigotry were presented by the union as the intellectual property of fascists and Nazis. Their elimination was now part of a national war effort.

Race and the War Years

The Teachers Union did not put the issue of Jim Crow on the back burner during the war but continued to highlight it in its publications, lashing out against institutional racism and the deliberate attempt to deny blacks the right of full citizenship. For example, in the October 2, 1943, edition of *New York Teacher News*, the union contended that American democracy was clearly flawed because of the existence of the poll tax. It noted that eight southern states used this infamous Jim Crow method to deny black citizens the right to the franchise. In fact, the practice of the tax denied in some southern places 99 percent of the population the right to vote.[7]

During the war, the Teachers Union did not limit its attack on racism and Jim Crow to the southern states. It also continued to hammer away at northern racism. It accused the Hillburn, New York, school district, for instance, of trying to create Jim Crow schools by assigning fifty-six black children to dilapidated segregated shacks serving as classrooms. The Board of Education in Hillburn was blamed for violating the law against segregation by gerrymandering and rezoning the black children to the broken-down building. The parents of the black children refused to send them to the schools and instead paid for private instruction during their struggle against the school district. The NAACP represented the parents in court against state commissioner of education George Stoddard.[8] Calling the situation "Jim Crow North," the union praised the parents for their courage in not caving in to school officials' threats to invoke the truancy law and other means of punishment.

The TU's ardent prewar language against Jim Crow did not dissipate during the war years; on the contrary, it remained just as intense. However, the union put the struggle against Jim Crow, both North and South, into a larger framework than in previous years. In the October 2, 1943, issue of *New York Teacher News*, Senator John Rankin of Mississippi not only was depicted as a racist but was specifically referred to as an "anti-Semite."

The TU argued that "the poll-tax will once more hamper our war effort." Fighting the poll tax was more than a matter of racial justice; it was also a strategy necessary to defeat the Axis powers. It was clear in the article that it was the patriotic duty of Americans to wage war against this undemocratic practice.[9]

The TU also labeled "northern Jim Crow" Nazism, and northern racists allies of Hitler. In its criticism of those who claimed that there was a crime wave in the predominantly black community of Bedford-Stuyvesant in 1943, the union argued that the claim was made in order to divert attention from the socioeconomic problems plaguing the community—poor housing, inadequate recreational facilities, dilapidated school buildings, and poverty. It specifically pointed its finger at the Hearst press, the *Daily News,* and the *Post* for concocting the notion of a crime wave. On several occasions the TU asserted that the Hearst press was pro-Nazi, at one point reporting that Secretary of the Interior Harold Ickes had named both the Hearst press and the Patterson-McCormick newspaper chain as among those "powerful and active forces in this country that would rather see Hitler win the war, if the alternative is his defeat by a leadership shared in by the great Russian (Premier Stalin) and the great American (President Roosevelt)." It also blamed Sumner Sirtl, head of the Midtown Civic League, for concocting the idea that there was a crime spree in Bedford-Stuyvesant. The union depicted Sirtl as a classic Nazi. He and his Midtown Civic Leaguers advocated a fascist agenda that included pushing blacks out of Bedford-Stuyvesant and relocating them to Jamaica Bay, Queens. He also called for the organization of armed white vigilante groups and gun clubs to protect whites against black people. The union compared Sirtl to a Nazi who wanted to create a Brooklyn branch of storm troopers and SS men. It was Sirtl's fascist organization that petitioned the Brooklyn grand jury to take steps to stop the crime wave in Bedford-Stuyvesant.[10]

The Hearst papers and Sirtl were not the only ones responsible for the crime wave concoction; *New York Teacher News* also named John B. Snow from Hillburn, New York, who, according to the union, never protested being labeled a "gentleman fascist." The TU pointed out that Snow used Nazi rhetoric when he accused Franklin Delano Roosevelt of being a Communist and blamed Jews for causing World War II. And if that were not enough, the union noted that he also fought for "Jim Crowism in Hillburn." The union contended that Sirtl, Snow, the Hearst press, and others who were pushing the crime wave story were creating disunity by using scare tactics to dissuade parents from sending their children to schools in Bedford-Stuyvesant, clearly a way of hampering the war effort. The TU did not mince words when discussing those who were heading the "Negro Smear." They were, it said, a "bigoted, fascist-minded interest and they have damaged the community and its schools."[11]

Couching its argument in the language of patriotism, the union asserted that "we believe that the American way is best." The "American way" that the union championed was its very own program. "Provide better housing, more playgrounds, more nurseries, improve school buildings, reduce class size, give the children the care they need, and juvenile delinquency will be reduced. Concern for our neighbors inspires love and not race hatred." The TU's prewar program no longer was only one for fairness but had been given a patriotic edge.[12]

Along with portraying Jim Crow as Nazism, the Teachers Union pointed to other overt acts of racism as evidence that a fifth column was functioning in the United States. Responding to the wave of anti-Semitic assaults that took place during the war, the union published an article in its weekly titled "Anti-Semitism—a Call for Action." It claimed that the recent anti-Semitic violence in Washington Heights, Brooklyn, and the Bronx was a "shocking reminder right in our own city that Nazis and their agents" operating in "our own country" were still trying to "change the outcome of the war by this most potent of Hitler's weapons [i.e., anti-Semitism]." Thus, the anti-Semitic attacks were depicted by the union as a means of dividing New Yorkers and improving the changes for an Axis victory. The union pointed to a 1940 investigation that disclosed that 407 members of the New York City Police Department were members of the Christian Front, an anti-Semitic, pro-Coughlin organization. As proof of the possible danger of further Nazi-type racist and anti-Semitic assaults, the union charged that twenty-three profascists who were indicted by the government for sedition were still at large and were "carrying on their activities." Mayor LaGuardia and police commissioner Valentine, the TU declared, should be forced to rid the police force of the profascist element and the U.S. attorney general should prosecute those who had been indicted for sedition.[13]

The union praised *Facts and Fascism*, a book by investigative journalist George Seldes, for not only pointing out that "small-fry fascists have been magnificently exposed" in such magazines as *Sabotage* and *Undercover* but also putting the spotlight on a group of men who financed American fascism and other "native fascist forces," including the American Legion, Charles Lindbergh, and the *Reader's Digest*, as well as the press. Using a patriotic vernacular, the union claimed that the book's "significance in the struggle for victory lies in its challenge to those who love democracy to exert every effort of mind and will to fight wherever it becomes manifest."[14]

The union saw anti-Semitism and anti-black racism as two forms of fascism. Its critique emphasized the common cause between a union with a large Jewish membership and a city with a large minority and Jewish population.[15] To bolster its argument that anyone in the United States committing anti-Semitic and racist acts was an agent of Hitler and that such acts undermined the war effort, the TU printed a drawing of a man in a Nazi uniform with a swastika on his face, operating two puppets. The first puppet was attacking a man wearing a yarmulke and the other puppet was desecrating a tombstone by drawing a swastika and painting the word "Jews" on the stone. The caption above the puppeteer read: "Berlin Pulls the Strings."[16]

In fact, many of the anti-Semitic actions in New York City were committed by young boys without any organizational affiliation. A special state investigation in 1943 of anti-Semitic attacks in New York headed by William B. Herlands, commissioner of the Department of Investigation, pointed out that forty-one of the fifty-two anti-Semitic incidents in the city involved youths ranging in age from nine to seventeen. The TU was well aware of the report. Despite the release of the Herlands report, the union continued to argue that attacks supported a fascist campaign to undermine the war effort. In a January 22, 1944, *New York Teacher News* editorial titled "Crush Anti-Semitism," the union warned of continuing racist attacks, including desecrations, assaults, and vandalism, and declared that these acts "have brought the leering visage of fascism close to us." Acknowledging the Herlands report and its finding that a number of children were committing these racist acts, it nonetheless linked these acts to a distant racist terror. It recognized the effort that many groups, including the Jewish, Catholic, and Protestant teachers associations, were making to fight anti-Semitism; however, it lamented what it saw as the absence of a sense of urgency among many regarding the necessity for unity to address the immediate danger. In fact, while there was a coalition of nations defeating Nazism overseas, "Hitlerism here at home may make our America the concentration camp of fascism."[17]

When Ralph Haller, principal of Andrew Jackson High School, issued a statement asserting that no student found guilty of taking part in racist activities would be allowed to receive a diploma from his school, the union publicly praised him for taking tough action. An editorial in *New York Teacher News* featured a lengthy quote from the Jackson High School principal's statement that he considered racist acts "totally in contradiction to everything that the America of today or the America which we hope to have tomorrow stands for." Haller said that he considered such activity "so completely un-American" that he would not give his signature on a diploma to any student guilty of any racist activity. The union expressed delight that a school let students know that racial intolerance was a "fascist weapon with which the enemy planned to conquer the world. It is against our own national interests, against our own safety to permit acts of violence against any minority group to pass unnoticed and unpunished."[18]

At the same time that the Teachers Union pushed those in power to take an aggressive position against fascist enemies from within, it adopted a rehabilitative approach, especially when it came to children. Clearly, the union had a dual message when it came to children. While it depicted youths committing anti-Semitic and racist acts as fascist sympathizers of Hitler and advocated punitive measures to stop them, it did not seek to completely criminalize them. Instead, it advocated the rehabilitative effects of education. Nazis were not born—they were made—and with the proper de-Nazification curriculum, they could be purged of their racist notions. Thus, teachers had a special role in the fight for democracy; they were to use the best weapon at their disposal, education, to win the battle for the hearts and minds of students. The union even adopted the slogan "Schools at War," and in March of 1942 it published a pamphlet titled "Schools for Victory." The piece emphasized the role that schools must play in the war effort, including teaching black history as a way to fight fascism and win the allegiance of African Americans. The union proposed using "textbooks and supplementary material recommended by the National Association for the Advancement of Colored People and the Association for the Study of Negro Life and History. It also called for the elimination from textbooks of all misinformation or derogatory statements about the Negro people."[19]

In its educational campaign to combat anti-Semitism and "other forms of Nazi-inspired racist activities" in New York, the union created a Committee to Combat Discrimination. The committee met on a weekly basis with the direct purpose of proposing ways the union could address racism in the city schools and neighborhoods, and in the nation. The committee circulated a petition calling on the board to create a program to fight racism. The committee also established a subcommittee to collect data, work with civic organizations, and create a speakers bureau. It also proposed a plan of action that called on the board to organize a conference of teachers, parents, and civic groups to work on a school curriculum that would inculcate ideals of equality and tolerance. The major objective of the committee was to build unity and, in that way, help achieve "victory over Nazism."[20]

Remaining committed to the Communist Party's line to prosecute the war, the union defended its program of improving working conditions for teachers by arguing that schools were the "bulwark of democracy," which required the unity of all "anti-fascist teachers and supervisors." Education, the union claimed, had been attacked by Hitler, and these attacks would "continue more sharply in an effort to extinguish enlightenment and culture and to pervert the schools to serve the needs of despotism and obscurantism." Teachers were obligated to ignore their "minor differences for the large objective to preserve and expand education as an integral part of the defense of American freedom and independence." The TU proposed that every aspect of school activity should be redirected toward achieving the maximum "contribution to the defense of freedom," including curriculum matters, administration, and supervision for the war. "By affording living examples of democracy in action our schools can truly function as effective weapons in the arsenal of democracy." One of democracy's most effective weapons was the health and welfare of children. The Selective Service Medical Board's rejection of a number of young men for physical deficiencies reinforced the importance of guaranteeing the health of children in the school system.[21]

The TU raised the issue of racial disparity by noting that health services were "particularly important in under-privileged communities such as Harlem, the Lower East Side, and other such communities." By singling out predominantly black and Latino communities, the union was accusing the board of neglect without proclaiming that the school board was racist. Instead, it couched its argument in the necessity for war preparation. It was also arguing that a strong democracy must assure all its citizens the same care and services.[22]

Besides pressuring board officials and government to take actions that would address racial disparities and pushing for racial unity during the war, the TU also called on individual teachers to contribute to these objectives. The "teacher as a citizen" could participate in "morale building" and rationing and "elect win-the-war candidates." The union revised curricula to "stress the meaning of democracy." This meant teaching "citizenship" by discussing and evaluating local problems, participating in get-out-the-vote drives, and contrasting "Hitlerism and democracy." The TU suggested that older students take a "census of nationalities" in their communities and note their "contributions to culture, as a basis for sponsoring a project on nationalities nights."[23]

The union sought ways to convince the public that its program was benefiting not only teachers but the entire nation. Even the language of the TU's annual conference reflected how the union placed its traditional concerns in the framework of winning the war. Its seventh annual conference, which took the theme of "Education for Victory," warned that a victory for the Axis "would destroy our national independence. . . . Conquered and enslaved by a ruthless invader, we would see swept aside every one of those pillars which [Thomas] Jefferson strove to establish and on which our way of life rests: equal justice, freedom of thought, of speech, of assembly and religion; and above all, the continuing heritage of public education." Moving away from the language of a collective bargaining agency, and substituting a war rhetoric, the union insisted that public schools were a "citadel and a fortress; a training-ground and a center of morale." The schools must "mobilize for victory," educating to "help in the training of thousands" who were going into the armed forces and war industry. Moreover, they had to "enlighten not only those within its walls, but the community which it serves" about the war.[24]

A crucial component of the TU's emphasis at its conference was the fight against racism. One of its forums at the conference, "Through Unity to Victory," discussed many topics, including "The Negro in National Unity" and "Combating Anti-Semitism." Another forum, "Developing Manpower in the Secondary Schools," offered a discussion on "How Can Schools Help Eliminate the Discrimination against the Employment of Negro Youth?" Its annual award went posthumously to Dr. George Washington Carver (he died in 1943), whose work was "one of the highest expressions of the strivings of the Negro people" and was a "granite monument" that would serve to disprove the "superior race theories and propaganda of the Nazis and inspire people everywhere to fight for victory and democracy."[25]

The Teachers Union insisted that the "Hitlerite poison of racism has taken a strong hold on our youth." But it was through education and providing students with information on blacks, Jews, and others that Nazi ideology would be defeated.[26] In November of 1943, a TU member and teacher at Mark Twain Junior High School in Brooklyn organized a school-wide student project called "Hitler's Secret Weapon—to Divide and Conquer." Topics featured in the project were "Race Prejudice—a Hindrance to Victory," "Propaganda Analysis," race and racism, and the contributions of various national and racial groups to America. The project examined whether the United States treated all its citizens equally. It praised America for being a "great democracy" but it raised the question whether all its people were treated fairly.

One way to ensure racial tolerance was to purge the system of intolerant teachers. The TU called on the Board of Education to launch an all-out offensive and to "clean its own house by investigating anti-Semitic employees," such as May Quinn and Milo McDonald. At rallies held in the Bronx, Queens, and Manhattan in January 1944, Teachers Union representatives and others called for the Board of Education to create programs "of racial tolerance and understanding in the schools as well as Congress to pass anti-hate legislation."[27]

Discussion of practically all evils affecting the school system was couched in the language of hindering the war campaign. Rallies were held by TU members, parents, and community organizations in the Bronx, Queens, and Manhattan at which teachers, leaders, and local legislators spoke out about the "threatening problems facing the community—anti-Semitism, anti-Negro discrimination, overcrowding and under manning of the schools." Overcrowding of schools and the lack of school personnel resulted in schools not being prepared to do their part for the war effort. Speakers for the union at the various rallies urge the Board of Education to create programs of racial tolerance and understanding in the schools and for those attending the rallies to support a number of hate crime bills, including the Steingut-Wickman bill in the state legislature, which made it a crime to publish race-hate material.[28]

The effort for national unity would ensure that America's greatest resource, its people, was behind the war effort to defeat the Axis powers abroad and the Axis-style supporters at home. The union had carved out a space for itself and the public school system in the battle to defeat Nazi aggression and fight racism by advocating an educational program that would promote racial and ethnic harmony among children, parents, and communities.

Intercultural Education

The emergence of intercultural education in the 1930s provided another yet important way the TU could challenge racism. This new field provided the union with a new language, new methods, and more innovative concepts for addressing bigotry in the schools and community.

During the war, the TU called on the Board of Education to adopt an intercultural education plan providing teaching units appropriate for each grade level and course, and conferences for teachers and administrators.[29]

One of the most important promoters of intercultural education was Rachel Davis DuBois, a white Quaker born in 1892 and raised in south New Jersey. Her politics and ideas were influenced by her friendly relationship with the African Americans who worked on her parents' farm, and by her Quaker religious values. She was active in social reform movements, including the Grange and suffrage movements.[30] After graduating from Bucknell College in 1914, DuBois began to teach at Glassboro High School in New Jersey and soon attended the First International Conference of the Society of Friends in London in 1920. There she heard speakers describe British imperialism in India and Jamaica and the cruel treatment of African Americans in the United States, including the 1919 race riot in Chicago and lynchings in the South. DuBois was so disturbed that she decided to take steps to heal the racial divide by seeking friendship across the color line.[31]

DuBois' views on race were also shaped by her travel in 1921 to the South, where she witnessed Jim Crow firsthand. In her autobiography she recalled seeing "white" and "colored" signs, reminders of how people of African origins were dehumanized in America. Her meeting with the great African American scientist George Washington Carver was an emotional revelation. She realized that she was in the "presence of not just a scientific genius, but a spiritual genius as well." She sat next to Carver at a dinner and tried not to show her "ignorance." She later wrote that she could never forgive her "white social worlds for having sent me through high school and college, never preparing me for such experiences." Her encounter with Jim Crow and with George Washington Carver convinced her of the need for intercultural education.[32]

Her final inspiration was the work of W. E. B. Du Bois. Rachel DuBois claimed that after reading Du Bois's "Race and War" in the *American Mercury*, she found the calling she "must dedicate the rest of my life to." She contended that "basic to the problem of peace and war is the problem of race." "I decided I must rid myself of my own ignorance about blacks in American life, not only reading books on the subject but by finding people in that group with whom I could become friends."[33]

Besides reaching across the color line for friendship, Rachel DuBois returned to teaching at Woodbury High School in New Jersey and she decided to emphasize cultural diversity in her school. She decided that an effective avenue to introduce cultural diversity was through the weekly assembly program. Bringing in an outside member of a particular racial and ethnic group to speak to an assembly and classrooms on the cultural contributions of that group would bolster the self-esteem of the various races and nationalities and also make others outside the group more aware and appreciative of their accomplishments. DuBois and the teachers in her school created the Woodbury Assembly Project.[34]

DuBois did not limit her concerns to African Americans. She also included other racially and ethnically oppressed groups: "I suppose my sensitivity to the feelings of the black youth made me more aware of the other minority pupils—Jewish and the Italian Americans." DuBois did not agree with melting pot ideas that focused on the assimilation and "Americanization" of nationalities and races. Instead, her assembly programs recognized that all groups made important contributions to American life. They also went beyond the notion of tolerance and instead wanted to develop "sympathetic attitudes toward various races and nations."[35]

DuBois' project of intercultural education stressed the "ethnic richness," the historical and cultural contributions of all. She was asked to develop intercultural assembly programs in other school districts, including New York City. In 1934 she created materials to teach intercultural education through assembly programs in fifteen New York City high schools and in that same year she established the Service Bureau for Intercultural Education. The bureau provided lesson plans and the opportunity to create intercultural education programs in the schools. The war brought her program additional support. She wrote in her autobiography that after the spread of "Nazi prejudice" in New York City, school authorities issued an order that schools had to create assembly programs and classroom lessons on "tolerance and democracy." Dr. Benjamin Greenberg, duty superintendent of schools, approached her and asked her to teach in-service courses. She agreed and had teachers contact her bureau for assistance in setting up programs.[36]

By the late 1930s the Teachers Union had embraced DuBois' brand of intercultural education. The union used both the methods and language. It agitated for assembly programs, developed materials on various racial groups, and spoke of the need for an intercultural perspective in the curriculum. The union also emphasized intercultural education as a means of building national unity.

As early as 1938 the TU was working with Rachel DuBois on intercultural education projects. In June of that year, the union's Harlem Committee organized "experimental series of lectures on the Negro in

American Civilization" to help teachers understand the problems of the community. Among those lecturing to hundreds of teachers were Doxey Wilkerson, professor of education at Howard University and a writer for *New York Teacher* (the union's monthly magazine); Max Yergan, the first African American to teach a course in black history at City College; and Rachel DuBois. The TU sought a broader audience for her program, saying that "through schools, churches and other community groups we can give people mutually appreciative experiences. To the schools it offers factual material on minority groups; as well as material on ways for promoting intercultural education, curriculum materials" and helping to create "world mindedness."[37]

In January 1939, two TU members, Marion Milstein and Jenny L. Mayer, published an article in the *New York Teacher* titled "Schools for Tolerance." The authors praised the radio program "Americans All— Immigrants All," a show that was aired on CBS in 1939 to promote tolerance in America of the various ethnic and racial groups. The radio program was the idea of Rachel DuBois. She believed radio was an important venue for countering the racist radio preaching of Father John Coughlin. She convinced the commissioner of education, John Studebaker, of the need for such a program. Studebaker, who was concerned about rising tensions among ethnic and racial groups in the United States, was thrilled by the idea and saw radio as a way of "institutionalizing in his agency the newly politically valuable field of intercultural education." Together with a representative from the Illinois Governor's Committee on Citizenship and Naturalization who was concerned about racial and ethnic tension in Chicago, Studebaker convinced CBS officials to air an intercultural education program.[38]

Milstein and Mayer called "Americans All—Immigrants All" a "significant achievement in the field of education for tolerance." Besides encouraging *New York Teacher*'s readers to listen to "American All— Immigrants All," Milstein and Mayer encouraged the use of plays and films to promote tolerance in the assembly program. They reminded readers that the Board of Education recognized the value of the assembly program because of the union's effort. The union had adopted a resolution "urging assembly programs to be used to inculcate the ideals of democracy and tolerance." Milstein and Mayer reminded readers that in response to the resolution, the superintendent of schools had sent a letter to principals instructing them to plan assembly programs to teach "these essential principles." They also suggested that language clubs "should make students aware of French, Italian, German and Hebrew ideals, ambitions, and creative efforts, and should help them see the human spirit underlying them all." They recommended that teachers and schools contact DuBois' Service Bureau for Intercultural Education for materials and bibliographies on various ethnic groups.[39]

While assembly programs and clubs were important vehicles for spreading intercultural education and promoting tolerance, they were not the only means. The union also encouraged academic departments to develop syllabi specifically for teaching tolerance. "English, the social sciences, foreign languages, even the official period, offer many opportunities for such teaching. The spirit of democracy should permeate every classroom at all times."[40]

Intercultural education had become a major influence and cause of the union, which began offering courses in intercultural education, and individual union members were involved in intercultural courses offered by community and civil groups. Lucille Spence, head of the TU's Harlem Committee, also became the head of an intercultural workshop, and TU members were responsible for assembly programs in schools offering dramatic skits on black history and films on African American history and culture. The principal of Morris High School praised the his teachers for creating an intercultural education program in his school in which students learned dances from various cultures and races.[41]

During the war, education was intertwined with patriotism. When people attending the Intercultural Forum at Andrew Jackson High School recited the Pledge of Allegiance, New York Teacher News reported that the salute to the colors was not simply a ritual but a vow to ensure the promises of the pledge. The major benefit of intercultural understanding and national unity was emphasized at the forum organized by the faculty of Jackson. The theme of unity was echoed by a host of speakers. James Maxwell, principal of James Madison High School, Brooklyn, and one of the speakers at the forum, declared that the "fascist enemy[,] both" abroad and "native born, seizes upon the normal human tendency to be suspicious of that which is different and turns that suspicion into fear and hatred." Dr. Alphaeus Hunton, educational director of the Council of African Affairs, claimed that justice for blacks was essential to the welfare of all Americans and necessary for world unity. The reason for racial fraction, according to Hunton, was the ignorance and indifference of many whites and newspapers, radio, and congressional figures who "preach the doctrine of a master race." Father Raymond Leonard of the Church of the Nativity, Brooklyn, emphasized that "man is one; civilizations are many." Dr. Paul Moody of the First

Presbyterian Church, New York, begged that people of various faiths and skin colors attempt to attain understanding of one another by having closer contact. The high school's Intercultural Club and the Faculty Interfaith Committee were active in organizing the forum.[42]

While national unity was an important theme, the promoters of intercultural education did not neglect its significance as a cure for racial animosity. To help teachers foster antidiscrimination intercultural education, the union created a reference room at its headquarters providing lesson plans, magazines, booklets, and other material on "intercultural understanding." It also created courses on intercultural education for teachers and it assisted in the formulation of the Board of Education's intercultural program and materials.[43]

As noted, the TU did not limit its focus on intercultural education to the study of black culture but examined a wide number of ethnic and racial groups. In the fall of 1945 the Association of Biology Teachers, the Association of Teachers of Social Studies, and the New York Association of Teachers of English (all TU affiliated) organized an in-service program titled "Minority Problems in American History," whose course schedule was to run from late October to early December. The program boasted a faculty of experts and scholars, including Columbia University professor of anthropology Gene Weltfish, who offered a course on "native abilities of different peoples of the World"; Doxey Wilkerson, who offered a course on "The Negro People in America"; Valia Hirsch of the Committee of Jewish Writers, Artists, and Scientists, whose course was titled "The Jewish People in America"; Robert J. O'Donnell, executive secretary of the Committee of Catholics for Human Rights, who lectured on the "Irish People in America"; and anthropologist Gitel Poznanski of Columbia University, who focused on Japanese, Chinese, Mexicans, and Indians. Other courses focused on minority problems in American history, the interaction between white and black Americans, and a history of immigrants in America. The final event was a group discussion among the teachers who participated in the program to develop intercultural cooperation in the classroom, the school, and the community.[44]

The TU's intercultural campaign extended beyond the school building. In March of 1944, the Citizens Committee of the Upper West Side of Manhattan, a group in which members of the TU were active, organized a Children's Unity Festival. *New York Teacher News* reported that it was the "most significant work that we have heard of in the city getting right down to rousing fervor for intercultural understanding." Celebrities from the worlds of baseball, boxing, and Broadway attended and a photo in the paper showed that whites, African Americans, Asians, Latinos, Jews, Italians, and Polish children participated in the affair.[45]

The union had some success in persuading the Board of Education to adopt intercultural education. In 1944 it persuaded school authorities to grant in-service credit to teachers who took intercultural education courses; in the same year, the superintendent of schools declared that it was the intention of the board to make intercultural education essential throughout the school system. The TU also pushed for legislation to make intercultural education mandatory in schools. In 1945, it submitted a resolution to the state assembly specifying that schools should teach scientific facts about race, challenge racial myths, eliminate bias in textbooks, and train teachers in intercultural education.[46]

By the time the United States had entered the war, the union had fully embraced the language as well as the aims of DuBois and intercultural education. In fact, intercultural education became the model for teachers to challenge racial intolerance. It was a means of gaining an appreciation for diverse cultures, challenging ethnocentrism and racism, and gaining unity to advance the war effort. DuBois' strategies to spread intercultural education into the schools had its strongest advocates in the membership of the TU.

Anthropology and the TU

Anthropology also became an avenue used by the Teachers Union to confront racism during the war years. By the early part of the twentieth century Franz Boas and other anthropologists challenged the notion that race was the decisive factor that determined intelligence and character. Boas saw culture as a set of customs, social institutions, and beliefs that characterize any particular society. These cultural differences were a result not of race but rather of environment. Culture was also a fusion of a variety of cultures as they interacted over time. Boas's approach was known as "historical particularism." He argued that anthropologists needed to carry out extensive regional studies in order to understand the processes changing culture. With enough regional studies, it would be possible to make broad generalizations about the development of culture.

Soon after Hitler came to power, Boas dedicated a great deal of his time to challenging Nazi ideas on race, or what he called "Nordic nonsense." Incensed by the removal of his books from the library of the University of Kiel, Germany, because he was Jewish and because of his views on race, he waged an effort to locate jobs and fellowships at American universities and colleges for scholars who were fleeing Nazi Germany. He led a campaign to persuade scientific learned societies, including the National Academy of Sciences, to adopt resolutions supporting academic freedom and condemning the events in Europe. Finally, after five years, he managed to get over 1,200 scientists at 167 universities and colleges to sign the Manifesto on Freedom in Science challenging pseudo-scientific findings of scientists who attempted to link race to intelligence. Boas came to the conclusion that the battle with fascism was ideological and that the one sure way of combating fascism was through science and education.[47]

By 1936, Boas had stepped up his anti-Nazi activities, including conducting scientific work to undermine Nazi ideology. He also traveled in the United States and abroad, presenting his findings and views on race. In fact, his anti-Nazi activity was so intense and straining it contributed to a fatal heart attack in 1942.[48]

Boas's political work won him the respect and admiration of many, including the New York City Teachers Union. In fact, the union was so appreciative of Boas's work that it awarded him its annual award at its 1940 conference and it recommended his work to teachers. In honor of his work, Herbert Chaimes, a TU member and biology teacher, organized the Franz Boas Workshop for teachers in 1943, a year after the famous anthropologist's death. The purpose of the workshop was to create programs for fighting racism. It also created courses on race problems for the Board of Education staff, parents, and civil organizations and organized workshops and forums on the contributions of racial and ethnic groups. The workshop also examined textbooks for biased materials, recommending to the board that it either revise these books or, in some cases, eliminate them from the curriculum.[49]

Relying on the arguments of Boas, the Franz Boas Workshop helped organize events addressing some of the very questions he studied. A school-wide event at Mark Twain Junior High School titled "Hitler's Secret Weapon" focused on anthropological questions such as whether language is hereditary or learned behavior and why groups develop language, as well as theories of race superiority. Leon Kaiser, principal at Mark Twain, gave credit to the Franz Boas Workshop for helping to organize the event.[50]

The Franz Boas Workshop was also given credit for creating a bibliography of books on Jewish immigration and the contributions of Jews as a group and individuals to "our American culture."[51]

Boas was not the only anthropologist influencing the TU. After his death, two of his students, Ruth Benedict and Gene Weltfish, both in the anthropology department at Columbia University, decided to "carry the banner on the race question." They wrote a pamphlet titled "The Races of Mankind" at the request of the USO for the armed forces who found themselves fighting next to people from different countries and different cultures. The pamphlet was also used in Germany's de-Nazification program.[52]

In October 1943, a nonprofit educational organization, the Public Affairs Committee Inc., published Benedict and Weltfish's thirty-two-page pamphlet for the American public. The pamphlet was as much a political manifesto as it was scientific literature. The two anthropologists argued that since race had become a central issue of World War II, then the findings of science on the subject should be widely studied. Indeed, this was the purpose of the pamphlet in what they labeled a "crucial moment in history." Like their mentor Franz Boas, they did not contend that race was a social construct but said they rejected the racist notion that race determines intelligence, character, and customs.[53]

Benedict and Weltfish showed that the various races have similar anatomical structures and that race had no bearing on height, the size of the brain, or blood type. They challenged the erroneous racial classification system of the Nazis by contending that groups such as the Jews were not races but religious groups. What separated these groups was culture, which was socially constructed. Degree of intelligence, they argued, has more to do with environmental factors such as education. They offered as proof scientific and historical examples, like the fact that northern blacks scored higher on intelligence tests than southern whites. Likewise, they noted Africans and Chinese had created advance civilizations and that "All races have made their contributions to human knowledge." Turning to the United States, they argued that various cultures contributed to the country's greatness. "Our country would be poorer in every phase of its culture if different cultures had not come together here, sharing and learning the special contributions each had to offer."[54]

Benedict and Weltfish contended that racial prejudice has a long history but its continued existence is not inevitable. In one of the most controversial sections of the pamphlet, they claimed that their proof was the Soviet Union. "The Russian nation has for a generation shown what can be done to outlaw race prejudice in a country with many kinds of people. They did not wait for people's minds to change. They made racial discrimination and persecution illegal. They welcomed and honored the different dress, different customs, different arts of the many tribes and countries that live as part of their nation." For the two anthropologists, no aspect of the Soviet Union has had "greater success than their racial progress."[55]

Although several groups attacked the pamphlet as subversive and it was banned from the library of the armed forces, the pamphlet sold like hotcakes. Civic groups, churches, and school districts bought thousands of copies. Thanks to the TU, it was a particular hit among New York City school teachers. In one Manhattan high school alone, three thousand copies of "Races" were distributed to the student body. Just a few weeks after it was issued, every copy had been sold and it remained unavailable for weeks. Finally, in December of 1943, *New York Teacher News* announced that the pamphlet had been reissued at only ten cents a copy.[56]

The union's campaign to promote the use of the pamphlet was one of the major reasons it sold out. In a February issue of *New York Teacher News*, the paper quoted the preface of the pamphlet: "We must know whether race is an inevitable barrier to any possible commonwealth of nations that guarantees the four freedoms to all men. We must know whether the diversity of races and ethnic groups in America must inevitably mean that this is a country divided against itself. No subject you study in school today is more fraught with consequences than this subject of race. We shall examine it from every angle." In another edition of the paper, the union contended that what made the pamphlet an invaluable work was that it presented "scientific" material on the subject of race. The paper also mentioned that a publication by the Council Against Intolerance in America used an illustration from the pamphlet and encouraged its use. It was a pin-up page of various races titled "Meet Your Relatives." Anthropology had become a field for the TU to challenge racist theories and in this effort, it even carried positive reviews of books, encouraging teachers to read them. For example, in its June 1938 issue there was a review of Bernhard J. Stern's *The Family: Past and Present*. This edited work consisted of essays by several well-known anthropologists describing property, marriage customs, and family relations of a number of nonwhite societies. The review praised the work for presenting, "vividly, the human factor."[57]

After the war, the union continued to stress the importance that intercultural education and anthropology could have on promoting a society devoid of racial and ethnic tensions. In the February 16, 1946, issue of

New York Teacher News, its weekly column Road to Peace (formerly Road to Victory) noted the release of new classroom materials for Brotherhood Week. Not only did the material work well for Negro History Week, but it also allowed teachers "the opportunity to broaden discussion so that students may become aware of the fact that Negroes, Jews, and other minority groups face common problems." The material consisted of fifteen posters by the American Missionary Association explaining "the physical origins of racial groups and stress the cultural contributions of all peoples." The titles of some of the posters were "Why Are There Different Races," "The Jews are Not a Race," "Inventions Have Come from All Races," and the "Negro Is an Integral Part of Our Culture." These posters, the union stressed, could be used for plays, pageants, and assembly programs.[58]

In addition to the posters, the TU pointed out that the National Conference of Christians and Jews had a number of radio and assembly plays for elementary, junior high, and senior high schools, "the theme of which are combating prejudice and improving intercultural relations." One program titled "The America of Tomorrow" takes place in a classroom where a teacher and her class decide following a discussion that "people all over the world, as well as the diverse groups in the United States, must learn to live in harmony."[59]

Conclusion

This chapter does not deny or ignore the Communist Party's influence on the thinking of the New York City Teachers Union. There is no doubt that the TU followed Moscow's line but also placed the fight for civil rights into a larger context. The move to support the policies of the Communist Party did not mean racial equality was no longer a priority. TU members sought ways of repackaging the goal of winning the war with the fight against racism. No teachers' organization in the city matched the effort of the TU when it came to the struggle for racial equality. Without a doubt, race and race relations were central issues in New York City schools before the Cold War because the TU remained just as passionate on this issue as it did during the prewar years. The union's contention that fighting racism was inseparable from winning the war was an attempt to get Americans to think about not only their ideals but their practices. The racist nature and objectives of the enemy provided the union with a means of winning people to the cause of equality at home as well as abroad. By juxtaposing the Axis's racist ideals to those of Americans, the TU asked Americans to distinguish themselves from Nazism abroad and from what the union called Nazi practices in America. The men and women who were members of this union should not be seen as dupes but as historical agents who addressed bigotry and sought ways of eliminating it. The chapter suggests that if the TU had been allowed to play a role in New York City schools and New York City, history might have been very different.

2

Cops, Schools, and Communism: Local Politics and Global Ideologies— New York City in the 1950s

BARBARA RANSBY

> I came into the social justice movements at the height of the repression of the Cold War period. . . . Organizations seeking civil rights, peace and justice had been crushed everywhere. . . . And although I discovered in those years that there was always a resistance movement, many people did indeed fall into silence. . . . But the one thing that could not be crushed was a burning desired of African Americans to be free.
>
> Anne Braden, 1999

In 1952, Ella Baker was elected president of the large New York City NAACP branch, becoming its first woman president. She had been active in the branch for several years, working with the youth council and several other projects, but her new post provided her with the latitude and authority to orchestrate some of the kinds of political campaigns she had long envisioned. After traveling around the country for two decades aiding grassroots groups to develop activist campaigns for change, she now had an opportunity to shape and direct such a movement in the heart of New York City. Her base of operations was Harlem, where she had great experience and manifold ties with diverse groups of black and white political activists and progressive intellectuals. Actually, she moved branch headquarters from offices downtown to the heart of the black community in Harlem to be more in the thick of things. Baker led the New York City branch the way she thought all NAACP branches should function: She identified issues of concern to black people—ordinary working people as well as professionals—and involved as many members as possible in building direct-action campaigns to address those issues. She also worked hard to build coalitions with other groups in the city. In New York, unlike many smaller cities where the NAACP was the only civil rights organization in town, the black political scene was eclectic and contentious. But Baker was able to deal with the personalities and navigate the territorial rivalries of various organizations with finesse. Part of the key to her success was that she relished rather than resented other organizational involvement. Every action did not have to be carried out in the NAACP's name. In fact, Baker maintained multiple organizational affiliations even as she presided over the New York branch.

During 1952 and 1953, under Ella Baker's leadership, the New York City NAACP branch built coalitions with other groups in the city and carried out aggressive campaigns focused primarily on school reform and desegregation and on police brutality.[1] In the course of these campaigns, Baker employed the whole range of protest tactics she had taught others to utilize: sending public letters of protest, leading noisy street demonstrations, confronting the mayor in front of the news media, and even running for public office after temporarily taking off her NAACP hat. Baker's photograph and her fiery words appeared regularly in New York City newspapers as she demanded quality public education for all New York students, along with active parental participation, and called for public accountability and fair treatment for people of color from the police. Often at the head of a crowd of supporters, acting in concert with other groups and individuals, Baker led the New York City NAACP into action alongside progressive whites and Puerto Ricans, the city's second-largest group of people of color.

In her efforts at coalition building, Baker tried to avoid the divisive Cold War politics that defined the national scene during the early 1950s and threatened to infect the debates over local issues. While Baker continued to have regular contact with Walter White, Roy Wilkins, and Gloster Current (her successor as director of branches, with whom she had a civil but strained relationship), she tried to function as independently as possible. She contacted the executive officers regarding fundraising efforts, membership strategies, and incidents that occurred in the city that both the New York City branch and the national office might respond to. It took a conscious, continuous effort for Baker to carve out her own path in the very backyard of the national office. The personality conflicts and the tension between the national organization and local branches that created long-standing problems in the association were compounded, during the early 1950s, by the growing influence of anti-Communism.

The national NAACP asserted its intention to step up the push for racial progress in the wake of World War II when it convened the National Emergency Civil Rights Mobilization in Washington, D.C., in January 1950. The tone and flavor of the event, however, suggested that the organization's national leaders intended to carry out that work safely within the bounds of Cold War rhetoric and ideology. The gathering brought together over 4,000 African American civic, community, and religious leaders in the national capital to press President Truman to take stronger action on pending civil rights initiatives. Demands included a permanent Fair Employment Practices Commission and voting rights protection.

The organization wanted to send another message to the Truman administration as well. Roy Wilkins and his colleagues were anxious to defend and reaffirm the NAACP's reputation against allegations of ties with Communism. Anti-Communist campaigners charged that the NAACP membership included those who presently or formerly belonged to the Communist Party and that Communist ideas therefore dominated the association. This was hardly the case, but in the volatile political climate of the1950s, and in the wake of the 1947 government decision to require loyalty oaths of federal employees, charges of Communist links seemed tantamount to charges of treason. The national NAACP responded by denying the allegations outright, despite the prominent role played by well-known leftists of various ideological bents, including Communists, in joint campaigns for racial justice over the previous thirty years.

The conveners of the National Emergency Civil Rights Mobilization went to great lengths formally and publicly to exclude radicals with any hint of Communist affiliation. The conference call explicitly declared the mobilization to be a "nonpartisan, non-leftist movement rejecting the persistent proffers of 'cooperation' and 'assistance' made by individuals and organizations long identified as apologists for communist doctrine and Soviet foreign policies." The mobilization in Washington was only the beginning. At its annual convention in Boston in June, the NAACP formally barred Communists from membership and following the lead of the CIO—which had recently taken similar steps—proceeded to purge leftists from its ranks.[2] This undemocratic stance was partly a defensive capitulation to the virulent red-baiting that was quickly permeating the political culture. At the same time, it was a continuation and deepening of long-standing tensions between the policies of the dominant leadership and the leftist politics of other antiracist activists, including some who were also NAACP members.

Like most black radicals living in New York City in 1950, Ella Baker had friends and colleagues who were Communists. She often disagreed with them but she had worked with them off and on for over twenty years. Baker had managed to stay clear of the debate surrounding the Emergency Mobilization in January, and she had not figured prominently in the arguments that took place at the NAACP's Boston convention. But as head of the New York branch, in a city known for its radical political culture, Ella Baker would not be able to dodge the issues indefinitely.[3]

In the early 1950s in New York and elsewhere, there was a vibrant and multifaceted campaign for quality integrated public education. Baker brought passion as well as great experience to the issue of educational reform. She was her mother's daughter, so education had always been near and dear to her heart. In contrast to Anna Ross Baker, with her conventional notions of teaching and learning, Ella was eager to explore more creative pathways to knowledge. In the 1930s, she had focused her energies on adult education. In the late 1940s and early 1950s, as the parent of a school-aged child, she turned her attention to elementary and secondary education. Her daughter Jackie was enrolled in a private Quaker school for most of her time in New York, a sign of Ella's commitment to raising her in an integrated, progressive, and nurturing milieu. But Baker knew that private solutions to public problems were not solutions at all. Her deep interest in public education led Baker to team up with the well-known psychologist and civil rights activist Kenneth Clark and his equally accomplished, less often recognized wife, Mamie Phipps Clark, to push for improved conditions for poor, largely African American and Latino schoolchildren in New York City. Through her relationship with the Clarks, Baker became a strong proponent of "community-based" models of learning, in which parents were empowered to help define priorities and design curricula for their children. In this struggle, she also worked alongside Stanley Levison's wife, Bea, who was a reading tutor at the child development center run by the Clarks and a strong supporter of their work.[4]

Ella Baker joined a growing community of education reformers who sought fundamental changes in public education and child welfare policies that went well beyond the simple demand for integration. Milton Galamison, an African American activist in Brooklyn, and Annie Stein, a Jewish Communist who was also active in Brooklyn, were pushing the national NAACP leaders as well as city officials to take more aggressive actions.[5] Baker led her Harlem-based group, Parents in Action, and the citywide NAACP branch into the campaign, and out of that struggle developed a relationship with both Galamison and Stein; the latter became one of Baker's dear friends and close comrades. These were the years in which the NAACP's long-term legal campaign to desegregate public education was about to bear fruit in the landmark Supreme Court decision *Brown v. Board of Education*, and community-based civil rights activists sought to lay the basis for change once litigation had opened the door to desegregation.

Baker officially began working with the Clarks during the early 1950s, although she may have known them earlier through her activities with the NAACP and other organizations in New York. In August 1952, she co-convened a meeting at the Clarks' home in suburban Hastings-on-Hudson, which frequently served as a gathering place for New York's black activist intellectuals, to talk about the issue of segregation in New York City schools. In March 1953, a follow-up meeting was held at the same location. These outreach meetings included activists, educators, and policy makers in the New York area and were directed at curricular reform in the city.[6]

Both Kenneth and Mamie Clark were the children of Caribbean-born parents, recipients of Ivy League doctorates in psychology, and staunchly committed social activists. Kenneth was the first African American accepted into Columbia University's graduate program in psychology; in 1942, he became the first black professor on the faculty of the City College of New York.[7] The couple's famous doll studies (which have since been questioned) sought to demonstrate how black children's self-esteem was damaged by racism, as evidenced by their preference for white over black dolls. The Clarks' doll studies were discussed at length in the NAACP's brief in *Brown v. Board of Education*, and the Supreme Court specifically cited the Clarks' work in its historic decision striking down segregated schools as unconstitutional. The Clarks had long careers as scholars and activists before and after the 1954 *Brown* decision. In 1946 they established the Northside Center for Child Development to provide "social work, psychological evaluation, and remediation services in the community."[8] They were visible and vocal participants in struggles over housing, health, and poverty, as well as education.

In 1954, Baker agreed to serve as a member of the Intergroup Committee, chaired by Kenneth Clark, which was set up by the New York Board of Education to address some of the problems African American and Latino children encountered in the public schools. On the eve of the Brown decision, in April 1954, the committee hosted a conference at the New Lincoln School in Manhattan, titled "Children Apart," which indicted the school system for instilling a sense of inferiority in black children and perpetuating the enormous disparity between the resources allocated to black and white schools. The meeting drew activists, social workers, educators, and parents from across the city and kicked off several years of intense protests and lobbying for school reform, school desegregation, and increased youth services in New York. Baker was a paid staff person for the conference and devoted several weeks of her time to planning the event, contributing her well-honed organizing skills to ensure its success.[9] She drafted literature and conference documents, lined up speakers, coordinated publicity, met with various participant groups, and strategized with other activists about how to make the event effective in reaching their larger objectives. The conference was perfectly timed: Those who attended were primed to act once the imminent legal victory in the *Brown* case created an opening for change.

Ella Baker and Clarks continued their work with the Intergroup Committee, but after several years of lobbying and working with city officials, Baker was ready to move from debate to direct action. She feared that her former colleagues at the national NAACP office would either oppose such a step or slow it down with red tape. So, instead of operating exclusively under the banner of the New York City NAACP branch, Baker helped launch Parents in Action against Educational Discrimination, a grassroots coalition composed primarily of African American and Puerto Rican parents that demanded integrated schools and greater parental participation in educational policy making. Years later, Baker recounted how the organization got started: "New York City didn't act right after the '54 decision. It didn't have any reason to act so you had to help it to realize it. I was asked to serve on the Mayor's Commission. They finally discovered the city wasn't integrated! And

Bob Wagner the second was then Mayor, and we ended up by having several sessions with him. In '57, the entire summer was spent in weekly parent workshops, helping parents become aware that they had certain rights."[10]

In the fall of 1957, the eyes of the nation were focused not on efforts to desegregate public schools in northern cities but rather on the pitched battle being waged in the streets of Little Rock, Arkansas, a confrontation so intense that it led to a standoff between Orval Faubus, the state's segregationist governor, and President Dwight Eisenhower, culminating in the deployment of federal troops. Daisy Bates, Ella Baker's friend and former NAACP colleague, was in the middle of the fray as the leader of the local NAACP branch. Bates negotiated with local school officials and police to try to ensure the protection of the nine brave black teenagers who defied vicious mobs to enroll in Central High School that fall. Bates's home was firebombed, and the newspaper that she and her husband ran was forced to close down because of economic pressures and harassment.[11] In the South in this era, struggles to secure basic legal rights were often met with violent reprisals.

Building on the attention that Little Rock had garnered, New York activists were eager to point out that racial disparities were not unique to the South and that militant challenges to government intransigence would be necessary in New York City as well. As was often the case, Baker found herself trying to push her civil rights colleagues— particularly the national leaders of the NAACP—toward a more militant stance at the same time that she was leading a popular struggle against those in positions of government power. The national NAACP office, afraid of negative publicity and of alienating its moderate liberal supporters, sought to discourage confrontation and advised the activists to "adopt a less provocative endeavor, pointing out that after all northern school officials, unlike the hostile segregationists of the south, had agreed to integration; it was just a question of how and when," according to Galamison.[12] Baker founded the grassroots parents' group in order to circumvent the NAACP's paralytic bureaucracy and "go slow" politics.[13]

On September 26, 1957, Parents in Action called a rally designed to up the ante and draw greater attention to the campaign. Baker led a spirited picket line of over 500 black and Puerto Rican parents in front of city hall in Manhattan to protest the beginning of another school year without a serious response to the complaints these parents had been making for years. The group was particularly angry with school superintendent William Jansen but on this day they took their complaints directly to the mayor. The parents group had planned this confrontation for months. When the day of the scheduled demonstration finally arrived, Baker was one of the angriest and most vocal of the protesters. Although many civil rights activists later described Baker as a quiet, behind-the-scenes organizer, she was by no means hesitant to exert her leadership in this instance. News reports, which quoted Baker extensively, described her as the leader and principal rabble-rouser in the group. The group's grievances included overcrowded schools, inappropriate curriculum content, the disproportionate allocation of more experienced teachers away from black and Latino schools, blatant racial segregation throughout the system, and the unresponsiveness of school officials to parents' concerns.

On that Thursday morning, the protesters picketed for nearly two hours, demanding an immediate meeting with Mayor Robert Wagner. Finally, when it was apparent that the group would not back down, Wagner was persuaded by one of his colleagues to leave a meeting of the Board of Estimates and see a delegation of twenty-one protesters, many of them local ministers and NAACP activists, led by Ella Baker. Sara Black, a reporter for the Harlem-based *Amsterdam News*, described the meeting as follows: "From 11:55 to 12:12 Mayor Wagner spent an uneasy 17 minutes facing the delegation. . . . Standing while the Mayor twitched nervously, spokesman Baker said: 'We parents want to know first hand from you just what is, or is not, going to be done for our children. . . . New York City, the world's leading city, should reflect the highest degree of democracy in its public school system.' "[14]

The group demanded a follow-up meeting with the mayor, to which he agreed. Baker then warned Wagner bluntly that he could not afford to alienate black and Puerto Rican voters two months before he would be on the ballot for reelection. After a few more sharp exchanges between Baker and the mayor, the group left city hall, exhausted and drained after their four-hour protest, but claiming a tactical victory.[15]

The campaign for quality integrated schools in New York during the 1950s is historically significant.[16] First, Baker and her allies went beyond the simple demand of racial integration, calling for greater parent and community involvement in running the schools. This campaign was the first stage in the longer-term struggle for community control of the schools, a volatile issue that reemerged during the late 1960s and early 1970s. To insist that parents be empowered to define their children's education was a more substantive and radical demand than simply saying that black and white children should sit next to each other in the classroom. Complaining about distorted media coverage of the New York school struggle in a letter to her friend Ruth Moore, Baker wrote: "The headlines especially are designed to give the impression that the only thing with which we are concerned is integration rather than the fact that integration is desirable because where there is separation, even in New York, the schools are too often inadequate."[17] Second, Baker helped to forge an important biracial alliance between the African American and Puerto Rican communities. Some of Baker's friends from the school struggles of the 1950s became allies once again in the 1970s, when Baker joined the Puerto Rican Solidarity Committee to push for Puerto Rican independence.

The other major cause that Baker championed during her tenure as New York City NAACP branch president was even more volatile: the campaign against police brutality. Police brutality was a problem in black communities throughout the nation, in the North as well as the South. Baker had tackled it in both small towns and big cities during her work as an NAACP field secretary. She was well aware that the issue had larger ramifications. Not only did police brutality against individual black people violate their civil rights, but the intimidation that the entire community faced from local law enforcement was a key way that oppressed communities were discouraged from political protest. From 1950 to 1953, the New York City NAACP branch office received nearly one hundred complaints about instances of police violence against blacks in the city.[18] The issue came to a head in the summer of 1952 when two men, Jacob Jackson and Samuel Crawford, were brutally beaten by two white officers in the West Fifty-fourth Street station house. One of the men was so seriously injured that he needed brain surgery.[19]

In February 1953, public anger was fueled by allegations made by the *New York Telegram and Sun* regarding a secret agreement between the New York Police Department and the U.S. Justice Department that discouraged the FBI from investigating brutality charges leveled against the department and simply allowed the department to handle such complaints as internal matters. The agreement rendered the police department exempt from federal oversight. In March, Attorney General James P. McGranery issued a statement that confirmed the existence of the agreement but claimed it had already been terminated.[20] In response to the initial revelation in the newspaper, Ella Baker issued a sharply worded open letter to the mayor demanding "the immediate resignation" of the police commissioner "to save the City of New York from further disgrace."[21]

The NAACP's national office and the New York City branch co-sponsored a meeting in early February on the subject of police brutality. Representatives from about a dozen other organizations in the city were present. The group formulated a list of demands for the mayor, including the dismissal of all federal and local officials implicated in the secret agreement, an immediate and thorough review of all pending cases, the establishment of a civilian review board, and immediate public disclosure of all allegations of abuse.[22] On February 29, 1953, the New York City NAACP sponsored a mass meeting at the Friendship Baptist Church to protest police brutality. The speakers included Baker, police brutality victim Jacob Jackson, Thurgood Marshall, Rev. Thomas Kilgore, and Earl Brown, a progressive member of the New York City Council.[23] Not, surprisingly, given his appetite for attention, Adam Clayton Powell, Harlem's flamboyant black congressman, held his own rally against police brutality at the exact same time as the NAACP event. Powell's plan may have been prompted by resentment that he was not offered top billing at the NAACP-sponsored meeting. Such ego rivalries and organizational turf battles were familiar but nonetheless wearying to Baker, and her tolerance for such political theatrics lessened as the years passed.[24]

Later, in March 1953, the Patrolmen's Benevolent Association and other police organizations tried to defuse mounting criticisms by denouncing the campaign against police brutality as a "Communist plot." The NAACP was one of the main groups attacked, along with Councilman Earl Brown. Baker's blunt reply was: "No communist plot can explain away that Jacob Jackson had to undergo two brain operations . . . nor does it explain how other able-bodied persons have walked into police precincts, but had to be carried out as hospital cases."[25]

As a modest concession and halfhearted gesture to the protesters, the police commissioner announced the inauguration of antibias training for officers in order to ease tensions and reduce the chances that police would treat black suspects in a way that might be regarded as using excessive force. The training was to be overseen by a human relations committee that included citizens who were not members of the police force. Ironically, school superintendent William Jansen, with whom Baker had locked horns over racism in the educational system, headed the police reform committee.[26] Baker was not satisfied with the outcome of the campaign and was determined to keep up the pressure with a vigilant scrutiny of the police. The struggle continued to ebb and flow for some years.

Ella Baker experimented with electoral politics in the early 1950s by running unsuccessfully for the New York City Council on the Liberal Party ticket. She first ran in 1951 and lost.[27] In 1953 the slate was led by her friend Rev. James Robinson, an independent candidate for mayor.[28] In the November 1953 poll, Baker was defeated handily by Earl Brown, the incumbent, her adversary in the election but an ally in the NAACP campaign against police brutality.[29] The defeat was probably not unexpected and may have been cushioned a bit by the support of friends like the ever-loyal Pauli Murray, who sent Baker an encouraging note on the eve of the election: "just to wish you a good luck at the pools tomorrow . . . affectionately, Pauli."[30]

Ella Baker's 1953 decision to resign temporarily from the NAACP branch presidency in order to run for the New York City Council seems an aberration within a career dedicated to grassroots organizing rather than electoral politics and career politicians. Within the context of her community-based activism in New York, Baker was openly skeptical of electoral politics and career politicians. Within the context of her community-based activism in New York, however, Baker's interest in city politics makes more sense. Not only did the NAACP regularly tangle with elected officials over issues such as school segregation and police brutality, but the broad, popular participation that was characteristic of New York City politics in this period made an electoral campaign seem a logical extension of issue-oriented organizing. Baker may well have realized that she could not win at the polls. The value of the campaign lay not in a vain hope of victory but in the broad-based educational effort that running for office entailed. In the early 1950s, as in later periods, some civil rights activists saw electoral politics as simply another mode of community organizing—a way to get issues in the spotlight. While the Liberal Party's campaign platform focused on the rather tame issues of cleaning up government corruption and inefficiency, the party did include a statement in support of more educational funding (through bond sales), opposition to bigotry and hate groups, and race-relations training for police officers. These may have been some of the issues that attracted Ella Baker to the party. But she was not the only African American activist to work with the Liberal Party in the 1950s. A. Philip Randolph, the socialist labor leader with whom Baker was closely associated in the 1930s, had a brief affiliation with the party, and Pauli Murray had been a Liberal candidate for city council in 1949. Murray's and Baker's willingness to run for office on the Liberal Party ticket suggests that it offered an appealing, although imperfect, alternative to the Democratic and Republican Parties.[31] So, clearly the party embodied some of what independent black activists were looking for in this period.

The Liberal Party was founded in 1944 by David Dubinsky, the leader of the International Ladies Garment Workers Union (ILGWU), as an offshoot of the more left-leaning American Labor Party, which Ella Baker was also briefly aligned with before it split. The Liberal Party drew an odd assortment of characters, a number of whom Baker had worked with before. Jay Lovestone, with whom Baker and Murray had been associated politically during the 1930s, was working with the ILGWU during the early 1940s and was involved in the Liberal Party's formation.[32] Although there is evidence that the Liberal Party had little more than a formal commitment to racial integration, even that was unusual during the 1940s. Running African American women and men for public office represented a clear and appealing departure from politics as usual. Why Baker allied herself more with the Liberal Party than with the American Labor Party was unclear. The American Labor Party is better known in progressive circles as a serious third-party experiment that began in 1936 as a way for leftists to back President Franklin D. Roosevelt without supporting the less progressive forces in the Democratic Party. The party, founded by Dubinsky and other socialists including Frank Crosswaith, began to splinter in 1936 over the Hitler-Stalin pact and the American Communist Party's pragmatic support of that agreement. Crosswaith and others then pushed to expel Communists from the American Labor Party, but the anti-Communist faction ultimately went its own way and formed the Liberal Party.[33]

Liberal-left coalition work took on a new meaning during the postwar period, when virulent anti-Communism spread through the organized labor movement, partisan politics, the U.S. government, and even the civil rights movement. At the same time, the move away from inclusive Popular Front politics and toward a more rigid sectarian agenda on the part of the Communist Party only exacerbated the situation. Comfortable alliances among people on the left who had divergent ideologies and affiliations dissolved under the dual pressures. Some independent socialists stood by current and former Communist Party members who had organized alongside them, while others sought to distance themselves from this increasingly suspect and stigmatized group by denouncing their former co-workers and, in some cases, "naming names" to government investigators to absolve themselves.[34] A few Americans refused to be intimidated, defending civil liberties and deploring McCarthyism. Many progressives, however, were silenced by fear and confusion, failing to fully appreciate the far-reaching dangers of the House Un-American Activities Committee's witch hunts or, on the other hand, understanding the dangers quite clearly and wanting to spare themselves by pointing a finger at others.[35]

David Dubinsky and the Liberal Party openly espoused anti-Communism. According to the historian Paul Buhle, Dubinsky became "fanatically anti-Communist,"[36] and the Liberal Party eventually followed his lead. Some members collaborated with the House Un-American Activities Committee to prosecute their Communist counterparts within the United States, while simultaneously working with the CIA to undermine Communist influence abroad. Baker would have certainly been aware of these politics, and the fact that she worked closely with the Liberal Party in spite of its undemocratic politics is wholly inconsistent with the views and values she articulated a decade later. It may be that her brief association with the Liberal Party should just be seen as yet another curious example of her eclectic and sometimes unusual political ties.

Although Baker's own relationship with the Communist Party was an ambivalent one, she never collaborated with government agencies to persecute alleged Communists. Ironically, throughout the 1950s, even as she positioned herself squarely among the non-Communists, if not the anti-Communists, Baker was being kept under heavy surveillance by the FBI as a potential subversive. Informants called her home and office under false pretenses to obtain information. Her apartment was watched, her phone bill intercepted, and her bank account monitored.[37]

In the late 1950s, Baker cooperated, however reluctantly, with NAACP officials when the national organization began to purge Communists from the organization. The 1950 decision to exclude Communists on the national level was implemented by Baker's old friend J. M. Tinsley, who headed the Committee on Political Domination, the goal of which was to end alleged Communist infiltration of the organization.[38] In September 1957, while serving on the executive committee of the New York branch, Baker was asked to serve on the newly established Internal Security Committee, headed by her former Liberal Party running mate, Rev. James Robinson. The committee met on October 14 at Morningside Community Center on West 122nd Street and drafted its mission statement and its report to the branch. Although the two-page report began with the unconvincing disclaimer that it was "not a 'witch hunt' committee but a 'watch dog' committee," it proceeded to lay out a rather rigid set of criteria for membership in the branch. "No individual having any affiliation with communists within the past fifteen years should be allowed on the Executive Board," the report stated. Any nominee for the executive board would be required to provide a "written and signed statement listing all past and present affiliations," and if "any officer or member is discovered to have any connection with communism within the past 13 years [15 years stated elsewhere], or to be presently so connected, they shall be expelled from the organization."[39]

The most public ouster was that of former Harlem city councilman Ben Davis Jr., an attorney and a well-known member of the Communist Party who had served time in jail under the Smith Act; his membership fee was returned by the branch president along with a terse letter "condemning atheistic communism."[40] Other New York City branch members were quietly coerced to resign under threat of a possible committee investigation. Baker must have felt enormously torn by this decision, since it was at variance with the personal choices she made. Around the time that she served on the NAACP committee to weed out Communists, she befriended Anne Braden and Annie Stein, two reputed Communists who were also militant antiracist whites and very principled people. In the case of Braden, Baker provided moral and political support, defending Anne and her husband, Carl, against the kind of persecution that the NAACP itself was replicating on a small scale within the organization. Looking back on her role in the NAACP's Internal Security Committee years later, after the most reactionary implications of McCarthyism had played themselves out, Baker confided to her friend Joanne Grant: "I followed a national office directive to the letter, and I should not have."[41] After her involvement with the Internal Security Committee, political independence became even more critical to Ella Baker.

During the postwar years and after she left the NAACP's national office, Baker was searching for a political home, an organization that embraced a radical and egalitarian practice and vision similar to her own, but she had clearly not yet found it. Finding that political community may have taken on even greater importance to Ella Baker after the death of her beloved mother, Anna Ross Baker, in December 1954 in Littleton, North Carolina, the family homestead. Anna Baker's presence there had been anchoring forces in Ella's otherwise fairly nomadic existence. During her travels for the black cooperative movement in the 1930s and her town-by-town organization of crusades on behalf of the NAACP in the 1940s, her mother's house had been a place for respite and for recouping her energy. The house was still there, but gone from it was the woman who had nurtured her early intellectual and political consciousness, toughened her up for the world, and consoled her when that world was unkind. Baker took the long train ride home to attend her mother's funeral and put her affairs in order. She returned north soon thereafter to her second home in Harlem with a renewed resolve to carry on the work that her mother had inspired her to embark on many decades before. A critical component of that work was building political bridges between struggles in the North and the front-line struggles in the South. One such bridge was the New York–based fund-raising organization In Friendship.

In Friendship was formed as a way to funnel resources to the activists who had launched and sustained the Montgomery Bus Boycott, which began in December 1955. Only a few months before, the brutal murder of young Emmett Till by white vigilantes in the Mississippi delta had galvanized national attention and black anger. These two events—new forms of resistance coupled with the continuance of racial violence—symbolized the promise and the perils facing southern blacks in the 1950s.

Baker was an important catalyst for pulling together the individuals and organizations that comprised the In Friendship coalition in 1956. Among them were dozens of individuals whom Baker had known or worked with on other campaigns and projects over the years. They included Walter Petersen, a leader of the New York chapter of the Liberal Party; Stanley Levison, a member of the American Jewish Congress; and Rev. Thomas Kilgore, the minister at Baker's own Friendship Baptist Church in Harlem. Other Baker associates were active in supporting In Friendship: Fay Bennett of the National Sharecroppers Fund; Rae Brandstein of the National Committee for Rural Schools; Cleveland Robinson of the AFL-CIO, District 65; and Norman Thomas, the Socialist Party leader. Ella Baker served as executive secretary of the group, and A. Philip Randolph was persuaded to chair the new coalition for its first two months. The Socialist-affiliated Worker's Defense League, led by Thomas, provided temporary office space. Initially, Baker's position was unpaid, but she managed the office, handled correspondence and book-keeping, orchestrated publicity and outreach, and did virtually all the tasks necessary to keep the organization afloat. The group was eventually able to piece together a modest salary for her.

On February 29, 1956, In Friendship launched its inaugural fund-raising campaign with an "Action Conference" held at the McAlpin Hotel on Broadway and Thirty-fourth Street in Manhattan. Randolph had issued the call for the conference in a letter, dated February 17, that conveyed a sense of urgency about the situation in the South: "Reports from Mississippi indicate that the White Citizens Councils have succeeded in choking off all sources of loans and other credits on which [black] farmers depend. We must show that those who are being attacked do not stand alone in their fight for decency."[42] He noted in passing the occurrence of a similar conference being convened in Washington, D.C., by Oscar Lee and Roy Wilkins. Randolph commented casually that the event would "add impetus to our work in this area," glossing over the competition implicit in the simultaneous formation of two organizations to serve the same purpose.[43]

Despite the strong commitment and good intentions of its founders, In Friendship had difficulties getting off the ground. Randolph abruptly resigned as chairman of the organizations shortly after its formation and before the New York fund-raiser even took place. He claimed that he was overextended in his obligations and felt it would be inappropriate for him to solicit funds on behalf of In Friendship, since he had already done so recently on behalf of other organizations. It is possible that something else may have prompted Randolph's action, since he was well aware of the existence of competing organizations from the outset, as indicated by his February 17 letter. Perhaps he was persuaded by colleagues in more established organizations to withdraw his support from the nascent group, or perhaps he feared that such an endorsement could become a political liability in his relationships with other groups. Since the initial supporters of In Friendship believed that a roster of prominent sponsors was necessary to give the group credibility, Randolph's resignation came as a particularly sharp blow. In a March 8, 1956, letter to Randolph, Norman Thomas pleaded with him to reconsider his decision, saying that it would "almost wreck a pretty promising beginning at worthwhile work."[44] Randolph resigned anyway. Perhaps in tribute to his long-standing friendship with and respect for Ella Baker, perhaps in order to exert some control over the campaign, he continued to work with the group after he stepped down as chair.

The founders of In Friendship were painfully aware of the competition and tensions with preexisting civil rights organizations, much of which arose from political turf battles and the clash of overinflated egos. Since a number of organizations were already engaged in similar efforts, the founders sought to avoid the appearance of needless duplication. As Fay Bennett of the National Sharecroppers Fund emphasized in a 1956 letter to Norman Thomas, "It should be made clear at the beginning that the contemplated work of the committee [In Friendship] will be handled through existing machinery and that its primary purpose, at least in its initial stages, would be to stimulate efforts on the part of other organizations to help those in the South who need help and in other ways to make an impact on the situation."[45] Despite In Friendship's attempts to avoid rivalry with other organizations, some prominent civil rights figures were still reluctant to view the group as an umbrella fund-raiser for the movement as a whole.

In the spring of 1956, three In Friendship leaders, including Baker, worked nearly full time for six weeks building for a mammoth civil rights rally that was held in Madison Square Garden in May. The other principal sponsor of the event was Randolph's Brotherhood of Sleeping Car Porters. Leaders of In Friendship naturally assumed that they would process all funds raised by the event, since they had formed the umbrella organization meant to pull together everyone else's efforts in civil rights activism. However, A. Philip Randolph had a different idea. As one of the top union officials involved, he opted to set up a separate special committee to direct, monitor, and dispense funds raised by the AFL-CIO. The committee was to have two labor representatives, handpicked by the head of the AFL-CIO, George Meany; representatives from several other organizations; and a single delegate from In Friendship. Although In Friendship acquiesced to the decision, it was clearly a slap in the face, given the organization's initiative in coordinating precisely the kind of tasks to be handled by the new special committee. Nevertheless, Randolph's powerful stature and the relative newness of In Friendship prompted the group not to openly criticize or oppose the decision. In fact, Ella Baker was at the July 11 meeting in Randolph's office when the new formation was set up. Not wanting to be divisive at the expense of the group's larger goals, she went along with Randolph's move, conceding that it was "understandable that the unions were reluctant to funnel moneys through an organization as young and untested as In Friendship," and In Friendship would willingly participate as one member of the larger committee.[46] The final insult was that the labor representatives on the committee would have veto power over all funding decisions, rendering the In Friendship forces fairly marginal to the whole deliberative process. These events illustrate the internal tensions, hierarchies, and competition for leadership that existed within the early civil rights movement, even among its northern supporters.

The conflict between In Friendship and the union leaders also illustrates the reluctance of established leaders to relinquish any of their power to, or even make room for, upstart organizations. Baker encountered this problem repeatedly over the years. National leaders in civil rights and other fields were protective of their prominence and status as the "official" spokespersons for their respective constituencies. Baker was vividly impressed by the deleterious effects of such rivalries and the stifling and coercive nature of the relationship between junior and senior partners in coalitions. She carried these memories with her into the political work she did in subsequent years. In particular, they shaped her desire to be vehemently protective of the independence and autonomy of the Student Nonviolent Coordinating Committee when it was founded a few years later. She defended the young militants' right to make their own decisions, despite their youthful inexperience, in the face of annexation attempts by some of Baker's well-established colleagues.

Difficulties and tensions with allies notwithstanding, the small core of In Friendship supporters persevered and made some important contributions. Randolph's resignation and his bid to control fund-raising did not "wreck" the organization, as Thomas had feared. In December 1956, In Friendship hosted its second successful fund-raiser, a major concert at the Manhattan Center featuring Coretta Scott King, Harry Belafonte, Duke Ellington, and others to commemorate the first anniversary of the Montgomery boycott. The event raised $1,800, an appreciable sum at the time. Part of the proceeds went to support the organizing efforts of the Montgomery Improvement Association, the main community group that emerged from the boycott. Funds were also set aside for other grassroots struggles as well. Specifically, In Friendship provided funds to two groups of black tenant farmers who were evicted from their plantations in Clarendon County, South Carolina, and Yazoo, Mississippi, because of their involvement in civil rights activities. The activists in these communities had tried to test the victory of the 1954 *Brown* decision by enrolling their children in previously all-white schools and had suffered harsh economic reprisals as a result.[47]

Civil rights campaigns in places like Yazoo and Clarendon County did not receive the widespread news coverage that the Montgomery campaign did, so the grassroots activists in these rural communities lacked the margin of protection that national media attention and sympathetic support from outsiders might have provided. Throughout the South, civil rights activists who were poor, poorly educated, and economically vulnerable were easy targets for retribution, for which they often had no recourse. In Friendship provided assistance to the grassroots leaders whom Ella Baker saw as the very backbone of the Black Freedom movement; they were likely, in her view, to be pivotal actors in whatever struggles were to emerge in the years ahead.

Baker's concept of progressive leadership was leadership that helped people to help themselves and allowed ordinary people to feel that they could determine their own future. When she lent her energies to In Friendship, her mission was grassroots empowerment, to tap and build on the activist spirit that the Montgomery boycott had unleashed and to nurture and encourage the emergence of strong indigenous leadership in communities throughout the South. That mission was an extension of the objectives she had worked toward in the NAACP during the 1940s. She not only wanted In Friendship to provide funds to meet the material needs of suffering families; she also wanted it to pay for local leaders to attend conferences, meetings, and workshops, which would boost their confidence as organizers and give them intellectual perspectives and tactical ammunition for the struggles they were engaged in. In other words, Baker believed in the adage that it is more important to teach people to fish and farm than simply to give them food. The funds that In Friendship raised were, in Baker's view, leadership development funds, not simply relief funds. For example, in the summer of 1956, while attending the annual NAACP conference in San Francisco, she learned about forty black farmers who were trying to form an agricultural cooperative. Instead of providing a direct grant to the co-op, Baker wanted the farmers to get a better sense of the scope and history of the cooperative movement, so she arranged to have In Friendship pay for a representative of the group, Orsey Malone, to attend a Cooperative Institute being held at Bard College in New York later that year.[48] Such inclusive politics and broad objectives differentiated In Friendship from a number of other support organizations.

In Friendship lasted officially for about three years and provided much-needed resources to sustain activists on the front lines of the southern battle against racism, but ultimately it could not sustain itself. As the civil rights movement grew in visibility and importance, larger organizations stepped in to offer funds, although sometimes with ulterior motives and camouflaged agendas. But the start-up and survival funds that In Friendship provided in the immediate wake of the Montgomery Bus Boycott were crucial. Even before its demise, its three founders—Bayard Rustin, Stanley Levison, and Baker—had begun to redirect their energies from fund-raising to direct consultation with movement leaders in the

South, namely, Dr. King and the emergent Southern Christian Leadership Conference.

From the very outset, Baker was thinking of ways she could get closer to the action, confiding to her friend and pastor Rev. Kilgore that she was literally "chafing at the bit to be down there as a part of the struggle."[49] Throughout the 1940s and 1950s, Baker was deeply engaged in local political struggles in New York around issues near and dear to her heart, but the new sparks of protest in Montgomery were too important to ignore. That potential ultimately inspired her to return to the South and resume the intense pace of organizing that had characterized her years with the NAACP during the 1940s.

3

"Taxation without Sanitation Is Tyranny": Civil Rights Struggles over Garbage Collection in Brooklyn, New York, during the Fall of 1962

BRIAN PURNELL

During the early 1960s, many residents of Bedford-Stuyvesant saw the neighborhood's filthy streets as a sign of their community's low status in New York City. The trash that accumulated on sidewalks and in streets crowded public space with its bulk and its stench. Children had to play around abandoned cars. Pedestrians on their way home from work dodged rats and vermin that darted from the asphalt to alleyways where bags of uncollected household garbage sat festering, sometimes for days at a time. Over the years, residents periodically complained to elected officials and appointees to the city's sanitation department, but the problem only worsened. Bedford-Stuyvesant inhabitants even organized periodic neighborhood cleanups through local block associations.[1] Their efforts brought temporary relief to certain areas but failed to remedy completely the overall problem. At its root, the abundance of garbage was linked to the scarcity of resources in this overcrowded residential area: Bedford-Stuyvesant required increased garbage collection and the city did not provide it. That this was a neighborhood with one of *the* fastest growing black populations in the entire city added a racial insult to an already odoriferous injury.

As the historians Harold Connolly, Clarence Taylor, and Craig Wilder and others have meticulously shown, Bedford-Stuyvesant was a community shaped by two different histories: the hope and optimism of its working-class families, of which blacks were at one point one group among many, and the racial ideologies and policies that slowly made the community an overcrowded, economically stagnant, and racially segregated black neighborhood. Over the course of the nineteenth century, transportation developments in the form of rail lines and trolley cars that crisscrossed Brooklyn's north-central thoroughfares transformed the area from a sleepy farmland hamlet to a bedroom community for working- and middle-class families. Irish, German, Scottish, and Dutch settlers, along with a sizable community of people of African descent, labored in Kings County's downtown business and commercial districts centered on the waterfront. African Americans made their home in the towns of Bedford and Stuyvesant Heights. During the antebellum period, black people established two independent communities in Bedford: Carrville, founded in 1832, and Weeksville, founded in 1838. Bedford's population continued to soar after construction of the Brooklyn Bridge was completed in 1883, and the nation's first elevated railroad stations stretched across Brooklyn in 1885. By the 1920s, the neighborhoods Bedford and Stuyvesant Heights were known as Bedford-Stuyvesant; and throughout the 1940s the neighborhood was racially integrated (49 percent white and 51 percent black), one of the few communities in New York City where African Americans and black immigrants from islands such as Barbados, Trinidad, and Jamaica purchased their own homes.[2]

All of that changed during the 1950s and 1960s. Economic and political policies that went into effect during the New Deal played on racial fears and prejudices, which caused middle- and working-class whites to abandon the community. Discriminatory policies that "redlined" the neighborhood were sanctioned by banks and real estate agencies under the banner of New Deal homeowners' development programs in the 1930s. They made it impossible for Bedford-Stuyvesant residents to finance home-improvement projects. Realtors practiced "blockbusting" tactics, which reaped handsome profits for them as they contributed to the deterioration of the neighborhood's housing. Real estate agents played on racial fears and plummeting real estate prices to convince white homeowners to sell their property. The area's brownstone and limestone houses became carved up into three, sometimes four apartments. On top of that, in other parts of Brooklyn, bigots refused to rent apartments or sell homes to blacks, which would have relieved overcrowding in the neighborhood and alleviated the strain on its housing stock. From the 1950s through 1960, Bedford-Stuyvesant quickly became the largest black neighborhood in Brooklyn, and by 1970 it was one of the most populous black urban areas in the United States.[3]

Bedford-Stuyvesant received some of the poorest levels of service from the city, especially in the area of garbage collection. Abandoned cars, rusted and stripped of their usable parts, were permanent fixtures on blocks. Abandoned empty iceboxes and refrigerators, death traps for youngsters, remained in vacant lots, even after residents made repeated calls to Department of Sanitation officials to have them removed. Bedford-Stuyvesant's garbage resulted in foul odors, attracted all kinds of vermin, and produced widespread filth, assaulting the senses and threatening health. When city government seemed reluctant to do anything about the situation, many residents in the community argued it was because the area's residents were overwhelmingly black and poor.

During the summer and fall of 1962, members of the Brooklyn chapter of the Congress of Racial Equality (CORE), which was one of the most active civil rights organizations in the borough, chose to address this issue. After two years of leading dynamic campaigns in Brooklyn against racial discrimination in housing and employment, Brooklyn CORE's interracial membership was ready to employ innovative nonviolent tactics to redress Bedford-Stuyvesant's "garbage problem." The chapter had already established its reputation as an activist organization through an aggressive campaign against landlords who discriminated against African Americans, which culminated in a lengthy assault against one of New York City's largest housing conglomerate, the Lefrak Corporation. Brooklyn CORE also made national headlines when it staged a dramatic demonstration during a campaign against employment discrimination at the Ebinger's Baking Company. In the Ebinger's protest, Brooklyn CORE members sat in front of delivery trucks and blocked them from exiting the bakery's depot, a tactic that broke the chapter's deadlocked negotiations with Ebinger's managers and helped win assurances from the company that it would immediately hire more black workers.[4] By addressing the garbage issues in Brooklyn's largest black neighborhood, Brooklyn CORE continued to make its mark as one of New York City's most recognizable grassroots activist organizations. The chapter already had a reputation for successfully turning everyday local political concerns into hot-button civil rights issues, and drawing attention to the problem of inadequate garbage collection in Bedford-Stuyvesant was a logical project for this small, audacious group of activists.

With its campaign against inadequate sanitation services in Bedford-Stuyvesant, Brooklyn CORE took its fight directly to the highest seat of political power in the city. Bedford-Stuyvesant residents elected representatives to the city council and the state assembly, but the mayor and his appointees in the Department of Sanitation controlled citywide garbage collection policies and only City Hall had the power to remedy problems with sanitation services. Still, the chapter pressed borough-level politicians to advocate for better services in Bedford-Stuyvesant, which helped gain publicity for the cause. Brooklyn CORE also hoped that everyday people in Bedford-Stuyvesant might become emboldened by a community-wide effort that fought City Hall for improvements in their quality of life. Chapter leaders imagined that mobilization around this issue would spark a wider movement against local forms of racial discrimination. Dubbed "Operation Clean Sweep," the campaign was a test of Brooklyn CORE's ambitiousness and creativity.

Moreover, Operation Clean Sweep challenged the mettle of Brooklyn CORE's members. Would they have the resolve to continue using non-violent, direct-action protest to fight against racial injustice even as they faced seemingly insurmountable obstacles? Operation Clean Sweep revealed how easily those in positions of power could use "culture of poverty" arguments to explain Bedford-Stuyvesant's poor sanitation conditions. These tactics absolved politicians of any responsibility for the neighborhood's inadequate services and deflected the onus back onto the very citizens who were forced to suffer the everyday effects of living in neighborhoods overrun by garbage. Blaming excess trash on poor people instead of inadequate policies also justified the continued practice of diverting resources away from communities that, over the years, had become the most in need of improved services and the most severely neglected by elected officials. In many ways, Operation Clean Sweep revealed one of the most imposing foes that civil rights activists in New York City faced in many of their campaigns during the early 1960s: an entrenched government bureaucracy shaped by influential power brokers, machine politicians, and political appointees who were largely unresponsive to the demands of poor and working-class communities for improved services. Instead of instituting policies that resulted in immediate and tangible changes in the quality of life in the city's emerging minority ghettos, politicians and power brokers often blamed problems that stemmed from racial discrimination and structural inequality on the behavior and culture of black and Puerto Rican citizens themselves.

This blame-the-victim understanding of urban racial inequality has also shaped the historiography of the civil rights movement. Because they lived in states with liberal antidiscrimination laws, urban blacks of the post-WWII period have been thought of as less susceptible than African Americans in the South to Jim Crow–style racism. Northern segregation was seen as benign, and even innocent or unavoidable, when compared to its southern counterpart. This distinction caused many movement contemporaries, and later scholars, to characterize the civil rights movement as a southern phenomenon that wiped away vestiges of racism from regions of the nation plagued by histories of racial slavery and legalized racial segregation. When historians began to write the history of the civil rights movement, northern racism and struggles against it were ignored, omitted, and forgotten. Historian Matthew Lassiter has argued that this "southern exceptionalist," view of American racism and "the de jure / de facto dichotomy trapped the black freedom struggle within a discourse of regional difference," meaning that civil rights struggles were southern by nature because the South was so out of step with the rest of the country. The nation needed national civil rights legislation, Lassiter points out, precisely because the South was thought to be so different from the North, and the South needed to catch up with the liberal consensus that shaped the rest of the country. Jeanne Theoharis has contended that the de jure / de facto formulations "naturalize the Northern racial order as *not* a racial system like the South's but one operating on class and culture with racial discrimination as a byproduct." For decades, these ideas effectively excluded postwar urban black political struggles from narratives of African American civil rights movements.[5]

The story of Operation Clean Sweep fills a gap in our knowledge of the post-WWII black freedom struggle by showing how civil rights history and racial discrimination were never confined to the South. Increasingly, academics, journalists, and public historians are highlighting the history of the northern, midwestern, and West Coast civil rights movements, and stretching the chronological parameters of the movements' histories backward to the Depression era and immediate postwar years of political organizing for increased black employment and housing opportunities, and forward to the late 1960s and 1970s advancements in urban black politics, pushes for affirmative action, and Great Society community development initiatives. Combined with the rich scholarship on local people and the role of armed self-defense in the South, these new histories will fundamentally alter our understanding of what the civil rights movement accomplished, the multiple social and cultural factors that influenced its participants' political ideas and social movement ideologies, who its principal actors were on both the national and the local levels, and what work still needs to be finished to reconstitute American democracy in the aftermath of its long history of slavery and racial segregation.[6]

But this revision of civil rights history carries a caveat: Readers who imagine that they will find a recapitulation of the southern movement in a northern urban setting need to adjust their notions of the movement's successes and failures, its leadership and grassroots participants. Jacquelyn Dowd Hall reminds us that "the dominant narrative of the civil rights movement . . . distorts and suppresses as much as it reveals."[7] Images of civil rights icons leading thousands of nonviolent participants into the jaws of police dogs and actions that inspired elected officials to pass monumental national legislation or forced segregationists to alter local Jim Crow policies in public places, do not appear in a place like Brooklyn, New York. In fact, the dominance of such narratives prevents us from appreciating the lessons that Brooklyn's civil rights history offers us, namely that one of the main challenges activists faced in the Jim Crow North was convincing elected officials, newspaper editorialists, and the masses of citizens that racial discrimination existed, and that discriminatory treatment of black individuals and communities created enclaves of second-class citizenship throughout America's liberal cosmopolitan cities. "Whites only" signs did not need to hang in public spaces for racial discrimination to be a powerful influence on political and social life.

That a small interracial group of activists in Brooklyn CORE orchestrated a dramatic nonviolent protest against patterns of racial discrimination in the city's sanitation services and generated noticeable media attention for this issue is indeed noteworthy. Such moments deserve examination, analysis, and, eventually, incorporation into the larger narrative of the nation's struggle for equality. We do ourselves a disservice if we romanticize this (or any) episode of civil rights movement history. But we also diminish our ability to learn from the past if we overlook or devalue Operation Clean Sweep and similar campaigns merely because they do not resemble our conventional understanding of the movement's successes, its heroic phases, and its principle leaders and participants.

The number of daily sanitation pickups in Bedford-Stuyvesant did not increase from the 1940s to the 1960s, a time when its population exploded and became overwhelmingly African American.[8] Over ten years before Brooklyn CORE began Operation Clean Sweep, citizens in Bedford-Stuyvesant complained to the Department of Sanitation and the mayor about the infrequent garbage collection. While investigating the problem during the spring of 1962, Brooklyn CORE chairman Oliver Leeds met with members of a block association in Bedford-Stuyvesant, who showed him a community newsletter from World War II that reported the sanitation department's wartime cutbacks in service to the neighborhood from six to three days. The cutback services were never restored after the war.[9]

The newsletter detailed how in November 1950, the sanitation committee of Bedford-Stuyvesant Neighborhood Council (BSNC) met with Commissioner Mulrain of the New York City Department of Sanitation and requested daily garbage collection in Bedford-Stuyvesant along with a change in the sanitation department's classification of the neighborhood. The sanitation department classified Bedford-Stuyvesant as a neighborhood of one- and two-family houses. Representatives from the BSNC informed Commissioner Mulrain that three or more families occupied most of the homes in the area. The committee also reported on the accumulation of "rubbish of all sorts" in the neighborhood's streets and argued that Bedford-Stuyvesant's garbage problem "requires attention not inherent in the physical size of the area." Commissioner Mulrain conceded that the group raised a valid issue with implications for other parts of Brooklyn, too, but he could not promise to increase garbage collection in Bedford-Stuyvesant. Commissioner Mulrain and the BSNC agreed that the neighborhood could expect "a steady improvement which should result in a cleaner neighborhood," but both recognized that there were factors at work beyond the department's control, namely, "the human element that is inherent and must be considered in matters such as these." Mulrain and the BSNC members recognized they could never completely stop people from littering. Both parties conceded that the "human element" would always affect the environmental conditions of urban neighborhoods, no matter what the Department of Sanitation did.[10]

Still, if people's behavior produced the trash, city government's policies did nothing to stop it from accumulating in Bedford-Stuyvesant's streets. By the 1960s the situation had worsened. Since about half of Brooklyn CORE's members lived in other parts of the borough and received different types of sanitation services, some blacks and whites within the chapter began to argue that Bedford-Stuyvesant's problems with garbage were brought on by discriminatory treatment. Arnold Goldwag, a part-time student at Brooklyn College who was in his early twenties when he joined Brooklyn CORE and became the chapter's community relations director, had a basement apartment in the Marine Park section of Brooklyn. He remembered the stark contrast in sanitation services between the two neighborhoods. Marine Park was predominantly white and composed of one- and two-family detached homes, each with small front lawns or backyard areas. In Marine Park, garbage was collected "at like six o'clock in the evening every single day," Goldwag remembered, "unlike Bedford-Stuyvesant, where it was twice a week," which did not meet the community's needs. "For the population in Bedford-Stuyvesant they should pick it up maybe (every) three hours, 'round the clock, compared to Marine Park," which had many fewer residents. Goldwag's memory slightly distorted the facts. Bedford-Stuyvesant received three-days-a-week garbage collection service and one of those days was supposed to be reserved for bulk trash, which included large items like refrigerators, scrap metal, and furniture. But since his work with Brooklyn CORE allowed him to travel around the borough, Goldwag knew that the neighborhood's garbage problem had less to do with residents' behavior and more to do with city policies: "Bedford-Stuyvesant, and some poor white areas, got [collection] twice a week if they were lucky, so the streets were always dirty, of course, because the garbage always overflowed."[11]

Following CORE's guidelines, an interracial team from Brooklyn CORE investigated the problem and scheduled negotiations with city officials. Goldwag, who was white, along with other chapter members such as Robert Law, a young African American college student, and Marjorie Leeds, a white woman who cut her political teeth in the Communist Party's Popular Front movements of the mid-1940s, compiled statistics on demographics and housing conditions in neighborhoods that received five- and three-day collection and contrasted those figures with conditions in Bedford-Stuyvesant. Their research indicated that Bedford-Stuyvesant had more people and poorer quality housing than other areas in their survey, even areas that received three-day garbage service.

Using data from the 1960 U.S. Census, Brooklyn CORE determined that areas with five-day collection were predominantly white and had lower housing densities. Besides Bedford-Stuyvesant, all other neighborhoods with three-day collection were largely white, with a black population of only 4.1 percent, and considerably lower housing densities. Compared with these communities, Bedford-Stuyvesant had almost

double the amount of housing, and 19.1 percent of Bedford-Stuyvesant's housing had over 1.01 persons per room, compared with 10 percent in all other areas that received three-day collection services.
Housing conditions in Bedford-Stuyvesant also contrasted sharply with
other neighborhoods that received three-day service. Only 75 percent
of Bedford-Stuyvesant's housing was classified as "sound," while 90
percent of housing was "sound" in all other neighborhoods with three-
day service. In Bedford-Stuyvesant, 18.6 percent of housing was "dete-
riorating," and 5.6 percent was "dilapidated," versus 8.6 percent and
1.4 percent respectively in all other areas with three-day service. The
data confirmed Brooklyn CORE's suspicion that there was a connection between Bedford-Stuyvesant's environmental conditions—
namely, its overcrowded housing and unsanitary conditions and its
insufficient collection services from the Department of Sanitation—
and its large, growing black population.[12]

At the start of their campaign, Brooklyn CORE members wanted
to address all the beleaguered community's social troubles. Bedford-
Stuyvesant's environmental problems, members of Brooklyn CORE
argued, went beyond infrequent sanitation collection and poor housing. The neighborhood suffered from poor city services, crime, under-
resourced public schools, joblessness, overcrowding, drugs, serious
housing deficiencies, and general neglect by landlords and residents.
Residents of Bedford-Stuyvesant, such as Rita Heinegg, who grew up
on Nostrand Avenue near Fulton Street, experienced these issues as a
part of their everyday lives.

Mrs. Heinegg's family was typical of the African Americans who came
to Bedford-Stuyvesant in the postwar period. Shortly after Heinegg's
birth in October 1944, her parents, who left school after the third grade,
quit farming in Seaboard, North Carolina, a small town near the Virginia
border, for work in New York City. Barred from the longshoremen's
industry by discriminatory unions, Rita Heinegg's father found similar
work loading and unloading cargo with the Pennsylvania Railroad.
Work in the "steamer doors," as Rita Heinegg remembers, was reserved
for blacks, who "did the same job" as longshoremen, "just for less
money." Rita Heinegg's mother found work in Brooklyn as a domestic.
She also worked in a local sweater factory and as a babysitter. The family
moved to Bedford-Stuyvesant in 1945, where for fourteen years they
lived on the top floor of a three-floor walk-up. Excessive trash was only
one of the things Rita Heinegg remembered about the neighborhood in
the late 1950s and early 1960s. "It wasn't a very nice neighborhood,"

she recalled. "You would wake up in the morning and we were seeing needles in the stairwell." To avoid embarrassment about where the family lived and to enroll the children in a better public school, Rita Heinegg's mother lied about their address. "We used to use our aunt's address so that we didn't go to P.S. 3, which was only two blocks away. She lived right outside Gates Avenue. It wasn't much better. It was still only a few blocks away but my mother felt that there was a little bit better school."[13]

Arnold Goldwag echoed these observations. He spent a great deal of time in Bedford-Stuyvesant on investigations of housing discrimination and illegal evictions and recalled how drug users and negligent landlords contributed to the problems caused by excessive garbage in the streets. Goldwag remembers how residents avoided junkies and rats that lurked in alleys by way of the "airmail express": "The landlord would not provide covers for the garbage cans. Now there were hot and cold running junkies, there were all kinds of things happening in the streets, and there were rats and cats in with the garbage. Well, why would you send your kids down five flights to put garbage next to an open can, and risk whatever? You open the window and it's the airmail express. It comes right down and splatters by where the garbage is. So one thing leads to the other."[14]

Indeed, garbage was just one of many environmental issues that affected everyday life in Bedford-Stuyvesant. Through investigating irregular garbage collection, Brooklyn CORE leaders began to recognize limitations in the fight against racial discrimination on a case-by-case basis. Oliver Leeds (who, like his wife, had a radical political background) was African American of West Indian background and the chairperson of Brooklyn CORE. He remembered when National CORE director James Farmer attended a Brooklyn CORE meeting as a guest speaker and Marjorie Leeds questioned him on the usefulness of individual protest campaigns. "Marge said to him, 'Look, where we are going with all these discrimination cases? The problems in Bedford-Stuyvesant are community-wide problems. They're not just the case of some landlord, or even an Ebinger store. The city is discriminating against this community.' "[15]

Until then, National CORE and CORE chapters throughout the country usually organized demonstrations with one clearly defined objective: desegregate a restaurant, or a pool; end race-based employment discrimination at a local business; or, with the Freedom Rides, force state compliance with federal laws. Brooklyn CORE argued that

Bedford-Stuyvesant's problems with sanitation collection were endemic social ills that both the city and local residents were responsible for correcting. Brooklyn CORE would mobilize the community to demand equal treatment from the city and, in the process, organize residents to take charge of their neighborhood's improvement. Although such an approach was uncommon for CORE, Farmer did not protest. "James Farmer said he was tickled pink that we would take on the city," remembers Leeds.[16]

Taking on the city began with a letter-writing campaign throughout the spring and summer of 1962. Marjorie and Oliver Leeds contacted the mayor's Rent and Rehabilitation Administration in April 1962 and petitioned for a variety of improvements on Gates Avenue between Broadway and Bedford Avenue, which covered an entire residential section running across Bedford-Stuyvesant. "This area," they wrote, was "completely and physically run down." Electrical fires occurred frequently in the winter because of old wiring in overcrowded buildings. They characterized garbage collection and street and sidewalk cleaning as "BAD." Houses on the block were in a "complete state of disrepair," and there was almost a "complete lack of recreational facilities in schools and [the] neighborhood." Street lighting was poor on Gates Avenue, which also had old, rusted traffic signs and inadequate police protection around the local school, P.S. 129. Marjorie Leeds was president of P.S. 129's Parent-Teacher Association and knew the school's needs. Enrollment, they wrote, was "100% de facto segregated," which affected the caliber of its teachers. "Poor conditions of the neighborhood," Marjorie argued in the petition, "leads [sic] to difficulties in staffing the schools."[17]

At the end of the letter, Marjorie and Oliver offered a two-part solution. First, the city should declare the area a " 'Special Service Area' for emergency rehabilitation" and have "all city agencies concerned move in for an 'Operation Cleanup.' " Then, the city was to provide people on Gates Avenue with "new housing in [the] neighborhood." Residents should not be evicted during Operation Cleanup. Instead, the Leedses suggested inhabitants have access to new housing regardless of income, marital status, or whether they were on welfare. "We regard this as essential," they underscored, "if the city is not to merely transfer these people to another ghetto slum area." The petition concluded with requests for "consideration and action" and an "early response." City Hall gave neither, and the summer passed without officials taking any "action" to correct these problems.[18]

In late August, Brooklyn CORE formed a delegation on sanitation conditions in the Bedford-Stuyvesant area and scheduled an appointment with Mayor Wagner's Citizen Complaint Office for August 24, 1962. This group included Vincent Young, a middle-aged African American city bus driver, and three young black college students: Audrey Law, Audrey Steward, and James Steward. When administrators in the mayor's Citizen Complaint Office tried to bury the issue by referring CORE's prepared statement to other departments, Audrey Steward demanded that the delegation be allowed to discuss the situation with someone in authority. The secretary for the Citizen Complaint Office called the Department of Sanitation's main office and made an immediate appointment for the group. Before leaving, the CORE representatives left a statement with the mayor's office demanding action by September 8, 1962, or else they would move ahead with their plans for direct-action protest.[19]

The delegation's statement differed from Oliver and Marjorie Leeds's earlier letter because it concentrated only on the problems of excess garbage and dilapidated sidewalks. Brooklyn CORE members realized they had to make their demands realistic and concentrate on one issue if they hoped to have any success petitioning city officials. Gates Avenue between Broadway and Bedford Avenue, they declared, had become "the most depressed street in the Bedford-Stuyvesant community . . . a completely rundown and filthy thoroughfare." Sidewalks were in disrepair and streets were constantly littered. Moreover, Brooklyn CORE charged that "the collection of garbage by the sanitation department is disgracefully inadequate." Sanitation inspectors did not enforce minimal standards, which allowed landlords to neglect their buildings' upkeep, and garbage collectors left lots, alleys, and stairwells filled with "discarded furniture and other refuse." Parent-Teacher Associations and block associations had previously brought this issue to the attention of city authorities, to no avail. Brooklyn CORE exclaimed that "this disgraceful situation" was "something that can only happen in a ghetto" and was caused by discriminatory treatment. The petition concluded with a request for "emergency measures," like daily collection of garbage, enforcement of sanitary regulations, and immediate repair of sidewalks, "no later than September 8, 1962."[20]

At the commissioner of sanitation's office, the delegation met with Henry Liebman and Marty O'Connell of the Community Relations Department, who assured them that the Department of Sanitation had requested funds for increased pickup service in Bedford-Stuyvesant.

They also confirmed what Brooklyn CORE already knew from its investigation: that because of difficulties maintaining trucks during World War II, the city instituted an "austerity" program and cut back from six-day to five-day pickup services in some parts of the city and to three-day pickup services in others, depending on the area's population.

In a condescending manner, Liebman suggested that Brooklyn CORE "form a committee to make the area 'cooperative' with the sanitation department" because the districts had orders to pick up any trash they saw on the street. He asked the delegates to "survey the district and report any filled lots." The city would clean them right away and issue summonses to owners of private lots who neglected the upkeep of their property. Liebman rejected the idea that trash baskets on each corner would lessen the amount of garbage in streets and on sidewalks, because, as he put it, "people misuse them."²¹ Exactly how they would misuse the trash baskets Liebman did not say. Most likely, he feared a spike in reported cases of people using the bins to start fires for warmth in the winter, or juveniles kicking them over for fun. In a neighborhood with such poor housing and so few recreation facilities, some residents misappropriated garbage baskets in these ways, which exacerbated environmental problems. Still, those issues did not cause Bedford-Stuyvesant's garbage problem, and Brooklyn CORE's sanitation delegation resented Liebman's attempt to blame the people in the community for his department's negligence.

Marjorie Leeds could not contain her anger. She exploded in the middle of Liebman's explanations with complaints about the horrendous sanitation service on her block. Oliver and Marjorie Leeds lived in Bedford-Stuyvesant at the time. They rented a small apartment in a brownstone at 272 Van Buren Street that belonged to Oliver's mother. The Leedses lived at the corner of Lewis Avenue, which was directly in the middle of Bedford and Broadway and four blocks north of Gates Avenue. Conditions on their street reflected the problems in the rest of the neighborhood. The sanitation officials, hoping they could distract the delegation from demanding widespread service changes, tried to redirect the rest of the conversation to Mrs. Leeds's situation, but she remained steadfast. "That was not what the delegation had come for," she reminded the officials. "We came about the dirty conditions throughout Bedford-Stuyvesant." James Steward then showed photographs of the conditions in the neighborhood—empty refrigerators, broken-down cars, heaps of rusty metal and splintered debris, children playing near caved-in sidewalks—and demanded action before September 8. The delegation left and went to Borough Hall in Brooklyn to try to see the borough president, Abe Stark. They were denied a meeting. They left a copy of their petition and requested an appointment before their deadline passed.[22]

September 8, 1962, was the scheduled date for Operation Clean Sweep. If there were no improvements in services by ten in the morning, Brooklyn CORE would mobilize citizens in Bedford-Stuyvesant to take matters into their own hands. Brooklyn CORE prepared for Operation Clean Sweep the week of September 1 by distributing leaflets in the neighborhood that summarized CORE's stalled talks with the city and announced the chapter's plans to stage a community demonstration the following week. They were purposefully vague in their descriptions of Operation Clean Sweep's details. Publicizing Brooklyn CORE's plans would have attracted unwanted attention from the police, who might have tried to thwart the action by arresting key members of Brooklyn CORE's leadership for planning an unsanctioned demonstration or illegal dumping. Also, according to Robert Law, some members of Brooklyn CORE suspected there were police informants in their ranks. To ensure there were no problems, organizers of Operation Clean Sweep kept secret the specific details of the action. They did not discuss where they planned to dump the trash at general meetings, so even some chapter veterans remained in the dark.[23]

Brooklyn borough president Abe Stark called for a meeting with chapter representatives on September 7, 1962, the day before CORE planned to implement Operation Clean Sweep. Members of Brooklyn CORE's Public Relations Committee met to speak with him about the unsanitary conditions of the Bedford-Stuyvesant Community, which they argued reflected "the woeful neglect of this area" by city and borough leaders. The committee reiterated the main arguments about infrequent garbage collection and emphasized that "this situation is a menace to the health and welfare of the residents . . . as well as degrading to them." At the same time, they again argued that infrequent garbage collection was part of larger community-wide problems brought on by "years of neglect."

Using Gates Avenue as an example, they complained to Stark that the area suffered from slum housing; inadequate transportation; segregated and overcrowded schools; a lack of nurseries, playgrounds, and libraries; unemployment; inadequate traffic lights and, of course, poor sanitation. The representatives assured Stark that Brooklyn CORE would remain interested and involved in the area's rehabilitation "until the Bedford-Stuyvesant community becomes a neighborhood to be very proud of instead of the eyesore that it is now."[24]

Stark promised to intercede with the Department of Sanitation on Brooklyn CORE's behalf and bring about a speedy resolution to this situation, but his timing for meeting with Brooklyn CORE was suspect. Most likely, Stark wanted to stall Operation Clean Sweep more than he wanted to improve conditions in Bedford-Stuyvesant. Residents of Bedford-Stuyvesant had practically no political clout. The neighborhood was not a tourist district that generated large revenues. Its citizens were not wealthy or well organized into political patronage clubs. This was one of the poorest areas with some of the highest crime rates in the city. In the eyes of politicians up for reelection or reappointment, monies that could have been put toward rehabilitating Bedford-Stuyvesant were probably better spent in districts that had more political and economic power.

Still, the delay in action did not last long. Brooklyn CORE moved quickly after it received the Department of Sanitation's response to the chapter's leafleting drive. Henry Liebman wrote a letter to the Brooklyn chapter explaining that Bedford-Stuyvesant was in the "alternate parking program," which meant that streets received machine cleaning service three days a week and garbage collection the other three days a week, so technically, the area received six-day sanitation service. Liebman noted that he would pass Brooklyn CORE's complaints along to area supervisors, who would ensure that "corrective measures be taken wherever necessary to maintain street cleanliness."

Liebman noted that nothing significant would change in the near future because Bedford-Stuyvesant's housing stock did not require additional garbage collection. "Refuse collection pickups," he explained, "are generally made in accordance with neighborhood requirements." Neighborhoods with tenements received five-day service, which, according to Liebman, was "the maximum that can be provided by our Department." All other areas received service three days a week. Unless the sanitation department received "budgetary authorization for additional equipment and personnel," Bedford-Stuyvesant would not receive additional service. "Please be assured," Liebman stated, "that the matter will be given careful consideration and study."[25]

In the minds of Brooklyn CORE members, more was at stake than garbage in the street. Dirty streets in an all-black neighborhood and politicians' reluctance to correct the situation revealed, at least to black members of CORE, patterns of racial discrimination in city services. Gilbert Banks, a black World War II veteran and skilled construction laborer, joined Brooklyn CORE during the Ebinger campaign after he experienced tremendous difficulties getting work on unionized construction jobs. Banks remembered that Brooklyn CORE justifiably took action with Operation Clean Sweep because the sanitation department's negligence and politicians' noncommittal attitudes were a reflection of how the city discriminated against poor people of color. "We were dissatisfied with the way the sanitation department was viewing the community," Banks recalled. "The sanitation department comes to pick the garbage up, but they have more garbage out in the street than they have in the damn truck. So we complained to City Hall, but they weren't hearing us."[26]

In fact, the city made the garbage problem in Bedford-Stuyvesant worse. According to Brooklyn CORE member Maurice Fredericks, "the garbage men would come by, supposedly to collect the garbage, but when they left, the place would be very filthy." Mary Ellen Phifer Kirton, an African American migrant to Bedford-Stuyvesant from Kannapolis, North Carolina, who became an active member of Brooklyn CORE during the fall of 1962, felt this practice was a clear case of racial discrimination. If garbage collectors spilled trash on the streets, "they didn't clean it up. They left it there. And that's what was so disturbing about them taking up garbage in black neighborhoods. . . . In other neighborhoods, if they spilled some garbage on the sidewalk or in the street, because they have brooms and shovels on the side of the truck, I'm sure they put that garbage in the truck. They didn't leave it lying in the street."[27]

If Brooklyn CORE had strictly followed CORE's "Rules for Action," it would have continued its letter-writing campaign and leafleting. Stark and Liebman conceded that the city would act on some of Brooklyn CORE's demands, but such actions would take time. Winning the hearts and minds of racially prejudiced people through education and mobilization was "the CORE way," and it seemed Brooklyn CORE was succeeding.[28] Brooklyn CORE members' anger, frustration, and impatience, however, prevailed over their adherence to CORE's beliefs in strict practices of compassion, discipline, and patience. Brooklyn CORE saw an opportunity to rally the Bedford-Stuyvesant community and instill a sense of political empowerment in residents.

The day before it planned to implement Operation Clean Sweep, Brooklyn CORE leaked some details about the demonstration to the press. On the morning of Saturday, September 15, 1962, newspaper readers from all over the city learned that "a city official is in for a surprise today" because "a load of garbage from Bedford-Stuyvesant is to be dumped on his doorstep." Arnold Goldwag, the chapter's public relations chair, did not reveal to the press where demonstrators would dump the garbage "for fear the police and sanitation people would show up first and send their truck away." He did, however, reveal that after Brooklyn CORE collected garbage that sanitation workers had passed up in Bedford-Stuyvesant, the demonstrators would take it by truck and "dump it at the office of one of the city officials who they say promised better garbage collection but did not keep his word." Demonstrators would then leave before police arrived. In his anonymous press release, Goldwag stressed that this action was necessary because city officials refused to provide Bedford-Stuyvesant with proper services. "The area is being discriminated against because it is a neighborhood in which mostly Negroes and Puerto Ricans live," and after a year of negotiations, CORE received only empty promises from Mayor Wagner, borough president Stark, and officials at the sanitation department.[29]

Brooklyn CORE launched Operation Clean Sweep on Saturday morning, which was when the sanitation department collected bulk trash in Bedford-Stuyvesant. The demonstration created quite a scene. An interracial group of about twenty CORE members waited until the garbage trucks finished collecting on Gates Avenue. Then, with their own U-Haul trailers attached to several cars, Brooklyn CORE collected trash that sanitation workers had left in the street. Maurice Fredericks, a black WWII veteran who joined Brooklyn CORE when it first formed in early 1960, remembered that "We went after the truck, and the garbage we picked up was the garbage that they should have picked up but for whatever reason they didn't. We collected what they failed to collect."[30] Women and men swept Gates Avenue with brooms and used shovels to load dirt and debris into the trailers. Men carted off large boxes, old mattresses, broken refrigerators, and hunks of metal. Marjorie Leeds and Barbara Weeks, an African American member of Brooklyn CORE, even wore aprons that featured Brooklyn CORE logos.[31] Robert Law described the festive atmosphere of the demonstration. After the participants collected the garbage that the sanitation department left behind, Law remembered that, "we marched down the street with the garbage in a parade."[32]

Residents came out and some stared with interest, others with amusement. Between twenty-five and thirty joined the group from CORE. One newspaper reported that close to fifty people, including children, participated in the demonstration. Law believed that, for the most part, the community supported Brooklyn CORE for its action, because "when we did things like that it said to the community for the first time, 'You don't have to accept this. You can actually do something about your condition.'" In his mind, Brooklyn CORE's Operation Clean Sweep was a turning point for many black Brooklynites who had grown up accepting second-class status and double standards. Before, they had never believed that "if you go down to the Department of Sanitation and say, 'Pick up the garbage,' and they won't do it, that we would have dramatized this with a demonstration."[33] Indeed, Operation Clean Sweep may have represented a brief moment when residents of Bedford-Stuyvesant witnessed a new way of using direct-action protest to make their political voices heard and force negligent politicians to listen to their demands.

The city anticipated CORE would dump the garbage at the mayor's office in City Hall. According to Oliver Leeds, police closed off the Brooklyn Bridge, which denied easy access to that area. Instead, after Brooklyn CORE members filled the trailers, they made their way to Borough Hall, the political and judicial center of Brooklyn and the location of the borough president's office. With no police or sanitation officials to stop them, demonstrators unloaded the broken mattresses, refrigerators, old rugs, splintered orange crates, and other garbage and placed it on the steps of Borough Hall nearest the corner of Court Street and Remsen Street. Shortly before noon, they formed a picket line and marched with placards that stated, "Taxation Without Sanitation is Tyranny," "Operation Clean Sweep," "Give Us a First-Class Bedford-Stuyvesant Community," and "Show Us Integration with Better Sanitation."[34]

Crowds formed to watch the demonstration and a few police officers arrived just as Oliver Leeds and others were unloading the last of the garbage. One police officer ordered the demonstrators to stop, but Leeds and others ignored him and continued the dumping. No one was arrested, but the police issued a summons to appear in criminal court on Monday, September 17 for "violation of littering sidewalk." Marjorie Leeds accepted the ticket. The crowds dissipated and demonstrators made their way home. Aside from the court summons, the only penalty was a ticket police officers gave to Oliver Leeds for illegally parking his station wagon and U-Haul trailer.[35]

Operation Clean Sweep had a strong impact on demonstration participants and local politicians. Brooklyn CORE's October 1962 newsletter had Operation Clean Sweep as its lead story. "Borough President, Abe

Stark, has felt the wrath of Brooklyn CORE and the entire Negro community," the piece began. "The action prompted Mr. Stark and City officials to tour Bedford-Stuyvesant where he found what he termed 'shocking conditions of poverty.'" Some participants, like Robert Law, were empowered by the demonstration. "Throwing that garbage was emotionally gratifying. It was like, here take this garbage back! You got the sense of fighting back." When Marjorie went to court that Monday, the judge found her guilty of littering and issued her a fine of ten dollars. When Leeds refused to pay and said she preferred jail, the judge summarily dismissed the case. Successfully evading fines and prison motivated Brooklyn CORE members and affirmed that Operation Clean Sweep was a just action. David Snitkin, a white garment worker and member of Brooklyn CORE, wrote to the editor of his union's paper and argued that Operation Clean Sweep should be mimicked by other neglected neighborhoods in the city. After summarizing the campaign and the demonstration, Snitkin declared, "Now the powers that be know what poor people have had to live with for many years." City officials probably wanted to avoid more demonstrations, but Brooklyn CORE members were prepared to continue Operation Clean Sweep if politicians ignored their requests. "We will come back again next week until you pick up this garbage," Law exclaimed. "Until you pick up this garbage, we will bring it back out here again and again." After Operation Clean Sweep, Brooklyn CORE leaders said the chapter would wait two weeks and see if the city took any action. If nothing was done, they promised to carry out another "dramatic action."[36]

Officially, Stark expressed more concern over the health and housing conditions in Bedford-Stuyvesant than over the threat of more Brooklyn CORE–led demonstrations like Operation Clean Sweep. Repudiating the dramatic demonstration, a defensive Stark told reporters that "there was no need of any action of this kind. Although I have no jurisdiction over garbage and refuse collection, I assured [Brooklyn CORE] that I would make every effort to obtain for this neighborhood the services it needs—and I am living up to my word." Operation Clean Sweep led the borough president to make some strong statements that he was politically unable to match with strong action. Stark agreed there was "an urgent need for daily collection of garbage" on Gates Avenue between Bedford and Broadway. "The condition is a bad one and I feel that action should be taken . . . at an early date."[37]

He also pressed Harold Birns, the city building commissioner, to tour parts of Bedford-Stuyvesant and Brownsville and witness the "appalling" living conditions of those predominantly black neighborhoods. Stark said he had been "concerned for some time with the terrible conditions under which some of our residents have to live" and described some of the houses in those neighborhoods as "unfit for human habitation." For all his supportive words, however, Stark was largely powerless in matters of public policy. At that time, the borough president's only formal political authority at the municipal level consisted of his vote on the Board of Estimate, which determined the city's annual budget. Stark declared that he would support any appeal for funds to increase garbage collection in congested Brooklyn neighborhoods, and he urged the Department of Sanitation to expedite those requests. Making suggestions and showing support with his one vote on the Board of Estimate, however, represented the extent of Stark's power and could not bring about the type of changes Brooklyn CORE demanded.[38]

Sanitation commissioner Frank J. Lucia stated outright that Bedford-Stuyvesant would not receive five-day pickup service without changes to the department's budget. Lucia claimed he needed funds to hire thirty-nine extra workers, and until the city approved his new budget, Bedford-Stuyvesant had to make do with three-day service. He did, however, have a two-part plan that he argued would decrease the amount of garbage in the neighborhood. First, Lucia planned to send more officers into Bedford-Stuyvesant to enforce the city's heath code and issue summonses and fines to negligent landlords. Second, he planned to work with Bedford-Stuyvesant civic groups to implement an education program that would discourage people from littering on the street and encourage them to deposit trash in garbage cans.[39]

The sanitation commissioner also contested Brooklyn CORE's allegation that the city racially discriminated against Bedford-Stuyvesant. Harlem and Brownsville, Lucia pointed out, were also predominantly black and Puerto Rican neighborhoods and those areas received five-day garbage collection service. Population density determined the frequency of a neighborhood's garbage collection, according to Lucia, not the residents' class or race. Bedford-Stuyvesant's garbage problem, he implied, resulted from its inhabitants' behavior, not racism or the city's negligence.[40]

Lucia's two-part plan and arguments of color blindness disregarded Brooklyn CORE's empirical evidence of Bedford-Stuyvesant's large population density and poor housing conditions, which warranted emergency attention. The sanitation commissioner seemed content, however, to characterize people in Bedford-Stuyvesant as representative of an urban "underclass," adherents to a "culture of poverty," and he implicitly blamed the residents for problems that reflected over a decade of political neglect.[41] Mayor Wagner was silent on the issue, which made the city appear unwilling to admit any responsibility for Bedford-Stuyvesant's complex problems. Lucia's solutions, while proactive, were insufficient and somewhat condescending. Summonses and fines were rarely an effective means of influencing slumlords' actions, and Lucia's proposed "education program" ignored the garbage already amassed around buildings, in empty lots and alleys, and on sidewalks. No matter how many behavior modification programs Lucia implemented, Bedford-Stuyvesant's population required extra sanitation services, which the city seemed unable or unwilling to provide.

Somehow, Brooklyn CORE misinterpreted Lucia's intentions and ran the headline "Five Day Pick-Up Achieved" on the cover of the October 1962 edition of the *North Star*, Brooklyn CORE's monthly newsletter. Later in the month, Oliver Leeds and others met with the sanitation commissioner, and Lucia reiterated the department's position: There was not enough money or manpower to switch from three-day to five-day collection. Lucia stressed that he had already made a request for more funds and expressed regret that the budget director had not taken action. He was hopeful, however, that despite "budgetary stringencies" it would be possible to obtain the necessary money for expanding services in Bedford-Stuyvesant. Indeed, Lucia recognized the area had a serious problem, but he refused to admit publicly that the city was responsible for both exacerbating the situation with inadequate services and correcting it with emergency increases in garbage collection.[42]

Brooklyn CORE ignored Lucia's explanations and continued to complain that there was no change in services on Gates Avenue. Apparently, the chapter misunderstood his promises and thought that at least Gates Avenue would immediately begin receiving five-day service. Befuddled and annoyed, Lucia responded in early December that he was "at a loss to understand (Brooklyn CORE's) complaint. . . . The schedule of services on this street was not changed nor was five-day service instituted." In the six weeks since the October meeting, however, the sanitation department had initiated some measures to alleviate the garbage situation in Bedford-Stuyvesant. Sanitation workers placed 237 additional litter bins on corners throughout the neighborhood and posted seventy-five "No Dumping" signs at vacant lots "to help curtail the illegal disposal of refuse." Lucia sent "additional supervision" into the neighborhood, which he claimed would "make possible increased control over the general situation."[43]

In November, sanitation patrolmen issued 1,124 summonses, "for various infractions of the Health Code." These steps—inadequate as they were—gave the impression that the city was not ignoring the predominantly black community. Lucia assured Brooklyn CORE that he would continue to advocate for increased collection in Bedford-Stuyvesant and that the department would service the community "to the fullest extent of our capabilities."[44]

The sanitation department did make one change to Bedford-Stuyvesant's pickup services: It increased collection of bulk garbage from one to two days per week. Lucia explained that the department added the extra day as a way to discourage residents from littering. The neighborhood's people, Lucia implied, were solely responsible for such high levels of trash, not the sanitation department or the city. Brooklyn CORE grew dissatisfied with superficial solutions that placed all the blame for the problem on the residents. The chapter remained committed to five-day collection as the only solution to Bedford-Stuyvesant's problem and took their complaints above Lucia to Mayor Wagner. "It is our view," Oliver Leeds and Robert Law wrote the mayor, "that a community as overcrowded as ours should get preferential treatment from the agencies of the city and not prejudicial treatment." They insisted that the sanitation department deliberately discriminated against Bedford-Stuyvesant by providing inadequate remedies to the neighborhood's garbage situation. Leeds and Law also admonished the mayor for his silence on the issue, which they found "quite shocking," since Wagner ran as "an independent fighting mayor" in the last election. Enclosed with the letter was a copy of a 1950 article in the *Stuyford Leader* that highlighted Bedford-Stuyvesant's fight for five-day collection service. Nothing had been done to help the neighborhood, Leeds and Law argued, for over a decade. Instead, all they received was "Twelve years of neglect! That's the story of Bedford-Stuyvesant. Years of allowing a good community to go to pot. Houses, schools, sanitation, bus service—even the local park—Tompkins Park is in shambles. If something isn't done about the sanitation—and quick—Brooklyn CORE and a few prominent ministers will circulate the (article) to every organization in this area."[45]

Similar correspondence continued throughout 1963. Brooklyn CORE members tried to recruit local residents to stage more direct-action protests but had difficulties gaining support. The chapter lacked

the personnel to initiate a door-to-door community organizing campaign, and a one-time dramatic action like Operation Clean Sweep did
not necessarily inspire everyday people to dedicate their time, energy, or
resources to a social movement. The one group directly in touch with
the black masses was the black church leaders, but most black ministers
in Brooklyn (except for the Reverend Milton Galamison, activist pastor
of Bedford-Stuyvesant's Siloam Presbyterian Church) were much more
politically cautious than Brooklyn CORE and tended to avoid direct-
action protest. The Brooklyn chapters of the NAACP and the Urban
League did not have memberships large enough to mobilize for future
"Clean Sweeps." Support from elected officials was also not forthcoming. State assemblyman Thomas Russell Jones, a staunch supporter of
local civil rights activism in New York City, was the only elected official
who wrote a letter to Mayor Wagner encouraging him to meet with
community leaders in Bedford-Stuyvesant and stating that he would support Brooklyn CORE in any conference, community-wide demonstration, or picket line that it may organize to bring about the desired
changes. This statement notwithstanding, Lucia made no attempt to provide the community with emergency services and remained steadfast in
his claim that the department needed to wait for increased funds.[46]

Despite the campaign's frustrating end, Operation Clean Sweep, successfully revealed the ways government bureaucracy and intransigent politicians maintained structures of inequality that disadvantaged people of
color throughout the city. The sanitation commissioner and the mayor
found it politically expedient to ignore this issue and present arguments
that blamed the victim rather than allocate the necessary funds to
improve garbage collection services in overpopulated neighborhoods.
That most of the residents in neighborhoods that suffered from such
political neglect were poor African Americans and Puerto Ricans only
exacerbated the palpable tensions that existed between them and the
city's power brokers, who were predominantly white. If these problems
were not addressed with tangible changes in services, they threatened to
explode in the face of politicians left to deal with the years of neglect
caused by their predecessors' inaction and indifference.

Indeed, this is exactly what seemed likely to happen when, in the
summer of 1969, Puerto Rican revolutionary activists in East Harlem
performed their own "Garbage Offensive" by depositing their neighborhood's uncollected trash in the middle of busy intersections and setting
it on fire. Similar actions followed several months later when, in early

1970, residents of Brownsville carried out the same type of action, which newspapers dubbed the "Brownsville Trash Riots." The Lindsay administration undoubtedly wanted to avoid more violence in Brownsville, but in the back of the mayor's mind was also the disgruntled sanitation workers' union. Two years earlier, sanitation workers had sent the city into hysterics with a strike that lasted nine days and allowed roughly 100,000 tons of garbage to pile up throughout the five boroughs. Wanting to appease angry residents and show workers he was allocating more spending for their overtime pay, the mayor handled the situation with an immediate call for sanitation workers to volunteer for extra shifts and work around the clock to clean up the garbage problems in these neighborhoods. The city could have dealt with this same issue years earlier when Brooklyn CORE quite literally brought their complaints to the steps of Borough Hall, but instead it chose to ignore those nonviolent protests and only responded when people resorted to using tactics that were much more antagonistic and potentially destructive.[47]

The history of Brooklyn CORE's Operation Clean Sweep offers a snapshot of the ways political bureaucracy and politicians' indifference contributed to poor quality-of-life conditions in Bedford-Stuyvesant brought on by years of overcrowding and little, if any, improvement in housing conditions. The dramatic nonviolent activism that Brooklyn CORE initiated made the problems of excess trash and poor services visible for all in the city to see. This tactic was essential when citizens and politicians summarily dismissed Brooklyn CORE's charges of neglect and discrimination with arguments that the citizens themselves were to blame for the excess trash.

Still, these ideas and the policies they influenced were difficult, if not impossible, to defeat with this one protest. Lucia's proposal to initiate education campaigns that would teach residents of Bedford-Stuyvesant how to properly dispose of their trash and correctly use garbage cans embodied the belief that dirty people, not poor policies and inadequate budgets, created the neighborhood's trash. Operation Clean Sweep represented one of the last-ditch efforts on the part of activists to demonstrate peacefully the ways that the borough's largest black community suffered from conditions that were created by specific governmental policies and practices. Garbage remained a problem in the city's most densely populated neighborhoods.

In the future, instead of using nonviolent tactics to express their grievances, people of color in Brooklyn and cities across the country protested in ways that mirrored the biblical prophecy that beleaguered African

American slaves had re-created in song. The slaves who had sung these words were people who, similar to many residents of Bedford-Stuyvesant, knew a thing or two about disrespectful treatment at the hands of indifferent power brokers: "*God gave Noah the rainbow sign. No more water. The fire, next time.*"[48]

4

Rochdale Village and the Rise and Fall of Integrated Housing in New York City

PETER EISENSTADT

When Rochdale Village opened in southeastern Queens in late 1963, it was the largest housing cooperative in the world. When fully occupied, its 5,860 apartments contained about 25,000 residents. Rochdale Village was a limited-equity, middle-income cooperative. Its apartments could not be resold for a profit, and with the average per-room charges when opened of $21 a month, it was on the low end of the middle-income spectrum.[1] It was laid out on a massive 170-acre superblock development, with no through streets, and only winding pedestrian paths, lined with newly planted trees, crossing a greensward connecting the twenty massive cruciform apartment buildings. Rochdale was a typical urban postwar housing development, in outward appearance differing from most others simply in its size. It was, in a word, wrote the historian Joshua Freeman, "nondescript."[2]

Appearances deceive. Rochdale Village was unique: the largest experiment in integrated housing in New York City in the 1960s, and very likely the largest such experiment anywhere in the United States.[3] It was located in South Jamaica, which by the early 1960s was the third-largest black neighborhood in the city. Blacks started to move to South Jamaica in large numbers after World War I, and by 1960, its population was almost entirely African American. It was a neighborhood of considerable income diversity, with the largest tracts of black-owned private housing in the city adjacent to some desperate pockets of poverty.[4] However, at least 80 percent of the original families in Rochdale were white, and the remainder African American.[5] The overwhelming majority of the white families were of Jewish background. I was a member of one of those Jewish families; we moved to Rochdale in 1964, when I was ten years old, and Rochdale was my home until 1973.

Rochdale was not isolated from its surrounding community. School-children from Rochdale and the surrounding neighborhoods attended racially balanced schools, and their parents shopped in Rochdale's malls and its cooperative supermarkets, the first in South Jamaica. Joshua Freeman notes, "Rochdale seemed to embody everything the civil rights movement . . . called for."[6] This was widely recognized at the time. A lengthy article in the *New York Times Magazine* in 1966 by the veteran radical journalist Harvey Swados sensitively analyzed the problems and promises of integration in Rochdale, concluding that Rochdale was providing the largest and most important practical test in New York City of the dominant question of the era—"could blacks and white live together?"[7]

This hope was very much of its time and place, as was Rochdale itself, built at the end of the superblock era in urban planning. And its cautious, hopeful attitude toward integration was also specific to its historical moment. Rochdale Village was one of the most tangible products of a period, from the mid-1950s through the mid-1960s, that can be seen, in both word and deed, as New York City's era of integration. Any argument to this effect would need to be hedged with reservations: Support for integration was often shallow and tentative, the opposition was often effective and tenacious, and the final results were in many ways frustratingly meager. Nonetheless, it was a time when there was a surprisingly wide consensus, starting from vastly differing perspectives, that concluded that integration was possible, practical, and necessary and was the best way to resolve the city's growing racial tensions. In the end, the imbalance between the high-minded rhetoric and the paucity of positive results helped bring this optimistic time to an end. For a variety of reasons, Rochdale Village was an important exception to this pattern, a concrete achievement of the era of integration.[8]

Integration was one of the dominant liberal ideals of the 1950s—and if it can be understood in various ways, at its heart was the conviction that an amelioration of racial inequality required fashioning ways that persons of different races could work, learn, play, and live together. If integration was not always viewed as sufficient for racial equality, it was generally seen as its necessary precondition. As such, it was commended by a wide and somewhat motley coalition, ranging from ex-Communists, independent leftists, and New Deal Democrats to Rockefeller Republicans, as well as some hard-nosed and utterly pragmatic government officials and business executives. If one is forced to categorize reforms as either "top down" or "bottom up," the push for integration was clearly both, a product of both grassroots organizing and deals struck in executive offices.

There were some general animating principles behind the conviction for integration, perhaps chief among them that prejudice was irrational, and its negative effects could be counteracted through education, counseling, effective legislation, and practical demonstrations of the efficacy of integration. That is, there was belief in the positive power of social engineering, and that effective governmental action could and should be used to overcome resistance to integration. Sociological studies provided the intellectual muscle for these arguments, such as this 1951 study that lauded early attempts at integrated housing by the New York City Housing Authority:

> We are in effect rejecting the notion that has characterized much of sociological thinking in the field of racial relations, the notion originating with William Grant Sumner, that "state ways cannot change folkways." The evidence of our study is that official policy, executed without equivocation, can result in large changes in beliefs and feelings despite initial resistance to the policy. Thus, it is clear from our data that although most of the white housewives in the integrated projects we studied did not, upon moving into the projects, like the idea of living in the same buildings with Negro families (and certainly the community as a whole did not favor it), a considerable change in attitudes and folkways has taken place as a consequence of their experiences resulting from a state way.[9]

There was a related belief that the state was beginning to do its part by stigmatizing and criminalizing segregation. Antidiscrimination legislation in New York City—the most expansive anywhere in the United States, which by the late 1950s covered public housing, publicly assisted housing, education, public accommodations, and multiple-unit private rental property—provided ambiguous support for this conviction.[10] This expanding scope of open-housing legislation could be read in multiple ways. The more complacent could imagine that history was on the side of integration, and if its triumph was not quite inevitable, as modern America moved slowly but ineluctably to realize its liberal potential, segregation would be eliminated. The more searching were angered that the antidiscrimination ordinances largely relied on moral suasion for their enforcement and were largely ineffective. Still, there was general hope that, in time, the laws would be strengthened, and the government would help lead the way to a more egalitarian society.[11]

Liberal support of integration is often opposed to radical defenses of racial equality that involved a fundamental quest for social transformation. The differences between the positions are real enough, but one needs to avoid viewing the 1940s and 1950s through 1960s lenses. The sentiment of the radical left had been overwhelmingly integrationist—think only of seminal works such as "Ballad for Americans"—and, for the most part, the commitment of those on the left to integration owed nothing to the exigencies of the Cold War but represented their deepest political convictions. If the events of the early 1950s tended to drive a wedge between liberal and radical alternatives on civil rights, by the end of the decade there was a new convergence. As the Communist left became increasingly moribund and irrelevant, old leftists with a special commitment to civil rights often joined non-Communist organizations pushing the liberal civil rights consensus, as Joshua Freeman and Martha Biondi have demonstrated.[12] In its wake there was a new Popular Front of sorts, but with the Communist Party left out. And in viewing this process one should not slight the contribution of the older non-Communist left, whose ranks included longtime civil rights stalwarts like A. Philip Randolph, and the social democrats who clustered in the American Jewish Congress. By 1960, old sectarian differences were not exactly forgotten, but for those who wished to move on, it was now far easier to do so.

To give an example of this from the history of Rochdale Village, Doxey Wilkerson was one of the most prominent black Communists of the 1940s and contributed an essay representing the Communist point of view to the seminal 1944 collection *What the Negro Wants*. By the early 1960s, his Communist days were behind him, and he was teaching at Yeshiva University, with a special interest in promoting integrated education.[13] In 1965 a group supporting integration in Rochdale, one typical of the time in its ideological inclusion, ranging from old leftists to mainstream democrats, arranged for Wilkerson to become a special advisor to the local school district, and he led frequent seminars on how to best implement integrated education in Rochdale. Doxey Wilkerson is one example of many: the push for integration in Rochdale and its schools in the early 1960s was marked not by a liberal-left fissure but by a liberal-left collaboration.[14]

But the founding act of Rochdale was another sort of collaboration, one between one of the city's leading social democratic organizations and an individual who had a reputation for ruthless pragmatism. The developer of Rochdale Village was the United Housing Foundation (UHF), the builder of some 33,000 units of cooperative housing from the early 1950s to the mid-1970s of increasingly gargantuan proportions, culminating in Rochdale Village's younger, much larger, and much better-known sibling, Co-op City in the Bronx. The UHF was a central organization in New York City's postwar social democratic establishment.[15] The UHF had its roots in the anarchist wing of the Jewish labor movement in the early twentieth century. The charismatic president of the UHF, Abraham Kazan, was the developer and for many decades manager of the Amalgamated Houses, one of a number of left-wing Jewish housing cooperatives that flourished in the Bronx in the 1920s.[16] His anarchism led him to favor the creation of practical, voluntary cooperative endeavors on a nonprofit basis that would provide a nonrevolutionary alternative to market capitalism, rather than political action to bring about social change, like the Amalgamated Clothing Workers of America's intensely political leader, Sidney Hillman. This and other differences with the union led him, in 1951, to form his own organization, the UHF, though it retained close ties to the Amalgamated and many other unions in the city, which remained its primary backers and supported its ambitions of building attractive inexpensive housing in the city.[17]

Kazan and the UHF always balanced a utopian confidence in a better world in birth with a very nuts-and-bolts practicality on how to achieve it. The name Rochdale Village is a tribute to the Owenite socialists and other assorted utopians who started the modern cooperative movement in England in 1844. The UHF always tried to impart the sense, with some success, that there was something special about living in a cooperative.[18] As for Kazan's acumen in driving a hard bargain, a brief story: One day, at about the time of the building of Rochdale, Kazan was meeting with Governor Nelson Rockefeller. The governor, impressed with Kazan's savvy, gave him the highest praise a Rockefeller could bestow. He told Kazan that he "could have gone into private business, and made himself a fortune." If Kazan was flattered by Rockefeller's remark, he remained true to his principles. "I am a co-operator," he replied, "interested only in building the cooperative commonwealth."[19]

The UHF saw cooperative housing as just the first step toward cooperative autarky, and Rochdale had two cooperative stores, a credit union, a pharmacy, and an optical center, and perhaps most impressively, and despite the determined efforts of Con Edison to prevent it, a cooperatively owned power plant that furnished all gas and electricity to Rochdale. There were unrealized plans for cooperative stores that would sell shoes, furniture, and gasoline, as well as a cooperative barber and beauty shop, a bowling alley, and a medical center and hospital.[20]

But at the same time, Kazan had hitched the fortunes of his cooperative commonwealth to a man whose name became a byword for ruthless pragmatism, and the bitter scourge of airy idealisms of any kind, Robert Moses. If Kazan and Moses were an unlikely duo who initially viewed each other with much suspicion, by the mid-1950s Kazan had become, in the words of Joel Schwartz, "Moses' favorite redeveloper."[21] Moses found in Kazan his equal in tough-minded resoluteness, who could build attractive housing quickly and inexpensively. Moses and Kazan shared an unswerving commitment to urban renewal and the need to replace tenements with modern housing, and Kazan, like Moses, did not flinch, when necessary, at tenant removals. For his part, as Kazan's protégé, the late Harold Ostroff asserted, "If you had Moses on your side, you knew that you didn't need anything more than a handshake to know that Moses would be with you through thick and thin."[22] Kazan recalled in his memoirs that "Rochdale Village owes its existence to Robert Moses."[23] This is so. Without Moses's advocacy and his complete mastery of all the bureaucratic arts, from threatening and cajoling to begging, Rochdale Village never would have been built.

Rochdale Village was built on the former site of the Jamaica Race Track, which in the early 1950s was the most popular sporting venue in New York City, drawing two million customers annually, more than any of the city's three baseball teams.[24] But the facilities were shabby, transportation was difficult, and there was little room for expansion. The close of Jamaica, with the proceeds from the sale to go to the refurbishing of the state's three other thoroughbred tracks, was rumored from 1953, was publicly announced in 1956, and finally happened in 1959, after much dithering and dickering between the interested parties.[25]

Needless to say, Moses was very interested in developing the site, and as city construction coordinator, he did his best to get his hands on the property from at least 1955 onward. His initial thoughts for the area included using the site for private houses; a city housing project; a mixed-use development with public, middle-income, and high-income rental housing; a campus for Queensborough Community College; and a new baseball stadium for the increasingly restless Walter O'Malley. Nothing came of any of these suggestions. By October 1956, Moses had decided the best use of the Jamaica site would be as a private middle-income housing cooperative, and he announced this intention at a speech at the headquarters of the UHF.[26]

Moses repeatedly said in the late 1950s that the development of the Jamaica site was his favorite ongoing project, and he gave several reasons for this. Like many city officials of the era, he was very concerned about building affordable middle-income housing in the city to staunch the flow to the suburbs, and Rochdale did something about this on the grand scale. He loved the size of the project. As he told a reporter in 1957, it "would be on a big-enough scale so that we could do a bang-up planning and building job there."[27] And most important for Moses, the lot, once the racetrack was razed, would be empty. He told the *Times* in 1959 that it was his favorite project because "we have 170 acres there with nothing on it at all. No people to move."[28] By that year political problems and bad press over tenant relocations were mounting for both Moses and the UHF. Kazan said of Moses that "the difficulties he had encountered in clearing the Lincoln Center site were still fresh in his mind when he learned that the Jamaica racetrack was going to be given up. He was very much interested in reserving that site for a low rental project."[29]

But the other reality about the Jamaica site was that if a middle-income cooperative were going to be successful there, it would have to be integrated. It would be welcomed by the neighborhood only if there was complete confidence that blacks could live there freely, and that Rochdale would not cut it itself off from the neighborhood. Local blacks were often suspicious of the Rochdale project, and black homeowners worried that Rochdale would lead to a decline in real estate values.[30] And at the same time, there was great worry within the UHF and elsewhere that whites would not be interested in moving in large numbers to South Jamaica. This proved to be unwarranted, in part because of the UHF's reputation, and in part because Rochdale proved, as Harold Ostroff wrote in 1968, "that if you offer such an attractive economic buy . . . people will not be able to afford their natural prejudices."[31] As Kazan told the UHF board in 1960, Rochdale "could attract a more integrated population, [with] more non-white families than have been participating in our previous activities."[32]

The UHF and Robert Moses had different reputations when it came to the support of integrated housing. The UHF in the early 1950s was one of only a handful of private developers in the nation that had a rigorously enforced open-housing policy in its cooperatives.[33] However this did not translate into large numbers of blacks in early UHF cooperatives, which, because of their ties to the Jewish labor movement, remained overwhelmingly Jewish in their populations. Nonetheless, blacks sat on the board of the UHF and its constituent and affiliated cooperatives.[34] Its publications regularly stressed the important role the cooperative movement had to play in ending residential segregation in the North, as in a 1956 article by Eleanor Roosevelt that complained that progress against housing discrimination had been "pitifully slow" and that cooperatives should be in the vanguard of change. With Rochdale Village, the UHF would have its chance.[35]

On the other hand, Moses had long before Rochdale staked out a reputation as a leading critic of civil rights legislation, and as was typical of Moses, his criticism tended toward the acidulous. He made no secret of his opposition to the landmark 1945 Ives-Quinn antidiscrimination law, which made New York State the first state in the nation to ban discrimination in employment, and in the late 1940s he was the most vocal supporter of the right of Metropolitan Life to bar black tenants from its Stuyvesant Town development.[36] In the mid-1950s he was still a critic of civil rights legislation, both in public—telling the *New York Post* in 1956 that his only regret about his fight to prevent antidiscrimination policies in publicly financed projects was "that he lost"—and in private—that same year, writing to a city official, he blasted a rather bland statement on civil rights from the mayor's Commission on Intergroup Relations as "contemptible," and as "stimulating racial, ethnic, religious, ideological and economic controversies."[37]

The favorite black leader of Robert Moses, into the era of Martin Luther King and Malcolm X, remained Booker T. Washington. In his racial and social beliefs he was essentially a late-nineteenth-century liberal. He had strongly opposed the effort to condemn the extension of civil rights legislation to the actions of private parties. If he condemned bigotry as a personal failing, he had his doubts about whether it should be made illegal. At the same time, he had long since made a peace of sorts with civil rights legislation. If he defended the right of private developers to discriminate at Stuyvesant Town, as he told the *Post* in 1956, he thought that Metropolitan Life's decision to exercise that right had been "grievously misinformed" and the attendant political controversy avoidable. He accepted the need to follow state and city antidiscrimination ordinances and grudgingly acknowledged in 1956 that the State Commission against Discrimination (SCAD) had "worked reasonably well," albeit because the "left-wingers" had been kept in check, and the work of SCAD largely remained in the realm of moral suasion rather than aggressive enforcement. Moses often worked with developers with special commitments to interracial housing such as the UHF, and on occasion tried to convince recalcitrant developers that fighting an open-housing policy would be more trouble than it was worth.[38]

In the climate of the late 1950s and early 1960s, Moses didn't hesitate to take credit for his support of integration in Rochdale. In early 1959 he wrote a friendly letter to Elmer Carter, the newly appointed head of SCAD, wanting to set up a meeting. He cautioned Carter that "handsome gestures are no good" in the field of civil rights or open-housing legislation. However, he called special attention to the Jamaica project as an example of a valid effort toward achieving integration in housing and sought Carter's support for the development, which had not yet been approved. One problem with the "era of integration" was that the evenly matched forces supporting and opposing integration often led to a stalemate, and the opponents of integration only had to play for the tie. Moses's advocacy of the Jamaica project showed what was possible when a powerful figure strongly supported the cause of integration. Even so, and even given his legendary powers of persuasion, this was far from an easy deal to close.[39]

The UHF had largely financed its previous cooperatives through union pension funds, though not a penny of union money went to the construction of Rochdale Village. The main reason for this was, as Abraham Kazan noted, that powerful union leaders, such as Harry Van Arsdale, president of the New York City Central Labor Council and a member of the UHF board, were "very cool" about the Jamaica project because they felt that white families would not move to South Jamaica. Kazan himself needed a lot of hand-holding and worried that Rochdale would become, in his words, a "white elephant," with the UHF left holding the bag on unsold apartments, unless the interest rates were suitably low. Moses wrote Governor Nelson Rockefeller in September 1959 that "I had the devil's own time to persuade the labor leaders to agree to sponsor this project."[40]

Moses was writing to Rockefeller, after the refusal of both unions and private lenders to provide financing, to persuade the state as the lender of last resort to pick up the tab for the construction of Rochdale, which, after some typical Moses-style browbeating, it did. In January 1960, various state agencies loaned the UHF all the outside funding for the cooperative, $86 million in all. Without the active support of Moses and Rockefeller, the two most powerful people in New York State, Rochdale Village never would have been built.

Moses was proud of what he accomplished in Rochdale Village. He saw the Jamaica site as a prototype, the first of a series of integrated cooperatives to be built in the largely minority areas of the city as a way of furthering urban renewal aims and building new middle-income housing relatively inexpensively and noncontroversially.[41] In 1963 Moses described Rochdale Village, in part because of its integrated character and its potential for improving the quality of life in the surrounding areas of South Jamaica, as "the most significant multi-family cooperative going on the city at this time." He planned bus excursions to Rochdale from the 1964 World's Fair in Flushing Meadows to show it off to the world and ranked it as one of his greatest achievements, comparable to Jones Beach and Lincoln Center. In 1966 he praised Rochdale as a place that "in a quiet way has achieved remarkable success in integration," and he hailed it, two years later, as "a model for the future."[42]

But ultimately, integration was created in Rochdale not by Moses or by Kazan, but by the people who chose to live there. If they were proud to live in such a community, most were quick to tell you if you asked that they were not civil rights activists. As Harvey Swados reported in 1966, it would be a mistake to assume that people moved to Rochdale "from conviction, eager to put their liberal, all-men-are-brothers belief to the test."[43] Overwhelmingly, they moved to Rochdale for economic reasons; for the large, inexpensive apartments; and for the prospects of good schools and a pleasant community life. For many blacks, like resident Lee Reynolds, what made Rochdale Village special was simply that it was a housing development that "we had a choice of moving into and not someplace that was left open to Negroes."[44] The Rochdale Village Negro Cultural Society hoped in 1965 that, because Rochdale was "a voluntarily integrated community, it can become an outstanding example of how this American problem of mutual distrust, fear and distortion can be resolved."[45]

However, even if the bulk of Rochdale's residents were not civil rights activists, they were willing to live in an integrated community, unlike the large number of white families who considered moving to Rochdale and then had second thoughts and backed out.[46] There were no racial quotas at Rochdale.[47] The UHF would have accepted whatever the final racial percentages turned out to be, and the number of white families who chose to move to Rochdale surprised many on the UHF staff. The UHF, which had not even had to advertise for previous cooperatives—word of mouth sufficed—had an extensive advertising campaign for Rochdale, which included notices in the black press.[48]

If most Rochdale residents were at least open to the idea of integration, there was also a group of activists committed to civil rights who moved to Rochdale as well. Old hands at political organizing and making their opinions heard, they probably played a disproportionate role in the political discourse in the cooperative. In addition, there clearly was a subtle process at work that drew some persons who had been previously largely apolitical or indifferent to civil rights into the excitement of building an integrated community.[49]

These groups—the longtime activists, those favorably disposed to civil rights, and largely apolitical persons who wanted the best for their community and families—started to coalesce and shape Rochdale's character as an integrated community even before they moved in. The local schools were notoriously substandard, including two of the very last wooden schoolhouses in New York City. Local blacks leery of the construction of Rochdale were in part placated by the promise that the old decrepit schools would be replaced by new ones within the cooperative. However, the Board of Education, notoriously skittish in any endeavor involving integrated education, was scandalously slow in building the new schools. By early 1962 it was clear to a group of prospective cooperators that the new schools would not be ready when families started to move in. They formed the Rochdale Village Committee for Public Schools, arguing that only by a thoroughgoing embrace of integration, and work with the local community, could Rochdale Village have quality schools. It was a broadly appealing message, and the committee, typical of the period, was made up of an ideologically diverse coalition of old leftists, social democrats, and many people who were essentially apolitical, just deeply alarmed at the lack of progress in building schools, as well as representatives of PTAs from the surrounding community. The committee's fight was largely successful and shamed the Board of Education into honoring its commitments, and this formed the basis of other struggles, notably the effort to integrate South Jamaica's intermediate schools.[50]

Integration was central to the vital social and organizational life of Rochdale. By design, UHF cooperatives were intended to foster a sense of community by participation in self-government and the flourishing of an active associative life. By November 1965, Rochdale had over 140 clubs, groups, fraternal orders, and other organizations.[51] Many of these organizations went out of their way to form integrated chapters. An integrated bridge tournament in Rochdale was the subject of a laudatory column in the *New York Times*.[52] One of the prominent organizations in the cooperative was the Rochdale Village Community Chorus; its annual concerts paid tribute to the fight for civil rights. In 1966 proceeds from the concert went to the Student Nonviolent Coordinating Committee. Accepting the donation award was Nathan Schwerner, the father of the slain civil rights worker.[53] The belief that Rochdale had a role to play as an exemplar of integration in housing was widespread. The weekly newspaper *Inside Rochdale* (mainstream to conservative Democrat in its orientation) wrote in 1966 that the cooperative "may easily become a national name as the advocates of Open Housing may look to Rochdale and say to the nation that integrated housing exists and works!"[54]

The internal politics at Rochdale, which were always vigorous and factional, were also integrated. The local politics, which often involved questions of whether the UHF exercised too dominant a role in the management of the cooperative, had no black or Jewish factions or blocs.[55] In 1966 the first person elected to the Rochdale Village Board of Directors by the residents of Rochdale (as opposed to being appointed by the UHF) was African American.[56] Interracial political cooperation extended beyond Rochdale's borders. In 1964, Kenneth Browne became the first African American elected to the New York State Assembly from Queens, with Rochdale providing the margin of victory over a white opponent. In 1966 Rochdale was part of the only electoral district in New York City with white and black co-chairs.[57] Rochdale was creating a citywide model for successful urban integration.

Alas, integration in Rochdale Village did not last. Many in Rochdale believed they had created community institutions and links strong enough to withstand the inevitable racial strains and pulls, but they were wrong. By 1969 the exodus of white families was pronounced, and it continued to grow in the years ahead. Black families, of course, moved out as well, but almost all the new families coming to Rochdale were African American. By the late 1970s the original 80 percent white–20 percent black racial percentages were reversed. By the end of the 1980s the cooperative was 98 percent nonwhite, which it remains today. Rochdale, having weathered some hard times, is still a flourishing middle-income cooperative, but it is no longer integrated.[58]

The reasons for the white exodus from Rochdale were complex. Rochdale was never a racial utopia. Most people who moved to Rochdale, it bears repeating, were not civil rights activists. In its early history one can find the complaints, both by whites and blacks, typical of the time—white fears of black crime, outsiders, and the problems of integrated education; black anger at curt and rude comments and treatment, and black fears that the Jews in Rochdale were "pushy" and were trying to unduly dominate the cooperative's political and cultural affairs.[59] Some projects, notably a proposed community swimming pool in Rochdale, clearly failed because of racial tensions within the building complex and hostility to the project's location among those in the surrounding community.[60] Probably the dominant view among Rochdale's residents was that by moving to Rochdale they had done more to advance integration than almost anyone else among New York City's millions, and asking them to do more would be unfair. As one man wrote in 1965, "we came to Rochdale, not as fighters for integration, but as people who have accepted integration as a way of life."[61]

One of the paradoxes of Rochdale was that though it was planned during the "era of integration," it opened just as the assumptions that guided that period were beginning to fracture. A new political climate in black communities was emerging even before the first families moved in, and these changes were apparent in the immediate vicinity of Rochdale. In the summer of 1963 the Rochdale Village construction site became one of two foci in the city—along with the site of the SUNY Downstate Medical Center in Brooklyn—for demonstrations against the blatant discrimination practiced by the city's 119 building trades union, most of which had few, if any, black members, and apprenticeship programs with long waiting lists that would have insulated them against potential minority membership for many years to come. (Kazan and the UHF, closely tied to the ALF-CIO, offered sympathy to the protesters but said that their hands were tied and argued that they were obliged to honor union contracts.)[62]

The demonstrations began on July 23, 1963, and lasted through October. Day to day, the number of protesters—generally between 50 and 100, and sometimes as many as 350—ebbed and flowed.[63] The protesters marched in front of the entrance to the construction site on New York (now Guy Brewer) Boulevard. Most chanted and carried signs, while some engaged in civil disobedience, primarily by physically blocking the passage of construction trucks. By the time the demonstrations had run their course, between 200 and 300 people had been arrested at Rochdale.[64] Three organizations shared responsibility for the demonstrations. The largest was the Jamaica branch of the NAACP, long active in the defense of civil rights in southeastern Queens, and, with some 6,000 members, a bulwark of the black middle class in Queens.[65] The two most prominent leaders of the Jamaica NAACP at the time of the Rochdale demonstrations, William Booth and Paul Gibson, would both go on to have considerable political careers.[66] The Long Island chapter of CORE (Congress of Racial Equality) was tiny in comparison, with no more than 100 members, but its determined interracial membership was a major presence at the Rochdale protests.[67] The third organization was the United Clergy of Jamaica, organized for this protest, which included many local clergymen (although some of the best-known churches in the area, such as the Allen AME Church, were conspicuously absent).[68] The churches provided venues for nightly rallies that would continue throughout the summer.

The demonstrations had as their purpose the increase in the percentage of the minorities at the Rochdale construction site to roughly the minority percentage in the city as a whole, around 25 percent, or what both sides in 1963 still referred to as a "quota" (the term "affirmative action" had not yet come into wide use). For this demand they were widely denounced by politicians. (For example, Governor Rockefeller, using the ultimate Cold War cuss word, declared that quotas were "un-American in concept and in principle.")[69] But that is not how the Rochdale demonstrators saw their efforts, and most viewed the protests as furthering the goal of integration. And future residents of Rochdale, white and black, were well represented at the protests.[70] William Booth, although adamant and resolute in his opposition to discrimination by the building trades unions, was excited about the prospects for Rochdale, and believed it would "further integration and help the Negro community." (His mother would soon move into one of Rochdale's apartment buildings.)[71]

However, the demonstrations also spawned a more radical alternative, a group of militants organized around the charismatic figure of Herman Ferguson, whose transition from a largely apolitical assistant principal in the New York City school system to a prominent Black Nationalist was catalyzed by the Rochdale demonstrations. Ferguson believed the other organizations at the Rochdale demonstrations were not sufficiently confrontational, and he engaged in the single most celebrated act of civil disobedience during the demonstrations, secretly entering the construction site late one evening with a small group of followers and chaining themselves to construction cranes, some sixty feet in the air.[72] When the Rochdale demonstrations began to wane, Ferguson was at the core of what became known as the Rochdale movement, an organization with a Black Nationalist orientation that demanded an end to all forms of discrimination against blacks in the Jamaica area.[73] Twice in 1963 Malcolm X addressed the organization, the second time of November 28, 1963, in what may well have been his penultimate public appearance as a minister of the Nation of Islam.[74]

For radicals like Malcolm X, integration was at best irrelevant to the quest for black equality. For mainstream liberals, too, there was a growing sense of defensiveness at the radical demands, and frustration that the plans for integration were proving inadequate. By 1965, the figure who perhaps was emblematic of liberal integrationism in New York City, the black psychologist Kenneth Clark, could write an elegiac study, *Dark Ghetto*, that cataloged his growing despair that those in power had the will to shape a genuinely integrated society.[75] Old issues continued to fester without solutions—when William Booth became human rights commissioner in 1966, he specifically mentioned the demonstrations at Rochdale, telling the press he had no more important goal than ending the still-rampant discrimination among the building trades unions.[76] If Rochdale was a counterexample to the growing sense of frustration, it was easily overlooked, and eventually overwhelmed by the growing turn away from integration. Longtime Rochdale school activist Sue Raskin has speculated that if Rochdale had not gone through the racial turbulence of the late 1960s, it might have survived as an integrated community.[77] But this was not to be.

Those who were in a position of influence in Rochdale Village in the late 1960s, across the political spectrum, are unanimous on the immediate cause of the failure of integration in Rochdale: the bitterly divisive 1968 teachers' strike.[78] Before the strike, an integrated group from Rochdale met with Al Shanker, the president of the United Federation of Teachers (UFT), begging him to give Rochdale a dispensation from the strike, fearing its potential damage. Shanker, who was on the board of the UHF and knew all about what was unique about Rochdale, predictably refused.[79] The strike, which across the city directly pitted blacks against Jews in ever-escalating volleys of rhetorical violence, irreparably destroyed the fabric of the integration. In Rochdale, black parents and some white supporters stayed in the schools around the clock, fearing, among other things, bomb threats. Black Panthers reportedly patrolled outside some of the schools. The strike was a brutal polarizer. Either you supported the strike or you didn't. There was no middle ground. Jewish liberals often found themselves despised by both sides. And those who opposed the strike, such as the liberal William Booth and radical Herman Ferguson, often found their other ideological differences less important than their shared opposition to the UFT. After the damage wrought by the eleven-week strike had cleared, there was no longer a constituency, or political future in supporting integration in Rochdale, or the city at large. The strike lingered as a wound, suppurating and unhealed.[80]

The problem was most acute in Rochdale's new intermediate school, which had opened in the fall of 1967. From the outset the school seemed to be in a state of disarray, with substantial discipline problems. The strike bitterly divided the faculty, and the weak administration of the school seemed unable to bring the faculty together or deal with the problems in their hallways or accomplish much of anything else. By 1969 problems with the school had led to the beginning of the white exodus. As whites left the public school system, for the first time black children were bussed in from the surrounding neighborhood. (Previously those from the adjacent neighborhoods, like the children from Rochdale, had been able to walk to school.) This further accelerated the loss of white students. The key to successful integration is quality public schools; without them, any attempt to create stable integrated housing will fail. A liberal integrated group wrote to the Board of Education in 1970, calling for maintaining the current racial balance in the schools, and arguing that Rochdale's residents were willing to make sacrifices for the sake of integration but "the one problem they cannot accept is a poor school situation. This above all is what causing many white and middle class families to move out of this community."[81]

There were other factors in the white departure from Rochdale. Crime was on the rise throughout New York City and was certainly on the rise in and near Rochdale. There was a heroin epidemic in South Jamaica in the late 1960s; the proximity to Kennedy airport and its abundant organized crime networks likely contributed to a rash of car thefts.[82] A deterioration of the physical condition of the cooperative; a rash of minor, but annoying, acts of vandalism; increases in carrying charges due to inflation and surging fuel prices; and chaotic internal politics within Rochdale, where one slate of candidates seemed to be trying on an annual basis to reverse the actions of the previous majority, were all contributing factors. In addition, many families moved to Rochdale for the express purpose of living inexpensively for a few years, saving money, and then purchasing a house in the suburbs. If education provided the catalyst to the white exodus, there was no lack of subsidiary reasons. Many works examining this period in New York City's history have portrayed lower-middle-class white families in the outer boroughs as simply "white ethnics" revolting against liberalism, following Jonathan Rieder's influential work on Canarsie.[83] Generalizations are difficult, and there certainly are people I interviewed who fit into the "New Deal Jews mugged by the 1960s turn conservative" narrative. Indeed, Meir Kahane, who would soon gain international notoriety as a right-wing rabble-rouser, was living in Rochdale at the time of the 1968 strike, rabbi to Rochdale's Orthodox congregation, and leading the newly founded Jewish Defense League.[84] But in general the people in Rochdale changed less than the city in which they lived. By all accounts Rochdale remained a very liberal place. It went heavily for Lindsay in 1969, and for McGovern in 1972, and strongly opposed the war in Vietnam in local polls.[85] But if people had practical reasons for moving to Rochdale, they had equally practical reasons for leaving. As one person put it, people's decision to move was less a rejection of Rochdale's founding principles, and more "because it no longer lived up to their expectations."[86]

Certainly those who remained in Rochdale in the early 1970s fought to keep it integrated. If it seems unlikely that, under any circumstances, it would have remained 80 percent white, there is no reason why it necessarily had to lose all its white population. But by 1973, fighting for integrated housing was no longer a fashionable issue. That year, WNET, Channel 13, the PBS station in New York City, the programming of which was broadly reflective of liberal opinion, had a documentary on racial tensions leading to the white exodus from Rochdale. The residents of Rochdale were deeply offended, and many complained of the exaggerations and sensationalism in the report. The producer responded that there was overwhelming evidence of serious racial tension in Rochdale, and that the message of the program was that "the possibility of successful integrated housing in New York City is a most difficult goal at best, if one examines the Rochdale experience."[87] The lessons drawn from Rochdale's experiment in integration were not those its founders and first residents had hoped for.

In many ways New York City and Rochdale Village have changed beyond recognition in the forty-plus years since the days when I was a ten year old roaming Rochdale's unfinished and unlandscaped grounds. Robert Moses and the UHF are long gone, and their ideas of planning seem past exhumation. And many housing experts argue that because of their costs, their tax structures, and their social impact, huge cooperatives like Rochdale are urban dinosaurs that long ago should have waddled to their well-deserved extinctions.[88] Perhaps. But Rochdale Village, having weathered some hard times in the 1980s and 1990s, is today strong and vibrant, the largest predominantly black housing cooperative in the United States. And if nothing else, the recent crisis in subprime mortgages, particularly acute in minority neighborhoods such as South Jamaica, and the trillions of dollars that are being spent to right our decayed housing system and mortgage markets should force us to re-examine the orthodoxy of recent decades that a reliance on the private market for housing is less expensive than alternatives such as government-sponsored, limited-equity cooperatives. Abraham Kazan's social vision and his cooperative commonwealth aren't dead, they have merely been resting.

And in 2010, as in 1964, New York City, in both its housing and its schools, remains one of the most segregated cities in the United States, especially in black outer-borough neighborhoods like South Jamaica.[89] The only difference between then and now is that segregation is now taken for granted and accepted as an unalterable facet of urban living. In his classic 1955 work, *The Strange Career of Jim Crow*, C. Vann Woodward wrote of the "forgotten alternatives" of America's racial history.[90] Woodward of course focused on the Reconstruction and post-Reconstruction periods, and his work scraped away layer upon layer of conventional wisdom that held that blacks and whites living together and sharing power as equals was a preordained failure. A similar veneer obscures the efforts to create genuinely integrated communities in the 1960s. History of course cannot be rewritten, and like Reconstruction, the effort to create an integrated Rochdale in the 1960s was ultimately a failure. Success is imitated; failure is shunned. But if Rochdale's efforts at integration were not a success, as one longtime activist told me, in different ways and in new guises, "it is an experiment that has to be tried again."[91]

5

Conservative and Liberal Opposition to the New York City School-Integration Campaign

CLARENCE TAYLOR

One of the most successful periods for New York City liberalism was during the mayoralty of Robert F. Wagner (1954–1966). During these years, benefits for workers rapidly increased, public housing was built, and more blacks and Latinos gained government jobs.[1] But at the height of liberalism, the city faced a great deal of racial turmoil. Despite its reputation as a bastion of liberalism and the mayor's efforts at making New York a place where harmonious race relations existed, many in the city failed to embrace black New Yorkers' fight for full equality. While New York politicians, union officials, and policy makers worked to eliminate racial discrimination in education, housing, and employment, they were unwilling to adopt a more vigorous agenda that would assure blacks and Latinos a greater share of public services, jobs, and resources. This failure led to civil rights activists organizing and leading civil rights protests. By the early 1960s, New York City's liberal mayor was under siege by numerous racial protests. In 1963 a coalition of civil rights groups, including the Brooklyn chapter of the Congress of Racial Equality (CORE), the NAACP, and the Urban League of Greater New York initiated a sit-in at Mayor Wagner's office demanding a halt to all construction sponsored by the city until all discriminatory hiring practices were "eliminated." CORE also led demonstrations at construction sites throughout the city, demanding that the state and city governments along with the Building and Construction Trade Council integrate the lily-white construction crew. In July of 1963, CORE teamed up with a group of Brooklyn ministers protesting at the construction site of the SUNY Downstate Medical Center. Named by one minister "jailbirds for freedom," over seven hundred people were willingly arrested at the Downstate Medical Center in an attempt to force the state to integrate the workforce by ensuring that at least 25 percent of the workers were black and Puerto Rican construction workers.[2]

One of the largest civil rights protests in New York City took place on February 3, 1964, when civil rights groups launched a one-day boycott of the public school system over the issue of school integration. The school-integration protest, led by the Reverend Milton A. Galamison, managed to keep close to a half-million children out of the public schools in an attempt to force the New York City Board of Education to come up with a plan and timetable to integrate the school system. The event was so dramatic that it caught the attention of Dr. Martin Luther King, who congratulated the demonstration leaders for their efforts in bringing New York City's racism to the attention of the nation.[3]

Galamison and the movement for school integration directly challenged the image of New York City as a shining example of urban liberalism. Civil rights activists consistently argued that racial discrimination

Demonstrators participating in the February, 3, 1964, school boycott.
(Copyright © 2009 The New York Times)

was not limited to the South; the largest school system in the country was also plagued by the problem of racial segregation. Black and Latino children were relegated to overcrowded schools, provided with fewer services than children attending schools that had predominantly white student bodies, and given the least experienced teachers. The goal of Galamison and others who led the school-integration campaign in New York City was similar to that of the southern wing of the movement— the creation of a harmonious community where racial barriers were eliminated and all were provided the opportunity to reach their full potential. New York City's Board of Education did not come up with a plan to integrate the school system because of widespread opposition to school integration. Some have argued that the failure of school integration was a result of the overly aggressive demands of black militants. However, this view does not take into account organized white resistance to school integration. A great deal of attention has been paid to southern white resistance to integration. But a fierce campaign using tactics from the civil rights movement and the southern white resistance campaign took place in New York in the early and mid-1960s, severely hindering plans to integrate the school system. Moreover, opposition to the New York City school-integration movement came not only from white parents but also from liberal circles. While white residents in some communities led a ferocious crusade against school integration, liberal forces who spoke in favor of racial equality also contested the school-integration movement. Liberal opposition led many in the school-integration campaign to distrust liberals, choosing to rely on their own actions to win school integration.

Wagner's New Deal Liberalism

The historian Joshua Freeman notes that during the mayoralty of Wagner, New York City labor reached its zenith of power. "Capitalizing on its long history of struggle and institution building, and the impressive display of worker militancy after World War II," Freeman contends, "organized labor wielded its influence in ways unrivaled in the city's history to make working-class life more pleasant and secure."[4]

The Wagner years were a period when labor was able to build an infrastructure of social security, housing, and health care. In addition, car and home ownership among the working class increased and vacations and college education became a reality for working-class men and women and their children. To be sure, labor was able to succeed in gaining political influence because it forged a coalition with liberal politicians that helped create a positive political atmosphere. It was labor's efforts that helped bring Robert F. Wagner, the son of the famous New York City liberal senator, to Gracie Mansion. Wagner represented the liberal wing of the Democratic Party that stressed political inclusion of ethnic and racial groups.[5]

The alliance between organized labor and liberal politicians, according to Freeman, helped erect a "welfare state in New York far more robust than the national norm." In 1958, Wagner issued an executive order granting municipal unions the right to collective bargaining. He also granted city workers lucrative contracts that increased salaries, extended health and medical coverage, and improved working conditions. The social contract in New York extended beyond worker and employer and encompassed government provision of affordable housing, health care, and other services to poor New Yorkers.[6]

To be sure, Wagner's liberalism was more than an attempt to create a working-class paradise; he also sought to make New York a place of racial and ethic tolerance by taking direct action to eliminate racial, ethnic, and other forms of discrimination. Wagner tried to keep his campaign pledge to improve race relations. In 1955 the mayor, along with the city council, established a permanent Commission on Intergroup Relations (COIR). COIR had the power to investigate complaints and to initiate investigations into racial, religious, and ethnic group discrimination. Its objective was to root out racial bigotry in New York City. In order to carry out its function, the group was granted the power to hold hearings, report its findings, and make recommendations to the mayor.[7]

As part of its investigatory duties, COIR was charged with studying the reasons for discrimination and social disorder among the various racial and ethnic groups of the city and to find avenues for developing an intergroup "dialogue." During Wagner's mayoralty, COIR's powers were extended (in 1958, thanks to the Sharkey-Brown-Isaacs Law) to investigate and hold hearings of allegations of housing discrimination. COIR became the first city agency of its kind in the nation to extend its powers beyond public housing and to include the private sector. In 1962 COIR was renamed the Commission on Human Rights and not only was granted the power to investigate discrimination based on race, creed, and color in employment, public accommodations, and housing but was also granted powers of enforcement.[8]

Indeed, as the historian Wendell Pritchett points out in his masterful work, *Brownsville, Brooklyn: Blacks, Jews and the Changing Face of the*

Ghetto, eliminating housing discrimination became a major objective of the Wagner administration. In 1957 the mayor ordered the city comptroller, Charles F. Preusse, to provide a study and make recommendations for reform in the New York City Housing Authority. Reflecting the liberal spirit of the city, the comptroller called for an end to the concentrating of "troubled families" in housing projects and for a "more balanced population economically." Under Preusse's plan, whites received preference for predominantly black housing projects, and blacks and Latinos for predominantly white housing projects.[9] While there were certainly problems with the comptroller's housing integration plan, it nevertheless represented a scheme to de-racialize housing projects by ending the geographical concentration of the poor. Preusse's plan reflected the city's racial liberalism during a time when the demand for integration and racial equality was on the nation's front burner.

Wagner's racial liberalism went further than establishing institutions to rid the city of racial and other forms of discrimination. Wagner increased the number of black and Latino city workers. By 1963 there were over 25,000 black and Latino city workers.[10] In an effort at racial inclusiveness in the arena of politics, the mayor also placed close black political allies in politically powerful positions. The Reverend Gardner C. Taylor is a case in point. Taylor, who was pastor of the 10,000-member Concord Baptist Church in Brooklyn, was one of the few Democrats among Brooklyn's powerful black clergy. In his first year as mayor, Wagner named Taylor to an advisory group seeking ways to improve city services. Four years later the mayor appointed Taylor to the New York City Board of Education. The best indication of Wagner's liberalism of inclusiveness came in 1962 when he named Taylor as part of a group of three to replace Joseph T. Sharkey as Brooklyn's Democratic leader.[11]

Wagner also empowered several other black clergy by putting them in charge of antipoverty programs. In 1964, with the help of federal funds, Wagner created the Youth in Action (YIA) program, granting the agency $223,225 to examine discontent among the youth and to develop antipoverty programs. The Reverends William A. Jones of Bethany Baptist Church and Carl McCall became members of the board of directors of the agency, while the Reverend Walter Offutt, assistant pastor of Bethany, became the chairperson of the board of directors. YIA became Bedford-Stuyvesant's official antipoverty program, offering job training for unwed mothers, remedial education, and adult on-the-job training. It also provided recreational services for teens. Indeed, several black churches received funds to house many of YIA's programs.[12]

Former New York City assistant budget director Charles R. Morris notes that Wagner, a man of integrity, had always been concerned about the poor, blacks, and Hispanics of New York. According to Morris, the mayor "tried valiantly to redirect city services. Federal juvenile delinquency money was tapped to provide summer jobs for young people from the slums. Money was found to pay for the Higher Horizons program for disadvantaged pupils—extra teachers, audio-visual aids, and bilingual or Spanish-language instruction." Morris points out that in 1964, Wagner created the city's Attack on Poverty, allocating fifteen million dollars "in flexible appropriation"; its major task was to coordinate the city's welfare, housing, educational, and job programs for the benefit of the poor. Wagner "was cut in the mold of the best of the 1950s mayors—committed to housing improvement and physical renewal."[13]

New York City's liberal efforts to challenge racial discrimination had the potential of making the city a model for other large urban centers. As the historians Gerald Markowitz and David Rosner contend, "New York, in particular, appeared well-positioned to become a model for a northern effort to address de facto segregation. Its traditions of liberalism, its strong labor movement, its historical mission of acculturating new immigrants, and the growing political importance of Harlem in the new Democratic coalition" placed the city in a strong position to attack "inferior education and segregated schools." Indeed, Mayor Wagner even addressed the school-integration situation by publicly supporting it. "Greater integration of our school children," the mayor declared in February 1955, "leading to a more wholesome integration of our citizenry, is worth the cost of providing safe guard crossings, overcoming traffic difficulties and a proper adjustment of school time."[14]

Milton Galamison and the New York School-Integration Campaign

Despite the appointment of black elites to powerful positions, and the New York's liberal elite's efforts to create a city where racial discrimination would be a thing of the past by establishing antidiscrimination agencies and by publicly supporting school integration, these efforts could not overcome the decades of customs and practices that maintained a system of structural inequality based on race. Notwithstanding the passage of antidiscrimination laws in employment and education in New York, racial discrimination was a reality for blacks and Hispanics. Although New York's State Commission against Discrimination (SCAD) had the power of enforcement, it decided to act more as a mediation agency instead of insisting on complete compliance with antidiscrimination laws. The historian Martha Biondi claims that SCAD did nothing to stop trade unions from using seniority and apprenticeships systems to deny blacks employment. Moreover, the American Jewish Congress reported in a survey it conducted in 1947 that 80 percent of the employers it surveyed were willing to racially discriminate and avoid hiring people of color.[15] The historian Craig Wilder points out that although the number of black and Latino city workers increased, "nonwhite public employees were grouped in the least lucrative and most tenuous jobs and categories. The mayor had not even achieved parity in his own office. In 1963, when the data was collected, most ethnic minorities were doing semiskilled, clerical, service or labor jobs." Of the 25,000 black and Latino city workers, 7,000 were doing clerical work in public agencies and departments.[16]

Blockbusting by realtors that led to segregated communities, redlining (banks and mortgage companies refusing blacks loans to purchase homes and businesses in certain neighborhoods), and industries that refused to hire blacks or relegated them to the lowest menial position were realities in New York City. Brooklyn's largest black community, Bedford-Stuyvesant, had become the poorest community in that borough. By 1957, the community's 9,825 welfare cases accounted for 23 percent of Brooklyn's public assistance cases. The infant mortality rate in Bedford-Stuyvesant in 1957 was 38.3 per 1,000, compared to the borough's rate of 25.2 per 1,000. Bedford-Stuyvesant's venereal disease and tuberculosis rates were the highest in the borough. Little was done by the city to reverse these trends. The city, according to Morris, needed better schools and hospitals, standard housing, libraries, and solutions to the growing problem of traffic congestion. Despite its attempt to provide public housing, the Wagner administration could not provide units fast enough to deal with the growing housing need.[17]

One issue that received a great deal of attention in New York was education. As the black and Latino population increased in the city, school segregation became a reality. Moreover, black and Latino children received inferior educational resources and services. In Harlem, the city's largest black community, there was only one high school, and no school building had been built between World War I and 1940. Schools also operated on a double schedule in order to relieve overcrowding, and the schools lacked libraries and gymnasiums.[18]

A New York City College professor, Dr. Kenneth Clark, directly challenged the image of New York City as a bed of liberalism when he accused the school system of not only being racially segregated but also of carrying out policies that ensured that the system would remain segregated. In 1954 Clark claimed that the Board of Education was aware that educational facilities, academic standards, and the curriculum in Harlem were inferior to those in predominantly white schools because no white students had been assigned to Harlem's vocational high school, despite the fact that it was the only school in the city that offered a particular course of vocational study. Moreover, Harlem schools had a disproportionate number of substitute teachers compared to the predominantly white schools, proving that the board assigned the least experienced teachers to the black community. Harlem schools had 103 classes for the mentally retarded and only three classes for the intellectually gifted.[19]

Clark's statements embarrassed the Board of Education and a city that saw itself as a fortress of racial tolerance and racial liberalism. The Public Education Association reported that segregation was widespread in the school system and that the board did little to correct the situation. Even before the release of the Public Education Association's report, Wagner appointed a committee to survey the utilization of school buildings to relieve overcrowding. Despite his efforts, he became a target of civil rights groups who accused him of doing little to integrate the schools. Civil rights activist Ella Baker, then chair of the education committee of the New York branch of the NAACP, met with Wagner and criticized him for his "hands-off" policy when it came to the board. Baker also organized a grassroots organization called Parents in Action against Educational Discrimination. The group consisted of black and Puerto Rican parents who demanded school integration and greater parent participation in school policy making, such as determining how resources were allocated. Baker claimed that Parents in Action had a number of meetings with the mayor and in September 1957 led a picket line of 500 parents in front of Wagner's office, noting that the city had not addressed the concerns of black and Puerto Rican parents.[20]

Without a doubt, Milton Galamison became the city's most visible and vocal critic when it came to the issue of school integration. Born in Philadelphia in 1923, and educated in the Philadelphia school system, Galamison received his bachelor of arts from Lincoln University and his master of theology from Princeton University. In 1948, at the age of twenty-five, he became the pastor of the Siloam Presbyterian Church, one of the most prestigious black churches in Brooklyn.[21]

Despite Siloam's middle-class orientation, Galamison's weekly sermons to the mostly black bourgeois congregation criticized American culture for what he labeled social sins: racism, militarism, and class exploitation. He was especially critical of Christianity for not playing a greater role in challenging these social sins. The historian Lisa Waller correctly notes that Galamison represented the left wing of Presbyterianism. According to Waller:

> This domination had moved away from an earlier focus on private morality and its emphasis on abstaining from drink, card playing, improper family life, and disrespect for the Sabbath. The "new agenda" for American Presbyterianism presented a highly politicized, leftist stance. This agenda articulated four primary goals for American Presbyterianism: they were the curtailment of militarism, the elimination of the disparity between both the wealthy and the poor in the United States and the wealthy West and the rest of the world, the abolition of racism, and the reformation of the family and gender roles."[22]

Galamison interpreted Jesus and other biblical figures as revolutionaries challenging social injustice. He felt that Christians had a duty to emulate Jesus and also take on the social sins of the world.[23]

Education became a key concern for Galamison because of his own experience of racial discrimination. As a child in elementary school, Galamison faced racial discrimination from a classroom teacher, and as a high school student he was relegated to a vocational training program, which denied him rigorous academic training despite his protest to school officials. He also recalled the harsh reality of racism when, as a child, he, along with other black children, was consigned to a Jim Crow section of the movie theater in Philadelphia and denied the privilege of competing for a door prize because he was black. These episodes in his life were important factors that motivated him to take on the fight against racial bigotry in the New York City school system.[24]

The pastor of Siloam Presbyterian Church consistently argued that the board's policies did irreversible harm to children of color. "We contend that within the framework of segregated education," Galamison once declared, "both white and Negro children are crippled emotionally and mentally irreparably and for life." Segregation reinforced the notion that black and Hispanic children were inferior and at the same time instilled a feeling of superiority in white children. Besides its psychological cost to children, Galamison also argued that segregation entailed political costs as well. According to the militant pastor, the practice was antidemocratic because it denied people their humanity and political freedom. Democracy meant equal opportunity to all, no matter their race, religion, or ethnicity. Segregated schools were robbing children of color of access to educational resources, thus denying them equal opportunity.[25]

In 1955, Galamison was approached by Annie Stein, a left-leaning member of the NAACP's Brooklyn branch, who appealed to him for his help to integrate the public schools. The activist pastor ran for and was elected the chair of the NAACP Schools Workshop. Unlike many civic organizations that were homogeneous in terms of race, class and ethnicity, the Workshop, which claimed over four hundred members, consisted mostly of women from various racial, ethnic, and class backgrounds. Black, Hispanic, and white parents, many members of local PTAs, came together to work for school integration. The Workshop claimed responsibility for persuading principals to establish intellectually gifted children's classes in segregated schools, forced schools to open libraries, and was responsible for many children receiving homework for the first time. But its main goals were to desegregate all schools in Bedford-Stuyvesant and Brownsville, Brooklyn's largest black communities, to improve both math and reading scores among black and Hispanic children, and to improve teaching standards.[26]

One of Galamison's greatest contributions to the struggle for school integration was his successful attempt at making many New Yorkers aware of the duplicity of New York City's established liberal elite. Although the board claimed that neighborhood determined the racial makeup of student bodies at public schools, Galamison and the activist parents pointed out at public hearings and in various publications that the Board of Education deliberately zoned children to schools based on race. They noted that in many cases, although black and white children lived close enough to be zoned to the same school, black children were assigned to predominantly black schools outside their districts. In one report, Galamison noted that predominantly black and Puerto Rican schools were overcrowded and in some cases were a "few blocks away from half-empty white schools on the other side of Broadway and also at Fulton Street." While the focus was on segregated schools in the South, Galamison maintained that the board kept "20,000 children in the Bedford-Stuyvesant and nearby areas" in segregated conditions. Although the 1954 Supreme Court *Brown v. Board of Education* decision had out-lawed segregation, and the board had committed itself to ending segregation in New York City schools, according to Galamison, the board refused to act.[27]

After one term as president of the Brooklyn branch of the NAACP, Galamison resigned because he wanted to dedicate himself to addressing school segregation, not conducting fund-raisers and fighting with the national leadership of the civil rights group over his political activity. Soon after leaving the NAACP, Galamison formed a grassroots parents' organization named the Parents Workshop for Equality in New York City Schools. This group offered ordinary people the opportunity to radically challenge school board policies. The group held rallies and demonstrations and directly confronted Board of Education officials. In one case, two hundred parents showed up to a meeting with the superintendent of schools on April 21, 1960, surprising the school head, who had only expected Galamison and a few people.[28]

By 1963, national civil rights groups had joined with grassroots organizations to form the New York City-Wide Committee for Integrated Schools and by the end of the summer of that year, the committee decided to launch a boycott to force the board to come up with a timetable and plan for integrating the public school system. In spite of the threat, Wagner refused to get directly involved in the school debate. Wagner's refusal to intervene led many black leaders of New York City's civil rights movement to accuse the mayor of doing nothing to stop the demonstration.

White Resistance

A puzzling question that scholars have addressed is why the liberal mayor didn't intervene in the struggle to avoid a citywide boycott, and why Wagner's liberalism didn't embrace a plan and timetable for citywide school integration. Some argue that the fault lay with black activists. Former New York City assistant budget director Charles R. Morris, for example, claims that Wagner was not at fault for the city's racial tension; he asserts that it was just impossible for the mayor's "good intentions" to keep "pace with the temper of the new generation of black spokesmen." The "new black leaders" were in no mood for compromise or "gradual transition. They wanted control over their own programs, and they wanted it right away." No matter what Wagner might have tried to appease the "new black leadership," it would have ended in disaster.[29]

In his biography of Mayor John Lindsay, historian Vincent Cannato similarly blames black militancy for overreaching. "Though Wagner had always been sympathetic to blacks and Puerto Ricans," Cannato contends, "the aggressive style of the civil rights movement clashed with Wagner's personality." Blaming blacks for wanting fair treatment, Cannato claims that

> The civil rights movement posited a form of black exceptionalism that put the problems of blacks in a special category. The Irish, Germans, Italians, and Jews never demanded that their children attend the same schools as more well-to-do "Americans," nor did they try to force their way into restrictive trade unions. Not only did the demands of blacks create resentment among whites, but traditional politicians like Wagner simply did not know how to handle such demands. Wagner knew how to build schools and deal with the teachers' union but he was at a loss as to how to integrate the city schools.

According to Cannato, white ethnics, who displayed a strong work ethic and moral values, fled from black crime and attempts by black parents to send their children to schools in white ethnic communities.[30]

Tamar Jacoby accuses Milton Galamison of making unfeasible demands. According to Jacoby, "militant minister Milton Galamison . . . escalated his demands, as now not for a timetable but for 'immediate' integration—an impossible request." She notes that the *New York Times*, "speaking for the liberal establishment," labeled Galamison "tragically misguided." Portraying him as a person out of control, Jacoby argues that the "more resistance he met, the more angry and insistent he became. He called on the board of education to produce and immediately implement a massive busing plan, even if this meant pitched battles with white parents." Jacoby places the blame for the failure of school integration on Galamison, Brooklyn CORE, and the "new breed of activists," who were "largely indifferent to white criticism." Galamison's theatrics alienated not only white but also black civil rights leaders. Civil rights moderates, who were the voice of reason to Jacoby, "could no longer carry the ghetto, and militants like Galamison were setting the agenda for the movement." Although Jacoby briefly mentions that white parents organized counterprotests, she says nothing about the intense white resistance against integration.[31]

The problem with Morris, Cannato, and Jacoby's argument of an overly aggressive black leadership demanding integration is that their analyses do not take into account the organized campaign on the part of white parents, or the liberal opposition to school integration. Despite the liberalism of New York's political elite, this political ideology did not filter down to many white communities and others outside those communities who by 1960s saw a civil rights agenda as opposed to their interests. One of the first efforts by the board to integrate the student body came in 1959 when it decided to transfer just 400 black children from schools in Bedford-Stuyvesant to schools in the white community of Glendale and Ridgewood, Queens. When word of the board's plans became public, white parents demonstrated in front of board headquarters, protesting the transfers. Parents took legal action to stop the transfer of the children. Under attack by white parents, superintendent of schools John Theobald told a crowd of white parents that the transfer of the 400 students was not an effort to integrate schools. It was simply to relieve overcrowding in a particular area.[32] White parents in the East Flatbush section of Brooklyn successfully prevented the transfer of their children from the area to a junior high school in Brownsville by suing the board for racial discrimination.[33]

White opposition to school integration intensified when the Board of Education implemented an integration plan, Blueprint for Further Action toward Quality Integrated Education. Schools in predominately white neighborhoods were paired with schools in predominantly black and Latino communities. Following criticism of the original plan, it was modified to send students in white areas to the paired schools in black areas while students in the mostly black and Latino neighborhood would be bused to white or integrated schools to achieve racial balance. When the plan was implemented in September 1964, it involved 13,000 students.[34]

In response to the plan, two newly formed organizations, the Parents and Taxpayers Coordinating Council and the Brooklyn Joint Council for Better Education, announced that they had a "full-scale battle plan to stop the transfers." The Parents and Taxpayers, which claimed to be made up of one hundred organizations representing 500,000 people, and the Joint Council, which claimed to be made up of seventy organizations representing 750,000 people, attempted to avoid the appearance that they were opposed to sending their children to school with black children. Instead, they proclaimed their support for the neighborhood school. They even adopted the tactics of civil rights groups. These tactics included using the courts and boycotting the schools.

In September 1964, 275,638 white children stayed out of the public schools. The elementary and junior high schools reported 235,087 absent—close to 31 percent of the elementary and junior high school attendance. In some cases, no children showed up to classes. In contrast, in one school all but one of the 475 students showed up for class that day.[35]

White Parents

Despite their attempt at covering up their fear of sending their children to school with black children, it was apparent that race was a motivating factor in the parents' reactions. One speaker at a rally of 15,000 people at City Hall sponsored by Parents and Taxpayers said, "I would sooner go to jail than see my child go to that school." Although they adopted protest methods from civil rights groups, they also drew on the southern white resistance to school integration. In response to the *Brown* decision, parents in southern states established private schools and academies to avoid integration. In 1959, for instance, white parents in Front Royal, Virginia, sent their children to the John S. Mosby Academy to avoid the integration of the public high school. Segregated academies were part of the massive resistance campaign launched by the southern whites.[36]

Anti-integration demonstration by white parents at City Hall. (Copyright © 2009 The New York Times)

Part of the massive resistance campaign against school integration in New York City was the use of parochial and private schools. Many of the children who were absent from school on September 14, 1964, had been enrolled in parochial and private schools. Moreover, private academies had been established by PTA affiliates in Queens. The Jackson Heights Day School operated in a room of a cooperative apartment building and had eighty students. The Konign Institute in North Jackson Heights enrolled two hundred students who were taken out of the public schools to avoid integration. The *New York Times* reported that some junior high school students in Eastern Queens who boycotted the schools because of pairing were being tutored by retired teachers until a school for them could be established.[37]

The resistance campaign of white parents had an impact. Although the Board of Education threatened to take legal action against parents for violating the law, President James Donovan also said that if the board found that any steps in the integration program were not effective, "you're going to have the same courage exhibited" in eradicating those steps as was demonstrated in implementing the program. Superintendent Calvin E. Gross also sent a message that the board was having second thoughts about its plan when he told reporters that pairing would be evaluated before a decision was made to extend it.[38]

The determination to resist the transfer of white children to integrated schools did not dissipate. In early October, the parents of sixty-five white first and second graders escorted their children to P.S 149 in Jackson Heights after the executive board of the cooperative voted against continuing to house the Jackson Heights Day School, where the children had been enrolled. Despite the objections of the principal of P.S. 149, Bernard Kessler, attorney for Parents and Taxpayers of Jackson Heights, threatened to send all the children from Jackson Heights Day School to P.S. 149. When the principal of P.S. 149 told the parents that they could not bring their children to the school because they were not registered, Kessler defiantly said: "Our children are now physically in the plant of the Board of Education. We are demanding that they be given instruction like their brothers and sisters who are also here." Daring the principal to have them arrested, Kessler declared that the "mothers will have younger children with them, with their bottles, diapers and strollers, ready to be taken away in the event of arrest."[39] The parents were borrowing from white southern resisters to school integration. But they also appropriated a civil rights tactic used by CORE and the Southern Christian Leadership Conference and also in New York City during the

Downstate Medical Center campaign. The tactic of mass arrests sent the message that demonstrators were willing to sacrifice themselves in their opposition to what they deemed to be acts that were morally unjust.

White parents won a major victory when, at a meeting Superintendent Gross held with civil rights groups, PAT, and the Joint Council for Better Schools, he asked all parties to make suggestions on how to evaluate pairing. He said nothing of expanding integration but instead gave PAT and the Joint Committee a way of trying to kill what little effort the board had taken in the integration effort. Only two representatives from the several civil rights organizations attended the meeting, and one of the two representatives, who was the northeast regional representative of CORE, walked out of the meeting in protest, saying: "This is a joke." Galamison, who refused to attend the meeting, criticized it as a charade.[40]

Claiming that no action had been strong enough to convince the Board of Education to integrate the schools other than boycotts, Galamison claimed that he was forced to use this tactic. Instead of a citywide boycott, Galamison advocated a boycott of junior high schools and schools for troubled teens, which he said amounted to "six hundred" schools. However, a sign that black parents were growing weary of boycotts was the shouting match that took place outside Junior High School 258 in Bedford-Stuyvesant, Brooklyn, between supporters of the boycott and parents who defied the boycott by bringing their children to school. The picketers' pleas of "Don't go to school today" were ignored by at least 1,000 of the 1,668 registered at the school who crossed the picket line. The PTA of J.H.S. 258 voted to oppose the boycott.[41] Members of the PTA met with a group of Brooklyn black ministers to help launch a campaign countering the boycott. Parents and the ministers organized counter picket lines. One pastor at the meeting reported that 128 churches would be assigned to assist parents in the "counterboycott."[42]

Despite the fact that the Galamison-led boycott spread to twenty-seven schools and 5,500 students participated in the action, he had little support. On February 17, the boycott became violent when 400 students who were boycotting the schools went on a rampage, breaking through a police barricade, throwing bricks through the windows of shops in the downtown area of Brooklyn, beating up some white high school and college students, and throwing food at police.[43] The following day the *New York Times* reported that 300 "rampaging Negro students from boycotted schools swept through streets in downtown Brooklyn . . . hurling bricks at policemen and breaking windows of stores." Several teens reportedly came to the downtown area with bricks and seventeen young people were arrested. Galamison also had been arrested and accused of violating state education law.[44]

Galamison was blamed for the violence and for doing irreparable harm to the school-integration movement. The *New York Times* declared that advocates of school reform who had given their support to the boycott had "misguidedly endorsed truancy masquerading under the guise of civil rights, [and] must by now realize that Dr. Galamison's course has severely hurt the cause of school integration. Dr. Galamison, whatever his intention, has lost his way."[45] Riverside Church, which housed a "Freedom School" for students who were boycotting, decided to close the school when the Board of Education convinced church authorities that the school violated state education law. By the end of February, the Board of Education estimated that 80 percent of the students who had been honoring the boycott had returned to school and attendance was normal at seventeen of the twenty-seven schools involved in the boycott. Superintendent Calvin Gross said that the "numbers speak for themselves." Indeed, the numbers did clearly indicate that the boycott had been ineffective. On March 9, Galamison said that the boycott was in a "state of suspension." He also claimed that he and his group had "given all we have to give," and that they would not continue the action without support from civil rights groups.[46] The inability of Galamison to win greater support and the fierce resistance on the part of white parents stopped the Board of Education from implementing citywide integration.

Liberal Opposition to the School-Integration Campaign

Blame for the defeat of the school-integration movement should not just be laid at the feet of the resistance campaign of white parents. The school-integration movement did not only face opposition from white parents; many in the liberal community opposed its objectives as well as its methods. Liberals who were critical to those launching the school-integration campaign argued that the school segregation was a complicated issue. There were many reasons for school segregation that were beyond the control of the Board of Education. Segregated housing, the increase in the number of black and Latino children in the city, and the movement of white families to the suburbs were some of the reasons for segregated schools. Liberal critics of boycott leaders argued that actions such as boycotts were no solution to the problem.

The New York chapter of the American Jewish Committee publicly opposed the boycott and announced its support for superintendent of schools Calvin E. Gross. The chapter ridiculed boycott leaders by claiming that "no one is fooled by playing games of deadlines, dates and numbers. There are no pat solutions, no panaceas, no specifics."[47] *New York Times* correspondent Fred Powledge warned those carrying out the boycott, "who are almost all Negroes," that they risked losing support among "white liberals who have supported them in the past."[48] Powledge's warning was not unfounded. Some of the city's most liberal organizations were on record opposing the boycott, including the New York Civil Liberties Union, the Anti-Defamation League of B'nai B'rith, and the New York Liberal Party.[49]

Influential liberal publications criticized the boycott. Although Norman Podhoretz, editor of the then-liberal publication *Commentary* supported the boycott "as a sort of ritualist gesture of Protest," he warned that he would oppose similar action.[50] The *New York Times* ran several editorials condemning the boycott. In a December 13, 1963, the *Times* declared that a boycott of the schools was a "futile and disruptive measure that does great educational harm to the children whom it pretends to help—and who need help most." While it supported integration, the paper claimed that "any pretense that integration, especially in deep areas of de facto segregated slum housing, can be fully and rapidly accomplished, is sheer fantasy."[51] In a tougher editorial on December 19, the *Times* asserted that the determination of some civil rights spokespeople to "declare war on Dr. Calvin E. Gross, the Superintendent of Schools, and on the Board of Education" was a "threat to the orderly processes of both education and integration." Labeling the boycott leaders' demand for involuntary transfer of students outside their neighborhood to achieve integration an "impossible demand" and an "invitation to chaos," the paper even asserted that the actions of the school-integration campaign leaders and activists were "expressions of irresponsibility which can only make more difficult a rational approach to a vital and difficult problem."[52] Admitting that the "misguided boycott" was a success because over one-third of the public school student body did not show up for classes, it nonetheless stated that "racial balancing of all the city's schools remains as impossible after the boycott as before."[53]

Liberal politicians publicly criticized the boycott. Although Mayor Wagner was silent on the conflict, Earl Brown, deputy borough president of Manhattan and former editor of the *Amsterdam News*, lambasted boycott leaders. In a letter to the *New York Times*, Brown claimed that black parents who would boycott the New York City public schools to force the Board of Education to come up with a timetable and plan to integrate the school system were no different from white southern parents who boycotted schools because of integration. Both groups would destroy school systems, and in "neither case can a boycott help." Brown contended that the solution of busing black children from their neighborhoods to schools in predominantly white areas was being implemented only to appease boycott leaders, because only a handful of children could participate. Both sides, Brown declared "lost sight of their objectives," which was to improve education for all children.[54]

While several clergy supported the boycott, some opposed it. The Reverend Dr. M. Moran Weston, pastor of St. Philip's Protestant Episcopal Church, one of the most prestigious black churches in New York City, asserted that "keeping children out of school is not an effective answer to poor and segregated public education." Rabbi Max Schenk, president of the New York Board of Rabbis, "appealed to both sides to resolve their differences by peaceful means."[55] New York's segregated school system was the "result of many factors within and outside the control of the Board of Education." One of the problems Weston noted was the quick movement of white children from the public schools to private ones.[56]

The United Federation of Teachers, which had won the right to collectively bargain for all New York City public school teachers, did not endorse the boycott. The City-Wide Committee for Integrated Schools issued "An Appeal to the Conscience of Teachers" urging them to respect the boycott. Galamison appealed directly to the UFT president, Charles Cogan, and the membership to respect the protest because integrated schools would allow teachers to work more effectively in the classroom. Galamison asked teachers to "participate in this lesson in citizenship which will enable us to more effectively put your knowledge to work through integrated education which reflects the real world in which our children live and grow." Instead of endorsing the boycott, the UFT claimed it would only protect any member who decided not to cross the picket line. The refusal to endorse the boycott made the board's threat to teachers who had planned to support the protest greater.[57] The union's refusal to support the groups carrying out the protest was not the first time that the labor organization was at odds with the civil rights community.

Years before the boycott, the New York City Teachers Guild, which would become the United Federation of Teachers in 1960, clashed with civil rights organizations over the issue of integration. While the Guild had a long history of supporting liberal causes, including civil rights, it opposed an involuntary transfer plan recommended by the Board of Education's Commission on Integration in 1956. The Guild did not deny that black and Latino children were not receiving fewer services than white children. However, it contended that the best way to promote integration was to improve the quality of the schools. Involuntary transfer of the teaching staff, the Guild claimed, would only lead to the mass exodus of teachers from the system, thereby exacerbating the problem.

Despite the Guild's view on involuntary transfers, civil rights and community groups interpreted the group's response as "racist," judging that it cared little about the needs of black and Hispanic children. Its major objective, according to critics of the Guild, was to protect the interests and privileges of white teachers. Edward Lewis, executive director of the Urban League of Greater New York, was shocked at the teachers' position. The Intergroup Committee of New York Public Schools, a group of twenty-six community, civil rights, civic, and union groups whose purpose was to put pressure on the Board of Education to integrate Harlem schools, opposed the Guild's and the High School Teachers Association's position on the transfer plan. In a letter to Charles Silver, president of the Board of Education, the Intergroup Committee urged the board to implement the teacher transfer plan without delay. The Guild, which was part of the group, refused to sign the letter to Silver. One member of the Commission on Integration said that the teachers lacked courage.[58]

In a fierce attack on the Guild, the president of the National Urban League, speaking to 400 people attending a conference of the United Neighborhood Houses, claimed that New York City teachers were involved in an organized campaign to avoid serving black and Hispanic children. In what *New York Times* reporter Murray Illson described as a "bitterly worded keynote speech," Lester Granger claimed that "one of the most disturbing symptoms that have recently appeared" among teachers was their "organized and sanctioned effort" to avoid serving in predominantly black and Hispanic schools. Granger argued that it was more than a coincidence "that these difficult schools are almost invariably those with heavy concentrations of mainland and territorial children of dark complexion. Call them Negroes, or call them Puerto Rican, the schools that these children attend are those which too many school teachers seek to avoid—and their avoidance in far too many cases is viewed by their superintendents and principals with a tolerant eye."[59]

The president of the Teachers Guild, Charlie Cogan, reacted to Granger's charges by accusing the Urban League president of confusing dark-skinned children with difficult children. He claimed that the problems of integration and difficult schools were two separate issues. Despite its defense, the Guild could not eradicate the perception that it cared more about the concerns of its teachers than it did about black and Hispanic children. Its sole focus on the "deficiencies" of black and Hispanic children lacked a critical analysis of the board's policies. To make matters worse, years of stressing professionalism that left little or no room for parents to become partners with teachers in their children's education and the unwillingness on the part of the union to establish community networks and other structures that could reach out to the black and Hispanic communities only alienated it from those communities.[60]

The clash between the Guild and civil rights groups demonstrated that influential liberals were in opposition to the New York City school-integration campaign. The Teachers Guild and later the UFT advocated a liberalism of equal opportunity, allowing people to compete on a fair playing field. Its defense of the "merit system" indicated its belief that such a system would protect people from discrimination based on race, religion, or ethnicity. On the other hand, civil rights activists believed that merit, when it came to the school system, was a myth. What was needed was an effort on the part of government and institutions to provide black children with equal resources.

Conclusion

The historian Thomas Sugrue challenges the conventional story that the late 1960s backlash was a result of the excesses of a political liberal agenda. "The 'silent majority' did not emerge de novo from the alleged failures of liberalism in the 1960s; it was not the unique product of the white rejection of the Great Society. Instead it was the culmination of more than two decades of simmering of white discontent and extensive antiliberal political organization." In his work on Detroit, Sugrue maintains that state and federal elected officials provided financial resources to the suburbs of Michigan while reducing funding to public education, antipoverty, and other social agencies in Detroit. Detroit, like other urban centers, also lost revenue from a declining tax base and "increasingly expensive social, economic, and infrastructural problems." Thus,

Sugrue points to deindustrialization, a long history of racial discrimination in unions and real estate, and local and national politicians' denial of needed financial assistance to urban centers.[61]

As in Detroit, white resistance to efforts at ending racial disparity has a long history in New York City. This widespread resistance ensured that the school system would remain segregated, and black and Latino children in Harlem, Bedford-Stuyvesant, and other black and Latino communities of New York would not receive the same services as children in predominantly white areas. However, white parents were not alone in their criticism of the attempt to integrate the schools. Liberal voices in New York who called for racial tolerance and outlawing discrimination also opposed the school-integration movement. In his book on Philadelphia, the historian Matthew Countryman argues that "Philadelphia's civil rights liberals badly misjudged their ability to maintain the support of the city's Democratic Party and its base of New Deal voters for racial reforms in local employment, housing, and education issues. To many black Philadelphians, the inability of civil rights liberalism to fulfill its promise of a truly colorblind city was a profound political betrayal. It was this sense of liberalism's failure that would lead many local black activists to begin a search for alternative approaches to achieving racial equality." These alternatives took the form of grassroots organizing and directly challenging the state.[62]

In New York City, civil rights leaders also proclaimed that the solutions proposed by liberals did not go far enough as long as structural barriers were the reality in the lives of black New Yorkers. Despite Wagner's efforts to deal with the school crisis, the dropout rate in New York City's high schools led to thousands of young people roaming the streets, while thousands of other children of color were being forced to attend substandard and overcrowded schools.[63] New York City liberalism helped provide services to organized labor but did little for those outside the institutions of the working class. The failure of city elites to address the concerns of the poor helped send the message to the grassroots civil rights movement that it could not count on broader support to end racial disparity. In particular, the movement became less concerned with compromising with New York's liberal establishment and concentrated on tactics to force it to capitulate to its demands. At times, more militant voices overreached. They had an exaggerated view of their ability to change the system. But the reason integration did not succeed had more to do with resistance campaigns from white parents and their grassroots organizations, political figures, and the lack of support from the UFT.

Indeed, Galamison challenged New York City's liberal elite by arguing that outlawing discrimination and using the rhetoric of opportunity liberalism did not go far enough. What was needed was a full frontal assault on discrimination. Small steps such as pairing that gradually changed the status quo were insufficient for Galamison. To eradicate inequality, government agencies needed to take dramatic steps and implement a full-scale program that would eliminate racial disparity in the school system. Wholesale change of the entire system was needed. Galamison's radical vision thus clashed with a modest liberal agenda unwilling to challenge its supporters, and at times its detractors.

6

The Dead End of Despair: Bayard Rustin, the 1968 New York School Crisis, and the Struggle for Racial Justice

DANIEL PERLSTEIN

> The loss of the dream
> Leaves nothing the same.
>
> Langston Hughes, "Beale Street"

On April 6, 1968, Bayard Rustin received the United Federation of Teachers (UFT) John Dewey Award, an acknowledgment by the New York City union of the civil rights leader's incalculable contributions to progressive social activism. A founder of CORE and close associate of Martin Luther King Jr., Rustin had helped invent the Freedom Rides and had organized the celebrated 1963 March on Washington. Throughout the 1940s and 1950s, he was a leading American pacifist and shaped the theory and practice of nonviolence. As the protégé of black labor leader A. Philip Randolph, Rustin also championed the victims of economic inequality. "More than anyone else in the postwar era," comments the historian John D'Emilio, Rustin "was a bridge linking the African American freedom struggle, peace campaigns, and a socialist vision of economic democracy."[1]

As much as the UFT Dewey Award acknowledged Rustin's activism, it also signaled his estrangement from the movement he had done so much to create. In the late 1960s, New York's white teacher unionists and black activists were locked in a bitter struggle over control of the city's mammoth school system. Black demands for "community control" followed a long, well-organized, and singularly unsuccessful campaign to integrate New York's schools, a campaign in which white liberal organizations, including the UFT, offered little support. As white resistance undermined black hopes of integrating education and achieving full participation in American life, black parents and activists turned to demanding power in running segregated schools. Whereas black activists saw community control as a prerequisite to democratizing school governance, eliminating racism in education, and opening school jobs to African Americans, teacher unionists saw it as a threat to due process, job security, and unbiased quality education. The conflict between black activists and white teacher unionists placed New York at the epicenter of America's racial strife.

Despite Bayard Rustin's long record at the forefront of the African American freedom struggle, in 1968 he distanced himself from black activists. The call for community control both reflected and propelled the growing power of nationalist ideas and ideals among African Americans across the United States. Blacks would gain more by aligning themselves with the labor movement, Rustin countered, than from protests reflecting their racial identity and particular concerns. Amid the rancor of the school conflict, this dual commitment to economic democracy and the integrationist ideal led Rustin to sever ties with old allies and become one of the UFT's few prominent black supporters.[2]

Rustin's arguments, grounded in decades of struggle, failed to stem the growing appeal of nationalist calls for Black Power and self-determination among school activists and the declining hopes for school integration among activists and policy makers alike. And yet, no less than advocates of community control, Rustin addressed the quandary that confronted all black activists once America's commitment to racial equality reached its limits and then began to recede.

The argument in this chapter that Rustin's estrangement from old allies reflected a profound shift in his politics and in the movements of the 1960s stands in contrast to much recent scholarship. Of late, historians have highlighted the essential continuity in Rustin's career and in the broader flow of recent American history. Their accounts have generated nuanced understandings of the interplay of integration and Black Nationalism in the African American struggle for social justice and of the enduring presence of both democratic ideals and racial inequality in American life.

John D'Emilio exemplifies the recent historiography. He portrays Rustin's politics as steadfastly grounded in "a bedrock optimism that the American political system was flexible and responsive enough to embrace change of revolutionary dimensions." This chapter, on the other hand, documents Rustin's growing pessimism that America would embrace full equality for its black inhabitants. Rather than a life of heroic continuity, Rustin's tragic recognition of American racism's enduring power led him to break with the allies and ideals that had shaped his life and to move toward racial accommodation.[3]

Not only does the heroic narrative fail to account for crucial elements of Rustin's biography, but it offers a poor guide to thinking about the choices activists must make: Militant protest or compromise coalition politics? Pacifism or pragmatism? Community-based politics or affiliation with organized labor? Bayard Rustin offered a sophisticated and compelling analysis of pedagogy, politics, and economic life, but one that black activists found increasingly unpersuasive. This essay examines that analysis, its sources, and its reception. Understanding the choices Rustin and other movement activists made and the social analysis that guided them can better equip us to make those choices we face.

Blacks, Schools, and the Civil Rights–Labor Coalition

As was befitting a talk to teacher unionists upon receiving an award named after John Dewey, Rustin attempted to synthesize pedagogical and social issues in his acceptance speech. Just as politics should address economic structures of inequality that transcend race, learning should focus on the search for universal truth. Rustin began by attributing to one of his own schoolteachers the expansion of childhood horizons circumscribed by "a home where there was no father" in a community where blacks were segregated. The role of the teacher, as of the political activist, he concluded, was not to affirm the particularities we inherit. Rather, where Dewey's democratic educational theory converged with "the creative labors of the American teacher," education had the possibility of "liberating one from the prison of one's inherited circumstances."[4]

Rustin based his assessment of teachers' work on the belief that all Americans could participate in a shared political life and culture. He discounted the notion that racism had created mutually incomprehensible and hostile worldviews that separated those outside the mainstream

from those inside it. Rather, by replacing "distorted, biased and ultimately racist" versions of American history with accounts that recognized the "notable contributions" of African Americans, teachers could
"foster the ideal of communication and compassion among all the young
people of our society," enabling them "to know the truth and to be
free." The act of teaching was thus "an integral part of the effort to bring
about social change and social justice in our society."[5]

Still, Rustin reminded UFT members, teachers' pedagogical responsi-
bilities were mirrored by their political obligations. Inadequate school
funding and sterile bureaucracies discouraged poor minority students'
academic success. Only "a coalition between teachers, trade unions, and
parent groups," he told the UFT, could "make educational . . . bureaucracies and . . . authorities more accountable."[6]

Moreover, echoing Dewey, Rustin argued that students learn to the
degree that they have the opportunity to use the knowledge they accrue.
Civil rights movement victories over legally sanctioned segregation had
not transformed the circumscribed lives of ghetto blacks, and the automation of industrial work was eliminating the jobs where blacks were
concentrated. Only by eradicating "poverty and the problems it creates"
would all students share the prospect of productive work and decent
lives, which generates the will to learn. Only with such changes would
teachers "achieve their full effectiveness and their full potential as professionals." Thus, the teachers' fate was inseparable from that of their dis-
possessed students; social reform would liberate them as well as their
pupils.[7]

Rustin believed that changes in the American economy magnified the
importance of educational reform. In an earlier age, he argued, immigrants with "a minimal public education" could "find jobs and become
part of the productive system." At the time of the school crisis, however,
the "automation revolution" left "no room for the uneducated or the
semi-skilled." An awareness of this unprecedented need for education,
Rustin maintained, "is why the schools have become a primary target of
the ghetto activist."[8]

If school reform was the right issue for black activists, community
control of curriculum and teacher employment was the wrong strategy.
It gave "priority to the issue of race precisely at a time when," with
the abolition of legally enforced segregation, "the fundamental questions
facing the Negro and American society alike are economic and social."
The allure of community control, Rustin argued, reflected the difficult
political conditions that confronted black activists in the late 1960s. After

a period during which civil rights advances had fed black hopes, America's commitment to racial equality had lost much of its force. As "the pendulum of history" began "to swing downward" toward reaction, black expectations for racial justice shriveled into despair. African Americans responded with "a turning inward" heralded by calls for Black Power.[9]

Community control, in Rustin's eyes, exemplified this new "politics of frustration." Grounded in the "psychological" need for pride in black identity, it offered the illusion of "political self-determination in education" to those "so alienated that they substitute self-expression for politics." Like the earlier separatist movements of Booker T. Washington and Marcus Garvey, the Black Nationalist campaign for community control "derives not from liberal theory but from the heritage of conservatism. It is the spiritual descendant of states [sic] rights." When stripped of the militant rhetoric that "so often camouflages its true significance," community control institutionalized "one of the worst evils in the history of this society—segregation"—and legitimized "the idea that segregated education is in fact a perfectly respectable, perfectly desirable, and perfectly viable way of life in a democratic society."[10]

Even within the black community, Rustin argued, the separatist fantasy impeded social equality. Discounting working-class proponents of community control, Rustin charged that the leadership of "the fight for the Negro to completely take over the schools in the ghetto is not the working poor. . . . It is not the proletariat. . . . This is a fight on the part of the educated Negro middle class to take over the schools . . . not in the interest of black children, or a better educational system, but in their own interest."

Much like projects of ghetto-based black capitalism, community control "deepen[ed] the class conflict within the Negro community" and thus subverted the very community it invoked.[11]

Community control was ineffective as well as wrong. Relying on a lumpenized "black slum proletariat" that lacked the leverage of an industrial working class to exact concessions from society, Black Power invocations of anticolonial struggle in the ghetto could not "create the preconditions for successful, or even authentic, revolution. . . . Before we are permitted to impose our will on the majority of Americans we will be crushed." Community control, Rustin concluded, constituted "a giant hoax . . . being perpetrated upon black people by conservative and 'establishment' figures." It epitomized "the opposite of self-determination, because it can lead only to the continued subjugation of blacks."[12]

Educators and black parents alike needed to realize that a local school board without "real power, democracy, and the funds to carry out new programs" could not "substantially affect the educational system." And even real power and money would not be enough. "Unless there is a *master plan* to cover housing, jobs, and health, every plan for the schools will fall on its face."[13]

The resources needed to initiate such a master plan, Rustin added, could only be secured "by a unified black movement joining with other progressive social forces to form a coalition that represents a majority of the population." Because quality of life is determined by "the economic and social nature of our institutions," blacks needed to ally themselves with the group that most forcefully advocated the democratization of economic and social life—organized labor. Whereas advocates of community control echoed the rhetoric of segregation and the logic of class privilege, teacher unionists, according to a pro-UFT advertisement organized by Rustin, demanded "the rights that black workers have struggled and sacrificed to win for generations." These rights, due process, job security, and "the right of every worker to be judged on his merits—not his color or creed"—were "crucial to Negro advancement."[14]

Bayard Rustin and the African American Freedom Struggle

Rustin's powerful defense of the UFT and critique of community control estranged him from most black activists in 1968. For decades, though, he had helped shape the main currents of the African American freedom struggle.

Born in 1911, Rustin was raised by his grandparents in West Chester, Pennsylvania. As a child, he was both immersed in black politics and culture and exposed to the most tolerant segments of white American society. His grandmother was a community leader and an early member of the NAACP. W. E. B. Du Bois, James Weldon Johnson, and Mary McCloud Bethune were among the prominent black activists who stayed at Rustin's childhood home when passing through West Chester. The town was also home to many Quakers, and elementary school field trips included visits to buildings that had once served as stations in the Underground Railroad.[15]

As a young man in the 1930s, Rustin moved to Harlem. Like the West Chester of Rustin's childhood, Depression-era Harlem exposed Rustin to the cutting edge of black political and cultural life and to the segments of white America most receptive to racial equality. Rustin acted with Paul Robeson and sang with Josh White. Through philosopher, progressive educator, and Harlem Renaissance luminary Alain Locke, he met such literati as Langston Hughes and Richard Wright. Locke more-over was a role model for Rustin, a gay man who did not advertise his homosexuality but made no effort to deny it. In New York, Rustin taught English to the foreign born at Benjamin Franklin High School, a center of progressive pedagogy, cultural pluralism, and antiracist educa-tion under the leadership of renowned educator Leonard Covello.[16]

Rustin's politics fused commitments to pacifism, socialism, and black equality. In the 1930s, when the Communist Party led the fight against racism, Rustin organized a Young Communist League campaign against racial discrimination in the military.[17] Then, following the Nazi invasion of the Soviet Union, the Party backtracked on its commitment to anti-militarism and racial equality. Disillusioned with the Communists, Rus-tin began working for black socialist labor leader A. Philip Randolph, whose Harlem offices were, in Jervis Anderson's phrase, "the political headquarters of black America."[18]

After Randolph introduced Rustin to the ideas of Mahatma Gandhi, Rustin wedded the philosophy of nonviolent direct action to his analysis of race and class relations. He helped found CORE, and even after the United States entered World War II, Rustin crisscrossed the country proselytizing nonviolence. Convicted of resisting wartime military con-scription, Rustin led direct-action protests against segregation within federal prisons.[19]

In the years that followed, Rustin was among the most militant and uncompromising agitators of the peace and civil rights movements. He helped direct Randolph's 1941 and 1948 campaigns against discrimina-tion in war industries and the military and then castigated Randolph for agreeing to a compromise that stopped short of complete victory. During the Montgomery Bus Boycott, Rustin emerged as an influential advisor to Martin Luther King Jr., and in the late 1950s he helped organize a series of school-integration demonstrations that drew thousands of pro-testors, in ever-larger numbers, to Washington.[20]

Rustin's organizing career climaxed with the 1963 March on Wash-ington, which he directed. The 1963 march echoed the school-integra-tion demonstrations of the 1950s in several ways. It simultaneously confirmed the vital role of unionized black workers in the African Amer-ican freedom struggle and marked the eclipse of organized labor's leader-ship of the movement. The growing role of churches, community groups, and liberal white organizations suggested that the achievement of racial equality was a moral rather than an economic problem. The protests thus expressed both the utopianism and moral transcendence of the nonviolence movement and heralded the eclipse of demands for economic justice.[21]

And yet, for all its continuities with earlier protests, the 1963 march signified a turning point in Rustin's relationship to black activism; even as the movement attracted an increasingly broad coalition of supporters, Rustin became increasingly convinced of the need to move beyond demands for civil rights. By 1963, he argued, the "legal . . . foundations of racism in America" had "virtually collapsed." Civil rights victories, however, could not address crucial aspects of black oppression. With economics replacing race as the most fundamental determinant of blacks' lives, black unemployment and de facto segregation in northern communities were growing, and the living conditions of the "great masses of Negroes in the north" were getting worse.[22]

In the face of these changes, Rustin's proposal for the 1963 march had focused solely on economic demands. Although these concerns were honored in the Washington protest's official demand for jobs as well as freedom, class issues faded from prominence during organizing. Martin Luther King Jr. and many other black leaders, together with liberal white organizations, were committed to the call for civil rights legislation, and civil rights inspired mid-1960s protestors far more than industrial policy. Moreover, march organizers included few unionists who might have seconded Rustin's efforts. Although the UAW supported the march, AFL-CIO president George Meany and eighteen of twenty AFL-CIO executive council members refused to endorse it, and when two hundred activists met to plan the protest, no AFL-CIO representative attended.[23]

Even though the March on Washington failed to highlight class politics, Rustin remained convinced that a progressive coalition could be built upon black demands for full inclusion in American life and labor's demands for economic justice. The African American freedom struggle, he reasoned, "may have done more to democratize life for whites than for blacks. . . . It was not until Negroes assaulted de facto school segregation in urban centers that the issue of quality education for *all* children stirred into motion." Moreover, in their own interest, unions would recognize that "capital is too strong for labor alone." Organized labor could not "hold its own in a reactionary society without embracing the interests of the minority groups."[24]

As Rustin hoped, the African American freedom struggle did flourish in the North in the 1960s. Instead of embracing coalition political activity, however, the northern movement adopted the disciplined, nonviolent protest approach of the triumphant southern one. Hundreds of thousands of African Americans in northern cities participated in a series of school boycotts from the fall of 1963 through the spring of 1964. Of these, far and away the largest took place New York City. Confronted with the monumental task of organizing the protest, boycott leader Rev. Milton Galamison called on Rustin to coordinate the action. More than 400,000 New Yorkers participated in a one-day February 3, 1964, boycott of segregated schooling. New York's newspapers were astounded both by the numbers of black and Puerto Rican parents and children who boycotted and by the complete absence of violence or disorder from the protestors. It was, as a sympathetic newspaper account accurately reported, "the largest civil rights demonstration" in American history. Rustin prophesized that the boycott was "just the beginning of a massive popular movement against the many forms of segregation, discrimination and exploitation that exist in this city."[25]

Arguing that "the movement to integrate the schools will create far-reaching benefits" for teachers as well as students, school boycotters had counted heavily on the UFT urging members not to cross picket lines. On December 18, 1963, Milton Galamison appeared before the UFT Executive Board to urge that the union join the boycott or ask teachers to respect picket lines. The union, however, promised only to protect from reprisals any teachers who participated. When militant protestors announced plans to follow up the February 3 boycott with a second one on March 16, the UFT refused even to defend boycotting teachers from reprisals. Later, at the time of the 1968 school crisis, Brooklyn CORE leader Oliver Leeds and African American Teachers Association president Al Vann would cite the UFT's refusal to support the 1964 integration campaign as proof that an alliance between the teachers' union and the black community was impossible.[26]

New York teachers, almost all of whom were white, were not the only professed allies of the civil rights movement who boycotted the boycott. The protest, with its demand for complete integration of the city's schools—a demand that would require white children to attend schools in black neighborhoods—severely strained the alliance between black integrationists and white liberals. White reaction in turn led to a split among boycott leaders. In a letter to black labor leaders, Rustin accused Galamison of extremism and, together with the national leadership of CORE and the NAACP, he left the boycott coalition. Meanwhile, militants blasted civil rights leaders for capitulating to the white establishment.[27]

Together with the civil rights moderates, Rustin made one last effort to promote school integration through mass protest. Coming in the wake of the boycotts, the May 18, 1964, March for Democratic Schools represented a move toward moderation in both its program and its form. White labor officials addressed the May marchers and representatives of established mainstream civil rights organizations, rather than the leaders of New York's grassroots black school-reform groups, who had directed protestors during the boycotts.[28]

Unlike the boycotts, with their demands for complete desegregation, the May action called for no more than "maximum possible" integration. This goal was to be achieved through such modest programs as the construction of larger schools and the replacement of junior high schools with middle schools. "Our purpose," demonstration organizers professed, was to "separate white people of good will from those who would camouflage their prejudices under the slogan, 'neighborhood schools.'" In response, such groups as the Jewish Labor Committee and the United Federation of Teachers, which refused to endorse the boycotts and their demand for complete integration, endorsed the May rally.[29]

For the upcoming rally, which came on the heels of a segregationist rally that had drawn 15,000, Rustin promised to attract at least as many. Instead, only four 4,000 protestors showed up, and the Board of Education was no more responsive to the conciliatory May demonstration than to the earlier, more confrontational boycott. Racial protest had reached a dead end; moderation, needed to win white allies, immobilized black activism.[30]

The school protests reinforced the impact of the March on Washington on Rustin's thinking. Community-based black activism had dismantled the legal apparatus of segregation and won southern blacks their civil rights, but such a strategy could not complete the struggle for equality once citizenship had been won. The "lessons of 1964 [were] clear: public protest alone will not wring meaningful innovations from the Board." The concerns of enfranchised blacks dictated the invention of new forms of activism and a move "from protest to politics." School reformers needed "a silent partner in this effort—the teachers' union."[31]

The American Federation of Teachers and its New York local, the UFT, had much to recommend them to Rustin. The union had actively challenged racial segregation of the schools and racism within the labor movement. Even before the 1954 *Brown* decision, the AFT had expelled segregated southern locals while the rival National Education Association maintained them well into the 1960s. When the UFT went on strike in 1967, it demanded changes in educational policy along with improved wages for its members. Although some activists claimed that UFT proposals would increase teachers' authority at the expense of black students' rights, when the strike concluded, Rustin argued that teacher unionists had achieved what black protestors had not, "a historic breakthrough in the area of parent-teacher participation in programs to improve our school system."[32]

Still, as a civil rights activist, Rustin seemed as much to have become a silent partner as to have found one. Whereas before 1964 Rustin had operated under the aegis of peace groups and black civil rights and labor organizations, after 1964 he headed the A. Philip Randolph Institute. Conceived by Rustin and social-democratic leader Max Shachtman, the black activist's new organizational base depended financially on the AFL-CIO and the UFT. In February of 1968, UFT organizer Sandra Feldman met with Randolph Institute staff to plan a conference of black teacher unionists. Although the UFT role was to be kept hidden, the conference's "ultimate goal," according to Feldman, was to get the union "some vital black leadership and loyalty." In the midst of the 1968 strikes, the Randolph Institute announced plans to move its offices into the UFT building, where it would be the union's only tenant.[33]

In his effort to build a civil rights–labor coalition, Rustin was caught between the demands of the grassroots activists he hoped to lead and the white allies he sought to nurture. Rustin, argues the historian Taylor Branch, "chafed under demands from new union employers" and "pleaded for leeway to salvage his ties with the civil rights movement." Meanwhile, many of New York's unions demonstrated hostility to racial equality. The building trades were particularly notorious for their exclusionary practices. No blacks or Puerto Ricans, for instance, were among the four thousand members of Pipefitters Union Local 638 working in 1963. Of the more than sixteen hundred members of New York's Metal Lathers Union Local 46, two were black.[34]

Efforts by black New York City activists to win economic concessions had constituted a dress rehearsal for the school boycotts. At the precise moment when the March on Washington celebrated the dream of a civil rights–labor coalition compelling federal support for integration, labor and government in New York had united against black economic and political demands. Black workers there were virtually excluded from construction jobs at a number of public and semi-public projects. In Queens, activists targeted Rochdale Village, a mammoth cooperative housing development that a number of unions were building, in cooperation with New York's municipal government. In Brooklyn, jobs protests focused on the massive Downstate Medical Center. While the project employed white construction workers who commuted from as far away as Pennsylvania, many black World War II and Korean War veterans living in Brooklyn and trained as surveyors and bulldozer operators were refused employment.[35]

The Ministers' Committee for Job Opportunities for Brooklyn rallied thousands of protestors and led hundreds in civil disobedience. In negotiations with New York governor Nelson Rockefeller, Milton Galamison and other ministers abandoned protesters' demands that blacks and Puerto Ricans get 25 percent of construction jobs and settled for the promise that the state would enforce existing antidiscrimination laws. Brooklyn CORE, which had initially led the protests, accurately predicted that the settlement would fail to produce jobs for blacks, and it denounced the ministers as "sell outs" and "Uncle Toms." Milton Galamison traced his militancy in the school boycotts in part to the bitterness with which he recalled his attempt at moderation in the Downstate campaign. For him and the thousands of activists who received their political apprenticeships demonstrating at New York construction sites, unions and white liberal officials were as likely to be targets of black protest as they were to be allies.[36]

The evolving racial stances of black and white Americans also threatened Bayard Rustin's dream of a civil rights–labor coalition. Rustin's publicly expressed optimism about the potential of a civil rights–labor coalition masked deep private concerns about the growing threat to progressive social reform posed by Black Nationalism and white backlash. He sensed the difficulties that activists faced as heightened movement expectations for black freedom hit up against the limited willingness of white America to allow it: "Negroes have been put in a desperate situation, and yet everyone—myself included—must urge them not to behave with desperation but politically and rationally."[37]

The full, tragic implications of the need to face racism "politically and rationally" became manifest in the summer of 1964. After a white police lieutenant killed a black ninth grader on his way to summer school, Harlem and Bedford-Stuyvesant exploded. Rustin witnessed the police riots that left hundreds of black New Yorkers bloodied, and he personally attended to the wounded. When he urged blacks to disperse and to resist with nonviolence, they spat at him and shot back, "Uncle Tom! Uncle Tom!" Rustin could have responded that common sense rather than the accommodation of racism recommended against unarmed blacks confronting brutal police. Instead, he answered the jeering crowd from a sound truck, "I'm prepared to be a Tom if it's the only way I can save women and children from being shot down in the street, and if you're not willing to do the same, you're fools."[38]

Behind the scenes, in protracted negotiations with New York mayor Robert Wagner Jr., Rustin adopted the same accommodationist approach. The son and namesake of one of the principal architects of the New Deal liberal coalition that had shaped American politics since the 1930s, Wagner responded to the unrest by condemning "mob rule" but not police brutality. Unable to convince the mayor to address the politically explosive issue of police violence, Rustin settled for Wagner's promise to seek ten million dollars from Washington for a jobs program. Fearful that New York's hotheaded black leaders would exacerbate tensions and block any settlement, Rustin recruited Martin Luther King to lend legitimacy to negotiations. The riots, like the school boycott, confirmed the limits that circumscribed black dreams of freedom and, Rustin told Urban League leader Whitney Young, left him "terribly depressed."[39]

Even as he implored black New Yorkers to avoid violent confrontation with the police, Rustin distanced himself from nonviolence both as a strategy to transform white consciousness and as an expression of utopian hopes for creating a just society. "Despite thousands and thousands who have gone to jail, despite bombings of churches and people, despite the millions of dollars tied up in bail and the millions paid in fines," he explained in a speech to the Fellowship of Reconciliation, "no breakthrough has occurred in the South and in the North Negroes are being increasingly pushed to the wall." Blacks were turning to violence, he argued, because the nonviolent "tactics that have been advocated and used [were] inadequate for dealing with the objective needs." No longer would he "tell any Negroes that they should love white people," Rustin concluded. "They don't love them, they have no need to love them, no basis on which they can love them."[40]

Before 1964, Rustin had imagined that civil rights activism would drive segregationists out of the Democratic Party and thus move the party and the labor movement to the left. The school protest failures, the Harlem riot, and the increasing visibility of white backlash in national politics forced him to reconsider. Repudiating his party's traditional racial values, Republican presidential candidate Barry Goldwater actively appealed to violent southern segregationists, at the same time that segregationist Alabama governor George Wallace attracted significant support among Democratic voters in northern primaries. Rustin and other moderate civil rights leaders feared that the Harlem riot would cost the civil rights movement crucial white political support. "New York City is the center of the Negro struggle for equality," Martin Luther King explained. "What happens here affects the whole country—from the share croppers of Mississippi longing for freedom to the followers of Barry Goldwater hoping to discredit liberalism."[41]

Together with NAACP leader Roy Wilkins, Rustin drafted a telegram to major civil rights leaders, arguing that "the tragic violence in Harlem" and Goldwater's nomination "may produce the sternest challenge we have yet seen." In response, they called for a moratorium on demonstrations during the 1964 presidential election campaign. Rustin himself severed ties with the peace and civil rights activists and organizations with which he had been associated for twenty years.[42]

Rustin further distanced himself from movement activists at the 1964 Democratic National Convention in Atlantic City. In the months leading up to the convention, the focal point of the civil rights movement had been Mississippi, where blacks excluded from the segregated regular Democratic Party had organized the Mississippi Freedom Democratic Party (MFDP). MFDP representatives petitioned the Democratic Party, seeking to replace the all-white Mississippi delegation in Atlantic City. "How could we not prevail?" Student Nonviolent Coordinating Committee activist John Lewis would still wonder decades later. "The law was on our side. Justice was on our side. The sentiments of the entire nation were with us." President Lyndon Johnson, however, opposed the activists. Seeking to appease segregationists, the Democrats refused to seat the integrated and integrationist MFDP delegation. For Lewis and countless other activists, Atlantic City was "the turning point of the civil rights movement. . . . Until then . . . the belief still prevailed that the system would work, the system would listen."[43]

Whereas Democratic Party actions at Atlantic City drove many young activists to a more radical stance, the realization that white America—even at the moment of the federal government's greatest commitment to civil rights—would not grant blacks full and equal citizenship drove Rustin away from radicalism. He worked to get the MFDP delegation seated but also discouraged demonstrations that might alienate "[the Negro's] friends in the labor movement and Democratic Party." For his efforts, Rustin earned the thanks of President Lyndon Johnson and vice presidential candidate Hubert Humphrey. On the other hand, militant organizers and grassroots activists were enraged. In the eyes of civil rights leader Bob Moses, Rustin had "flip-flopped" and thereafter remained steadfastly on the "conservative side."[44]

For Rustin, the 1965 Watts riot intensified the political quandary of 1964. The riot "had brought out in the open the despair and hatred that continue to brew in the Northern ghettoes." There, "a truly hopeless and lost generation . . . can see the alien world of affluence unfold before them on the TV screen. . . . Mistreated by the local storekeeper, suspected by the policeman on the beat, disliked by their teachers, they cannot stand more failures." Although Rustin condemned senseless destruction by black rioters, decades confronting southern segregationists had left him unprepared for the hostility of Los Angeles officials. The two political alternatives Rustin could offer—coalition politics and moral witness—both depended on the goodwill of liberal whites. Watts rendered them equally implausible.[45]

Blacks, Rustin lamented, were "in a situation similar to that of the turn of the century, when Booker T. Washington advised them to 'cast down their buckets' (that is to say, accommodate to segregation and disfranchisement)." The extent of Rustin's retreat from the quest for black equality and freedom was manifest in a 1966 debate with militant Student Nonviolent Coordinating Committee activist Stokely Carmichael. In response to Carmichael's critique of individual white prejudice and institutional racism, Rustin argued that blacks needed to align themselves with a white majority committed to progress. Pushed by Carmichael as to why he had supported the Democratic Party in 1964, Rustin said that President Johnson "was the lesser of two evils." Coalition politics, which had once offered Rustin the promise of promoting black liberation, was reduced to making more palatable an immoral society.[46]

Bayard Rustin acknowledged the reasons why his endorsement of coalition politics was so tepid. "It took countless beatings and twenty-four jailings—and the absence of strong and continual support from the liberal community," he noted, "to persuade [Stokely] Carmichael that his earlier faith in coalition politics was mistaken, that nothing was to be gained from working with whites." And beyond political betrayal by white liberals, white liberalism itself offered no adequate solution to life in America's ghetto "dead ends of despair."[47]

Finally, political analysis was not the only reason Rustin distanced himself from ideologies of racial identity and from the peace and civil rights movements. Being black in white America circumscribed Rustin's life and shaped his politics, but just as America refused to accommodate fully black demands for equality, the peace movement and black community refused to embrace Rustin fully. He was gay, and for his homosexuality, he suffered the scorn of movement comrades as well as the taunts of Dixiecrats.[48]

A. J. Muste loved Rustin like a son but considered the embarrassment caused by what one peace activist labeled Rustin's "personal problem" grounds for dismissing him from a position at the Fellowship of Reconciliation. When Rustin was convicted of having sex with two white men in 1953, he dutifully resigned from the Fellowship of Reconciliation. Scandalized by Rustin's homosexuality and Communist past, black ministers squelched Martin Luther King Jr.'s efforts to hire him at the Southern Christian Leadership Conference, at a time when Rustin, almost fifty, was counting on King for a regular salary. When Adam Clayton Powell, embroiled in a political dispute with King, threatened to tell reporters that King was having an affair with Rustin, King broke off all contact with his advisor.[49]

Earlier, New York's anonymous streets had offered Rustin a setting in which, despite occasional police harassment, he did not feel a need to hide his homosexuality. Still, he did not conceptualize cruising as an act of living the truth analogous to freedom riding. Then, his 1953 arrest and the reaction of movement comrades to it convinced Rustin of the need to stay in the closet. If one wanted to be an activist, he concluded, "sex must be sublimated." Homophobia thus provided Rustin with a dress rehearsal for racial accommodation.[50]

As Rustin cut his links to the peace and civil rights movement, longstanding personal, intellectual, and political ties with social-democratic activists blossomed. Social democracy embraced the Marxist concept that the means of production determined social organization but stressed the gradual achievement of industrial democracy through constitutional means. Theorizing that politics reflected universal laws rather than cultural particulars, social democrats argued that racial discrimination reflected class relations and should be addressed through the class struggle. In the famous phrase of Eugene Debs, "The Socialist Party is the Party of the whole working class, regardless of color," and therefore had "nothing special to offer the Negro." Efforts to promote working-class solidarity often reflected and contributed to assimilationist cultural values. Social democracy was particularly attractive to union officials, and its adherents dominated the leadership of the UFT.[51]

Bayard Rustin discounted neither the impact of racism on American life nor the rich cultural traditions created by African Americans. He was fully convinced that "freedom in America applies to all but Negroes," that "in a million quiet ways, the majority of white Americans go about insulting the manhood of Negroes every day."[52] An accomplished singer of black spirituals as well as of opera, he had "preached the dignity of black skin color" and taught "Negro history" long before such things became popular.[53]

Still, only a thin line separated attentiveness to the cultural heritage or particular history of African Americans and the reproduction of racist stereotypes. Rustin challenged the rationale of educational programs based on particular qualities or pathologies imputed to the black family, underclass, or culture. "A Negro coming out of Mississippi," he argued, is not "disadvantaged" compared to the masses of immigrants who came to American cities from Europe. The newly arrived white ethnics "did not know American culture; they did not know the language." But because American "society was prepared to use [their] muscle power," these earlier migrants found "jobs and become part of the productive system." By contrast, the blacks who populated America's deindustrializing ghettos in the 1960s remained outside the political, cultural, and educational mainstream "even though they [knew] the language and culture of the United States."[54]

Educational programs that sought only to remediate the deficiencies in ghetto youngsters mistook the cultural consequences of poverty for its economic causes. Drawing on social-democratic race-blind theory, Rustin argued that social and economic forces rather than the presumed attributes of black children explained the educational failures of African American youth.[55]

Social democracy provided a basis for Rustin's politics as well as his pedagogy. "Wearing my hair Afro-style, calling myself an Afro-American and eating all the chitterlings I can find," he maintained, "are not going to affect Congress." Confronted with the inability of black protest to address the economics of inequality and fearful of unleashing the vengefulness of America's white majority, Rustin found in social democracy theoretical justification for moderate, race-blind egalitarian organizing. At the same time, the social-democratic vision allowed Rustin to respond to and transcend his own multiple identities in his political work.[56]

"Until we face the need for a fundamental reordering of our priorities," Rustin reminded educators, school reforms would constitute no more than pseudo-solutions to the crisis of ghetto education. The years leading up to the New York school conflict, he noted, had witnessed the introduction of the middle school, pairing, open enrollment, community control,

and more useless maneuvers, one after the other. Meanwhile the objective situation gets worse and worse. . . . Until we are prepared to eliminate slums . . . we are going to have inferior education for Negro children. If we turn the schools over to parents and community leaders, they will be no different. As long as we have slums, as long as we have the kind of housing we have, as long as people are not working, the schools will be inferior. It is amazing to me that anyone can think it possible to create an effective way of teaching a child who lives in a ghetto. He simply will not be educated, no matter what gimmicks you use. It's a matter of fundamental change here or nothing.[57]

Community control, in Rustin's analysis, only distracted African Americans from real reform.

Coalition Politics in Post-liberal America

Despite Rustin's social-democratic invocation of proletarian solidarity and "fundamental change," he recognized that revolution was not on the horizon in 1968.[58] Congress was no more concerned with economic democracy than it was with racial equality. What distinguished organized labor from militant black activism was not its power to secure full social justice for African Americans but rather its willingness to accommodate the domestic and foreign policy agenda of Cold War America. At a time when race relations and U.S. actions in Vietnam, rather than industrial conflict, were the defining issues of American politics, Rustin and other social democrats cloaked acquiescence to militarism and racial inequality in the mantle of working-class radicalism.

Rustin, for instance, condemned antiwar protestors, while urging Martin Luther King to be silent about Vietnam and improbably asserting that the government's unlimited resources allowed it to fund fully a real

war on poverty without cutting military funding. As the antiwar movement increasingly questioned the ideological underpinnings of U.S. foreign policy, Rustin became increasingly vehement in the anti-
Communism that had been part of politics since he left the Young Communist League. Similarly, he fervidly denounced Black Nationalism
while displaying little emotion in the face of racial bias in the labor
movement. For Rustin, as for white social democrats, calls for blacks to
align themselves with the labor movement marked an abandonment, not
an affirmation, of radicalism. As Rustin became isolated from old allies,
he ever more strongly allied himself with the very conservatism he
denounced.[59]

Bayard Rustin was well aware of the limits that confronted the black
freedom struggle and of the conflicts that separated black New Yorkers
from teachers and the rest of organized labor. His efforts at coalition
building had exposed the ambivalence with which white labor greeted
black allies. Still, conditions in America and its cities, Rustin argued in
his UFT award speech, left blacks no real alternative to alliance with
organized labor.[60]

Rustin's attempt to build a civil rights–labor coalition in his John
Dewey Award speech came at an inopportune moment. Days before he
was to address the UFT, a white sniper assassinated Martin Luther King
Jr. in Memphis, and for many black activists, hopes for integration died
along with King. When Rustin was called to Memphis, Michael Harrington, a white social-democratic comrade, stood in for him at the Hilton Hotel, site of the UFT's award ceremony. As Harrington read
Rustin's speech, protestors gathered outside the Hilton. They demanded
that Rustin sever his ties with the UFT and condemned the union's
opposition to community control, its "racist attitudes [and] policies
against black and Puerto Rican children and communities," and its
"refusal to oppose the racist war in Vietnam."[61]

The Hilton Hotel protestors were not alone in their hostility to the
civil rights–labor coalition Rustin advocated. The conflict between
white teacher unionists and black community organizers led to a series
of three extraordinarily bitter teachers' strikes in the fall of 1968 that
dominated racial politics and municipal affairs in New York. As the
school conflict reached its climax, increasing numbers of black unionists,
as well as educators, ministers, and community activists, opposed the
UFT. Harlem Labor Council and UFT official Richard Parrish, who had
worked with Rustin on the 1950s Washington integration rallies, was

among the black labor leaders who embraced community control. Parrish believed that by remaining in the UFT, black teachers could help
heal the rift between the union and the black and Puerto Rican communities. Still, in a September 15, 1968, television interview, he labeled
the UFT walkout over community control "a strike against the black
community . . . a collusive action of supervisors, teachers and custodians
against black parents and students."[62]

As the 1968 teachers' strike wore on, leading black and Puerto Rican
unionists repudiated labor solidarity in favor of a racially defined notion
of community. Late in October, two hundred labor leaders, including
Parrish and Negro American Labor Council president Cleveland Robinson, identified the families of black and Puerto Rican workers, rather
than teacher unionists, as "the victims of this vicious system." The group
supported community control "as a means of ending this nightmare that
for too long has existed in our communities without redress." Rather
than advancing a civil rights–labor coalition, the actions of teacher
unionists precluded it.[63]

The conflict over community control ended in a victory for the
teachers' union and a defeat for black activists. A 1969 union-endorsed
"decentralization" law gave the central board of education far-reaching
control of textbooks, curriculum, school construction, and teacher hiring, and complete control over New York's troubled high schools. The
law created between thirty and thirty-three "community" school districts with limited powers, each containing a couple hundred thousand
residents and thus difficult to influence through community organizing.
UFT president Al Shanker called the new law "a good piece of legislation," while Brooklyn civil rights leader Milton Galamison claimed,
"We couldn't have gotten a worse bill in Mississippi."[64]

Designed to insulate the school system from black activists, the law's
"Community School Board" elections worked as planned. In Ocean
Hill–Brownsville, voter turnout fell from 25 percent in 1967 to 4 percent
in 1970. In a school system where only a minority of students were
white, whites formed a majority on twenty-five of thirty-two "community" boards, including that of Manhattan's District 3, where 19 percent
of students were white, and Brooklyn's District 13, where only one student in twenty was white.[65]

The cost of allying the African American hopes to organized labor
proved even greater than Rustin imagined. Although its triumph guaran-
teed the UFT a prominent role in school affairs and municipal politics,
the defeat of community control left a residue of bitterness, alienation,

Bayard Rustin (*right*) and Albert Shanker (*center*). (Copyright © 2009 The New York Times)

and distrust that would poison New York and its schools for decades.[66] The 1968 conflict helped reshape New York's electoral politics. As the historian Jerald Podair has observed, the more conservative candidate has won almost every New York mayoral election since the school conflict; the city of LaGuardia, Wagner, and Lindsay became the city of Koch, Giuliani, and Bloomberg. More broadly, teacher unionists demonstrated how a standard of race-blind equal treatment could shift from justifying racial equality into a rationalization of white domination.[67]

Rustin's efforts foundered amid the very ghetto conditions and urban conflicts he hoped to address. Although he argued persuasively that the new urban conditions created by automation propelled black demands for equal education, Rustin ignored the need to rethink race relations and labor activism itself in light of economic changes.

Marjorie Murphy notes that at the very time when the newly founded UFT was winning concessions from the school system, black school activists, mobilizing as large a percentage of their constituency as the UFT had, "had little to show for their efforts." The contrasting results

of teacher organizing and black activism reflected the evolving conditions of urban and national life.[68]

From the 1940s through the 1960s, "urban renewal" and highway
development projects such as the addition of a second level and new
approach roads to the George Washington Bridge and the construction
of the Verrazano-Narrows Bridge destroyed hundreds of thousands of
working-class New York homes while fostering real estate booms in
New Jersey and Staten Island. Over two million New Yorkers—the vast
majority white—moved to the suburbs, while the number of black and
Latino New Yorkers grew in proportion to the number of whites who
left the city. Meanwhile, the city's industrial job base declined steadily.
In the garment industry, for instance, two-thirds of jobs disappeared in
the second half of the twentieth century. Government responsiveness to
the poor gave way to responsiveness to business interests.[69]

As white laborers, including the city's teachers, fled the city, it distanced itself politically, culturally, and indeed physically from alliance
with the black freedom struggle.[70] This movement to the suburbs both
reflected and propelled UFT's growing role in school politics and black
activists' defeats. The very power of the UFT on which, in Rustin's
view, blacks ought to depend was thus embedded in the racial inequality
black activists confronted. Rustin's phantom of a black-labor alliance, no
less than dreams of black separatism, constituted an accommodation with
the persistence of racism as well as resistance to it.

The dilemmas that Rustin and his adversaries confronted in 1968—
separatism versus integration in the black quest for racial justice, the relationship of race and class in American society, and the possibility of
finding white allies in the quest for black freedom—were not new. At the
same time, declining industrial production in American cities, declining
support for liberalism in American politics, and the growing gulf between
expanding white To ignore the break in Rustin's politics requires ignoring as well the thoughtfulness and courage with which he made that
shift. And it requires ignoring the ever-evolving balance of democratic
aspirations and social inequality in American life. Celebratory accounts
of the movement can give us encouragement in arid times but they offer
little guidance. To ignore the choices that Rustin made and the reasons
he made them does him no honor.

The issues Bayard Rustin faced—about the relative power of race and
class in shaping American life, about the quest for racial justice at a
moment when historic victories in the struggle against racism led many
Americans to conclude that white supremacy was a thing of the past—

continue to perplex Americans committed to social justice. Neither Rustin nor the advocates of community control he opposed offer an ideological role model or map. The very choices that Rustin and his adversaries made demonstrate that, despite the continuities of history, we must make our own consequential choices in the context of our own day.

7

The Young Lords and the Social and Structural Roots of Late Sixties Urban Radicalism

JOHANNA FERNANDEZ

Against the backdrop of America's spiraling urban crisis in the late 1960s, an unexpected cohort of young radicals unleashed a dramatic chain of urban guerilla protests that riveted the media and alarmed Mayor John V. Lindsay's New York. From garbage-dumping demonstrations to a series of church and hospital occupations—termed "offensives" after the dramatic Vietnamese military campaign against U.S. forces in 1968 known as the Tet Offensive—this small interracial group exploded into the country's consciousness, staging its social grievances with infectious irreverence and distinctive imagination. They had enormous ideas, a flair for the dramatic, and a penchant for linking international crises with local concerns; within a few years this group of young men and women would reshape social protest and win an astounding number of victories. They called themselves the Young Lords.

This chapter explores the character and influence of protest movements in the late 1960s through a review of the emergence of the Young Lords Party (YLP) in New York, a self-proclaimed Puerto Rican revolutionary nationalist organization that consciously fashioned itself after the Black Panther Party (BPP) and ardently championed the independence of Puerto Rico.[1] Through most of its active life between 1969 and 1974, the YLP led militant community-based campaigns that addressed issues of racism, incarceration and police brutality, employment, and inequality in education and public health, including sanitation, lead poisoning, access to decent health services, and hunger in the lives of poor children. The Young Lords was led by first- and second-generation Puerto Rican radicals raised on the U.S. mainland, rather than on the island. Its members were youths who were radicalized by the civil rights and antiwar movements of the 1960s and whose political outlook was shaped by the social and economic crises that began to grip northern cities in the postwar period.

The history of militant urban activism in the late 1960s suggests that organizations like the Young Lords and the Black Panthers were spawned by the deep and unprecedented social and economic changes taking place in northern cities in the postwar period, and that their practices and politics were also tied to these developments. The history of the Young Lords Party challenges mainstream depictions of the civil rights and Black Power movements. It suggests that although racial inequality in America impelled the movement's emergence, the objectives and character of protest were integrally interwoven with grievances of social and economic import and driven by a strong class impulse.[2]

Before its emergence as a political organization, the Young Lords was a gang that had been active in Chicago since the 1950s and that emerged politicized in that city in the tumult of 1968.[3] The primary architect of the Young Lords' political conversion was its chairman, Jose "Cha Cha" Jimenez, who became politicized in prison after reading *The Autobiography of Malcolm X* and the story of religious transformation told by Thomas Merton in his best seller, *Seven Storey Mountain*. Upon his release from prison, Jimenez was targeted by a War on Poverty program designed to bridge the transition from jail to civilian life for former inmates; he was also approached by a local activist, Pat Divine, who convinced Jimenez that he should join the struggle against urban renewal in the Lincoln Park section of Chicago, where the Lords were active. After a number of failed attempts at politicizing the Young Lords, members of Jimenez's gang heeded the call of activism following the fatal shooting of one of their own, Manuel Ramos, by an undercover police officer, James Lamb. In the weeks that followed, the Young Lords would be politically transformed by the campaign they would mount to bring Officer Lamb to justice.

In consultation with Panther leaders Fred Hampton, Bobby Lee, and Henry "Poison" Gaddis, Jimenez proceeded to turn the Young Lords into the Panthers' Puerto Rican counterpart.[4] Because of their established gang network, hundreds of young men and women joined the Young Lords Organization (YLO) and partook in their militant neighborhood protests against police misconduct and urban displacement in Chicago under the guise of urban renewal.

The example set by the Black Panther Party provided a compelling model of organization that was instrumental to the evolution of the Young Lords. Following the first wave of urban upheavals beginning in Harlem in 1964, the BPP's founding members resolved to organize the radicalized sections of poor and working-class African Americans. The BPP initiated a series of "survival programs" to address the immediate causes of the riots. The first of these was a civilian patrol unit to monitor police arrests and defend community residents against police aggression in east Oakland, California. Later, the Panthers added a children's breakfast program, an ambulance service, and a lead-poisoning detection program to their compendium of activities.[5]

Between 1968 and 1970, the Chicago YLO led a series of militant campaigns with a community-service approach akin to the Black Panther Party's survival programs. In Chicago, a city targeted by Lyndon B. Johnson's War on Poverty initiative, the YLO established tactical alliances with social service organizations, community advocates, and government antipoverty programs. The Young Lords' protest actions included the occupation of the Armitage Church in Chicago following several failed attempts at convincing church leadership to allow the group use of the space to set up a day-care program and health clinic. Collaborating with other radical organizations and social service groups, the Chicago YLO successfully stopped an urban renewal plan for construction of middle-income homes in the city's west Lincoln Park neighborhood that would have displaced Puerto Ricans and other Latinos.[6]

The Puerto Rican radicals inspired the formation of sister organizations in other cities, the most influential of which was based in New York City. The New York Young Lords subsequently duplicated the organizing efforts of the Chicago group in Puerto Rican neighborhoods, including East Harlem and the South Bronx. In New York, the Young Lords Organization—later renamed the Young Lords Party—was initiated by politicized students in 1969. It flourished alongside the conflagrations of New York's city and labor politics in the late 1960s. These young men and women full of passion came of age during the racially divisive NYC teacher's strike of 1968, the school decentralization movements in Ocean Hill–Brownsville, recurrent housing struggles, the welfare-rights movement, the prison rebellions at the Tombs and Attica, local street riots, and the rise of Puerto Ricans and other Latinos as an electoral force in the city.

The New York chapter of the Young Lords was founded by a bright and dynamic core of first-generation college students. While generations before them had been excluded from higher education on the basis of race and ethnicity, in the 1960s African American and Puerto Rican students began to matriculate at universities across the nation in record numbers, following the institutionalization, between 1964 and 1966, of special admissions opportunities for minority students.[7] As newcomers into an inhospitable environment, many students of color found campus life to be politically formative as they were confronted with issues of campus discrimination, financial aid, and the narrow scope of their colleges' core curricula. The young people who founded the Young Lords Party in New York all formed part of a network of Puerto Rican and African American student activists across the city who were involved in campus struggles. Young Lords Iris Morales and Felipe Luciano were members of the Puerto Rican Student Union, which served as a clearinghouse of activity, coordinating the efforts of the various Puerto Rican student groups emerging in colleges across the city.[8] One of the major strategists of the organization, Juan Gonzalez, was a member of Students for a Democratic Society and a leading member of the coordinating committee of the Columbia Strike of 1968.

The core group of young people who initiated the launch of a New York chapter of the Young Lords were brought together and transformed by the experimental project in college education at State University of New York at Old Westbury, which rigorously pursued diversity, an innovative curriculum, and a structure of democratic practice that incorporated faculty and students in college governance. A number of them, including Denise Oliver, Mickey Melendez, and David Perez, had been identified by recruiters at Old Westbury because of their roots in socially conscious community work and associations with the Real Great Society, a government antipoverty program in East Harlem. Eventually, these young men and women became part of a network of activists who formed a precursor to the Young Lords called the Sociedad de Albizu Campos (SAC). Organized and led by Mickey Melendez, SAC was a reading circle named after the father of the Puerto Rican national independence movement, Don Pedro Albizu Campos, and composed of students who were interested in Puerto Rican history and the politics of Puerto Rico's national liberation movements.[9]

Through their readings and activities with the SAC, these students entered a markedly different stage in their political evolution that would eventually lead to a full-fledged embrace of revolutionary nationalism. Within this tightly knit network of budding revolutionaries of color, many were Puerto Rican but a number were African American. What they shared, however, trumped race: They knew each other intimately, they had grown together politically, and they were looking to make their mark where they were. At the same time, a number of SAC members, including Robert Bunkley and Pablo Guzmán, who was a recent arrival from a study-abroad program where he witnessed the tragedy of student protests in Mexico in 1968, were increasingly interested in the Black Panther Party.

As tens of thousands of students began to question the logic and structure of American society, many groups began to look outside the university to poor communities for more permanent sites of struggle. The SAC was especially influenced by the concept of "community control" in New York following the Ocean Hill–Brownsville school controversy, which, combined with the black movement's ardent call for independent black political power bases, inspired its members to connect ideological discussions with activity in the Puerto Rican community of East Harlem. At the urging of Mickey Melendez, the SAC made contact with prominent Puerto Rican student activists in the city, including Columbia University Strike Committee member Juan Gonzalez and Felipe Luciano, a member of the Last Poets, the Harlem-based group of Black Power-era artists whose politically charged live-music and spoken-word poetry performances in the 1960s prefigured the emergence of hip hop and rap in the 1970s and 1980s.

In the spring of 1969, an interview with Jimenez in the Panther newspaper, *Black Panther*, drew the attention of a number of members of the SAC.[10] Of particular interest to SAC members was Jimenez's statements concerning the colonial relationship between Puerto Rico and the United States.[11] In response, a small group of SAC members decided to drive to Chicago to learn more about the Young Lords. After convening with Cha Cha Jimenez and securing permission to launch a chapter of the YLO back home, the New York radicals, who were eager to connect theoretical understandings of power and politics with urban community organizing as the next phase in the movement, reported back with excitement on the mission and work of the Chicago group.

After learning from Jimenez about other radical New York groups attempting to make inroads among Puerto Ricans in that city,[12] members of the SAC called on a preexisting Lower East Side YLO and an East Harlem photography workshop for inner-city youths with whom the East Side group had been collaborating to discuss merging the three groups into a New York chapter of the Young Lords Organization.[13] The New York Lords announced their formation on Saturday, July 26, 1969, at the East Village's Tompkins Square Park.[14] Before long, they were duplicating the organizing efforts of the Chicago group in East Harlem and the South Bronx.

Although the stated political goal of the Young Lords was the liberation of Puerto Rico, the group's first two years were consumed with the social and economic grievances of Puerto Ricans in urban communities on the mainland. The group's nationalist orientation and Puerto Rican identification obscured the Young Lords' diversity: Approximately 30 percent of the organization's membership was composed of African Americans and non–Puerto Rican Latinos.[15] The fact that the Young Lords garnered support outside their ethnic group for their nationalist agenda is testament to the legitimacy of their claim and its parallels in anticolonial postwar struggles. In New York, the ethnic crossover imprinted in the Young Lords' membership was also incubated in the shared experiences of African Americans and Puerto Ricans in the city. These groups came to develop a unique relationship shaped by both groups' condition before the dominant society as racialized and colonial subjects.[16]

Their most famous campaign was their audacious garbage-dumping protests, which forced the city to conduct regular neighborhood garbage pickups. A quieter but more significant victory was their anti-lead-poisoning campaign, which was instrumental in the passage of anti-lead-poisoning legislation in New York during the early 1970s. At Lincoln Hospital in the Bronx, the Young Lords were among the first activists to challenge the advent of draconian spending cuts and privatization policies in the public sector.

Because Puerto Ricans were relatively new arrivals in New York, the emergence of an organization as dynamic as the Young Lords became the subject of hundreds of articles in local news publications, including the *New York Times*. As recent arrivals, Puerto Ricans were not expected to assert themselves in such a dramatic fashion. In fact, according to various *New York Times* articles, in the postwar period, Puerto Ricans were viewed as a "mild mannered" people. One of the questions raised by mainstream depictions of Puerto Ricans as mild mannered is, What accounts for the discrepancy between the way they were perceived upon their arrival and the aggressive and radical examples of protest that emerged within a section of Puerto Ricans in the late 1960s?

Riots were the single development that most influenced the emergence of northern urban radicalism in the 1960s. In 1966, over twenty-four cities went up in flames. That same year, Puerto Ricans rioted in Chicago. And the day before the Detroit riots of 1967, Puerto Ricans rioted in East Harlem.[17] In addition to the riots, the failure, in the 1960s, of liberalism and its inability to posit solutions to social problems that corresponded to their magnitude also opened the door to revolutionary critiques of the urban crisis.

In 1966 and 1967, Puerto Ricans were the major protagonists in riots that swept through East New York and East Harlem. Detonated in each case by the police shootings of Puerto Rican civilians, these riots marked a turning point for Puerto Ricans in New York. They revealed the extent of civil rights injuries for minority groups other than African Americans. So shocking was the violence that it opened up the possibility of reformulating a public debate that the mainstream media had largely cast in black and white.

On the night of July 23, 1967, approximately twenty-four hours after the most extensive riots of the 1960s began in Detroit, the predominantly Puerto Rican neighborhood of East Harlem was roiled in violence. That night the police intervened in a common weekend brawl between two men in East Harlem. Renaldo Rodriguez, one of the men involved in the knife fight, was shot and killed by police officer Anthony Cinquemani. According to the police report, when Cinquemani and his partner approached the scene, Rodriguez lunged at the off-duty officers in street clothes with his knife. In response, patrolman Cinquemani drew his revolver, identified himself, and shot an allegedly unsubdued Rodriguez repeatedly in the chest.[18]

In East Harlem during the 1960s, the fatal shooting of a civilian by a police officer was not uncommon. What was unusual was the violent conflict that immediately ensued between residents of East Harlem and the police. While poor communities in many northern cities were at the breaking point, East Harlem was a neighborhood of relatively new migrants. Nonetheless, in the three days of unrest that followed the shooting of Rodriguez, thousands of mainly Puerto Rican youths took to the streets. On the night of the shooting, about four hundred African American and Puerto Rican residents congregated at the intersection of 111th Street and Third Avenue, hurling rocks and bottles at the police.

The melee led to the sealing of traffic in twenty-four city blocks, and to the deployment of approximately 160 helmeted police and three bus-loads of officers from the Tactical Patrol Force, a special riot-control unit notorious for its abuse of power in Harlem, East and West.[19]

As mandated by state law, the mayor visited the scene of the riot, attempting to defuse the violence by talking to crowds of youths who were rapidly congregating on street corners. In these impromptu forums, the mayor asked the community to form a committee of Puerto Ricans with whom he would meet at Gracie Mansion to hear their grievances. In the meetings later that day, a group of young Puerto Rican leaders affiliated with various antipoverty programs achieved a compromise with the mayor and the chief of police. The leaders would help restore order in exchange for the temporary decommissioning of the infamous Tactical Patrol Force.[20]

However, the truce was called off when a second wave of more intense rioting began less than twenty-four hours after the first eruptions. From tenement windows, Molotov cocktails and all manner of refuse were pitched at the police, while youths hurled bricks and garbage cans in open street confrontations with over one thousand police reinforcements dispatched to disperse the rioters.[21] Day two brought approximately seven straight hours of rioting. The young people involved exhibited a naked and taunting hostility toward the police. On the third and final day of the crisis, the riots spread to Puerto Rican neighborhoods in the South Bronx. In total, four Puerto Ricans were killed, all with the .38 caliber bullets used in police guns.[22]

During and following the East Harlem riots, a consensus emerged among civic groups, the mayor, the media, and even sections of the police department that the upheaval was not simply an eruption of lawlessness. In their actions, participants isolated particular grievances, and demands were sketched out spontaneously by the insurgents. The reality of these events challenged mainstream interpretations of the riots of the decade as anarchic. Although there was some looting, the violence in East Harlem was unequivocally directed at the police. Moreover, media coverage of the event suggests that fighting often intensified when the Tactical Patrol Force patrolled the streets. Reports of rioters congregating on street corners, of improvised soapbox speeches at different junctures in the course of the riots, and of groups of youths running through the streets with Puerto Rican flags point to the complex political character of the East Harlem riots. In one instance a man mounted a lamp pole, "made a short speech in Spanish about Puerto Ricans fighting in Vietnam and said, 'Something is owed to us.' "[23] Moreover, in the course of the upheaval, residents continually pressured politicians, police officials, and antipoverty workers making appeals for peace to order the removal of policemen stationed on rooftops. But this was not enough. The mood in the streets suggested that people wanted meaningful control of their neighborhoods and their institutions, a sentiment captured earlier in the decade by the idea of Black Power. One group drew a line in chalk just above 110th Street and over it wrote: "Puerto Rican border. Do not cross, flatfoot."[24]

The rebellion was as much an indictment of the police as an assertion of Puerto Rican rights. Yet as recent arrivals, Puerto Ricans were not expected to assert themselves in such dramatic a fashion, especially in light of their inexperience with New York City life. However, Puerto Ricans settled in the poorest sections of northern cities in the 1950s and 1960s at a moment of heightened racial segregation and economic displacement, and such conditions certainly fueled the riots of 1967. Moreover, such an audacious act of protest was made possible by the rebellious mood of the times. Puerto Ricans settled in northern cities as the civil rights movement successfully infused the national political debates on poverty and race in America with a new urgency. The timing of Puerto Rican migration, and the spread of the civil rights movement to northern cities, among other factors, would have an impact on the political identity of Puerto Ricans and their disposition for protest.

The Puerto Rican riots pointed to the growing disconnect between Puerto Rican leaders in the War on Poverty programs and the rank and file of the Puerto Rican community, which was moving increasingly to the left amid the struggles of the 1960s and in light of its own direct experience with the urban crisis. News reports suggest that there was a discrepancy between the political outlook of rioters and that of the antipoverty community organizers who attempted to quell the violence. Amid the rioting, one antipoverty worker remarked, "Tell a kid you're putting $1 million [in the poverty funds] and he says 'that's got nothing to do with me.' "[25] While traditional Puerto Rican leaders called for moderate measures—such as the integration of the police department and racial sensitivity training—the sentiment of deep discontent on the streets demanded a more far-reaching social platform, such as that offered by, among other radical organizations, the Black Panther Party, which linked economic conditions with political agency. Determined to establish a foothold in the antipoverty bureaucracy, however, many Puerto

Rican leaders failed to appreciate that the ire in the Puerto Rican community was fueled by social and political problems requiring much deeper reforms than those offered by the Great Society programs.

But local politicians were not in a position to prescribe enduring solutions to broad social problems. Their immediate work often revolved around managing volatile situations and outbursts of discontent. In New York, Mayor John Lindsay established "Little City Hall," which sought to bring organic leaders at the neighborhood level into City Hall and municipal government. According to the mayor, disturbances could be avoided through the cessation of "alienation [of various groups and communities] through greater contact" with responsive government officials. The "purpose was to tap street-level activists, including gang members, and enmesh them in a series of relationships with the administration."[26]

Mayor Lindsay's attempts to address urban discontent came also in the form of his famous walking tours of poor neighborhoods. These tours were intended to earn him the goodwill of the city's growing and increasingly isolated African American and Puerto Rican residents, to counteract feelings of "powerlessness" among the poor, and to give them a sense that the mayor was personally invested in solving their problems. In 1967, the mayor's office established "the summer task force," raised close to $1 million from corporate sponsors for summer programs, identified thirteen official trouble spots, and assigned members of his staff to coordinate responses to minor neighborhood complaints requiring the fixing of potholes, building of parks, removal of abandoned cars, and the like.[27] The very names of these programs were an indication of how the city's liberal administration understood the problems before it and how grossly inadequate they were in addressing the city's deep social problems. Mayor Lindsay's summer task force included the following programs: Operation Bookmobile (in Bedford-Stuyvesant); Harlem Cultural Festival; Operation Puerto Rican Repertoire Theatre; Operation Summer Jobs for Youth; Operation Sports Rescue (with the New York Knicks); Operation Plane Ride; and Operation Beat the Heat, which offered two thousand weekend bus trips to beaches, airports, and state parks in the summer of 1967.[28]

These programs fit with the liberal notion that at core the problems experienced by urban communities of color were tied to lack of opportunity and exposure to aspects of a white middle-class lifestyle. Missing from Mayor Lindsay's assessment of and prescription for the problems confronted by communities of color was an understanding of northern poverty and racism that identified its structural and economic dimensions: increased segregation in housing, consciously segregated public schools, an ailing public health care system, a disfigured landscape, structural unemployment, and poverty wages in the sectors that were employing people of color (as nurses' aides, orderlies, porters, cooks, elevator operators, and laundresses) in the hospitals, restaurant and hotel trades, and New York's declining postwar manufacturing industry.[29]

The urban riots that exploded across the country in the latter half of the 1960s were a bold reminder of the class divisions in American society. These rebellions were a raw manifestation of the anger and political disenchantment of racial minorities in the postwar North. They dramatized the conditions of de facto racial apartheid, police brutality, and economic depression in communities of color. Moreover, the riots demonstrated that racial conflict was not solely a southern phenomenon and were a stark symbol of the crisis of credibility suffered by northern liberals. The riots expressed the sentiment already developing among civil rights workers in the South: that racial and economic inequality were a structural feature of American society, and that nothing short of a full-scale rebellion would bring about an equitable social order.

In many ways, this logic was right. In the South, white supremacists were at the helm of a renegade and anachronistic system of racist segregation that had, by the 1950s, become marginal to the American political and economic structure and therefore could now be defeated after a century of struggle. However, in the North, problems were more structural and entrenched in the very fabric of the system and therefore required changes of revolutionary proportion. After World War II, northern cities became more segregated by race and more divided by class than ever before in the history of the cities.[30]

First, World War II encouraged a mass migration of people of color into the cities because during the war the economy was cranked up to maximum capacity for the war effort. African Americans from the South, Puerto Ricans from Puerto Rico, Mexicans from Mexico, and Chicanos and Native Americans from the Southwest traveled to northern cities in search of wartime jobs. The process of suburbanization, which happened simultaneously, encouraged the departure of whites from the cities. In many ways, the urbanization and proletarianization of otherwise rural people gave them confidence, improved their wages, and gave them a sense of their power in numbers. This migration to the cities fueled the civil rights movement.[31]

In the case of Puerto Ricans, the transfer of more than one-third of Puerto Rico's population to New York, Chicago, and Philadelphia between 1943 and 1960 engendered a unique generation of mainland-identified Puerto Rican youths. As sons and daughters of the postwar migration, their consciousness was shaped by an unlikely combination of politicizing experiences, from the rise of the civil rights movement and the Vietnam War to their own experience in an urban setting beset by industrial decline and greater economic and racial segregation. The convergence of Puerto Rican migration with the rise of the civil rights movement, in particular, had a profound impact on the racial consciousness of the children of Puerto Rican migrants. Among other developments, this process gave birth to an organization with the kind of politics held by the Young Lords Party, which would insist that Puerto Ricans and African Americans shared common political and economic interests.

However, with the end of the war came a long-term process of structural changes in the economy of northern cities. A process of deindustrialization took hold that created a sizable class of *permanently* unemployed and discouraged young workers—a completely new development in modern urban history. The consequences for the newcomers were devastating. The industrial base of the cities, which until then had provided stable and consistent employment to new arrivals, was now evaporating just as African Americans, Puerto Ricans, Mexicans, and Native Americans began to migrate into the cities in large numbers as a result of the wartime labor demands of WWII. People of color were disproportionately affected by these new changes. The situation was such that the Bureau of Labor Statistics began to publish a series of reports in the 1960s on the changes underfoot in the labor force of New York City. These reports articulated a concern over groups of predominantly African American and Puerto Rican men in their prime working years who were living in New York's poorest slums. Among Puerto Rican, African American, and white men, lack of job activity was highest among Puerto Ricans. In 1966, 47 percent of Puerto Ricans in New York were either unemployed, underemployed, or permanently out of the labor force for lack of success finding employment.[32] In Chicago, 22 percent of industry moved to the suburbs between 1950 and 1977.[33] And city conditions were further worsened by tax-base erosion, which exacerbated the disrepair of the urban environment after the Depression.

These conditions, combined with police brutality and northern racism on the one hand, and on the other the raised expectations of change produced by migration and by the southern civil rights movement—

alongside very little real progress—led to the riots. The riots were a call to action for radicals. They suggested to many that the anger of the riots, if organized, could lead to social change.

These conditions also influenced the character of organizations like the Young Lords. It is no surprise, in the context of a postwar urban economy that for the first time in modern urban history had created a class of permanently unemployed urban dwellers, that radical organizations like the Young Lords and the Black Panthers would launch a critique of this development. Nor is it surprising that, at the same time, they would decide to organize what they called the "young lumpen proleterian cats," referring to a term coined by Karl Marx to describe the permanently unemployed and discouraged workers living on the margins of society. Radical grassroots movements that were cohering in the second half of the decade reflected the distinctive social features of the urban environment in which these movements emerged. The urban movements built by the Young Lords and BPP, and others, emerged out of and were a response to the new technical structures of capitalism in the form of automation and modernization in the second half of the twentieth century. Thus, these young militants were reacting to special conditions at the same time that they were trying to make sense of them.[34]

In the cities the burden of the kind of poverty that was being produced in the postwar period was disproportionately borne by people of color, especially the young men among them. Yet in the public discourse of the 1960s, urban poverty was increasingly seen as a racial phenomenon rather than as a product of the postwar, structural transformation of the cities. Increasingly, racist theories about the dysfunctionality of the African American family and the propensity for violence among African American and Latino males came to explain the causes of the new urban crisis. In their papers and in their public meetings, organizations like the BPP and the YLP challenged quite sharply the bankruptcy of these theories.

In fact, contrary to the static narrative of the postwar urban crisis as a force that prostrated communities of color, the local histories of the Young Lords and the Black Panthers suggest that they were among the first to identify the causes of and launch a fight back against what we know today as the urban crisis. At the same time, the increased racism in mainstream political debates about the origins of the urban crisis, coupled with the increased racial segregation in the cities—that people of color were moving in and whites were moving out—made an interracial struggle with white Americans very difficult to imagine.

The material basis of the traditional call for black and white solidarity was evaporating. Instead, dramatic action was created by polyglot groups birthed by the increasingly multiethnic character of the American ghetto. Moreover, demographic changes shaped the nationalist political orientation of people of color in the cities. The organizations coalesced on the basis of race and ethnicity, reflecting the residual racial configuration and ideology of the old racial structures in America, but on the ground in their racial makeup and composition, they were a harbinger of things to come: The Young Lords reflected the diverse racial and ethnic makeup of the postmodern city, of which Los Angeles is the best example.

Despite its largely Puerto Rican membership and professed Puerto Rican nationalism, the organization possessed a rare multiracial and multiethnic composition. Operating in the interstices of the late 1960s and early 1970s, the YLO attracted Chicanos and African Americans, as well as other Latinos. According to Iris Morales, former member of the YLP and producer of the documentary film on the Young Lords, *¡Palante, Siempre, Palante!* "activists who had participated in the civil rights, Black liberation, and cultural nationalists movements joined." Puerto Ricans were a majority of the members, but African Americans "made up about 25 percent of the membership. Other Latinos—Cubans, Dominicans, Mexicans, Panamanians, and Colombians—also joined. One member was Japanese-Hawaiian."[35]

Most importantly, non–Puerto Rican members were not merely passive participants in the organization but were integral to its lifeblood. Denise Oliver, an African American, was the first woman elected to the Young Lords' central committee. Pablo Yoruba Guzmán, one of the founders of the New York group and member of the central committee, was of Afro-Cuban parentage, and Omar Lopez, the major strategist of the Chicago YLO, was Mexican American.

With a formal leadership in New York largely composed of Afro-Latinos, and with African Americans making up fully one-quarter of its membership, YLP members launched one of the first Latino political formations that identified with the Black Power movement, that saw itself as part of the African diaspora, and that was instrumental in theorizing and identifying the structures of racism embedded in the culture, language, and history of Latin America and its institutions. Iris Morales, Felipe Luciano, and Denise Oliver were among the members of the organization who initiated the work of analyzing racial identification and racial formation in Latin America and the specific historical circumstances and comparatively different economic and political contours within which racism emerged in that continent.

But material conditions alone do not a radical movement make. The conditions outlined above, combined with northern racism and police brutality on the one hand and on the other the example set by organizations such as the Black Panther Party, were instrumental in fueling a radical movement. The riots functioned as a call to action for radical activists. After the riots, radicals understood that militant action alongside a radical analysis of the problems of American society could influence a wide spectrum of working people. The emergence of the Black Panther Party in 1966 was the most dramatic example of this development.

The Black Panther Party was compelling because it articulated in simple and uncompromising language the totality of political and economic grievances with which African American northerners had been concerned since the start of the civil rights movement during World War II. Their platform read as follows: "We want the power to determine the destiny of our Black Community. . . . full employment for our people . . . an end to the robbery by the white man of our black community . . . decent housing, fit for shelter of human beings . . . education . . . an immediate end to police brutality . . . clothing, justice, and peace."[36] The BPP's survival programs and their dramatic civilian patrol unit was a brilliant application of their politics because these addressed the causes of the riots in both economic and political terms. What was different about the BPP was that it combined concrete community-based organizing with an overarching critique of capitalism and a critique of the role of the state, a combination that had not previously been articulated decisively by any civil rights organization. Their critique of the state was critical because it tapped into a major trend within the movement wherein the state was a key focal point and target of protest. Sixties activists criticized and protested against government repression, against poor municipal services, against urban renewal, against the warfare state, against the state's control of women's bodies, against legal and state-sponsored forms of racial and ethnic oppression, and against the forms of punishment instituted by the state, as with the prisoner takeover of the Attica prison.[37] This moment gave birth to a rights-consciousness movement, in which the state was challenged on its violations of the rights of individuals.

The BPP also proposed an alternative view of how society might be organized on the basis of more humane priorities. They called themselves socialists. The Black Panthers then, did three important things: They engaged in a kind of organizing that connected with the anger and conditions of African Americans and other minorities in urban centers; they articulated a theoretical analysis of the urban crisis; and they put forth an alternative vision of society. Because the BPP accomplished these three things, the organization gave northern protests a deeper purpose and meaning at precisely the time when radicalization was becoming widespread.

In essence, the BPP established a model of organizing that captured the imagination of urban dwellers and that awakened many other radical movements, especially among groups with a history of racial oppression in this country. Today, however, the Black Panther Party is maligned and not accorded its proper place in history and we know very little about the movements that it inspired. These included not just the Young Lords but also the Revolutionary Union Movement, the Brown Berets, the Health Revolutionary Unity Movement, I WOR KUEN, the Young Patriots, the American Indian Movement, and many others.

Building on that momentum, in the late 1960s, the Young Lords captured the political imagination of a growing number of Puerto Ricans in New York and dramatized the problems of poor African American and Puerto Ricans. Beginning in 1969, the Young Lords in New York engaged in a fast-paced course of dramatic and media-savvy campaigns and established branches in the Bronx, East Harlem, Brooklyn, the Lower East Side, Hartford, Bridgeport, Newark, Camden, and Philadelphia.[38]

The first campaign was the Garbage Offensive, a campaign protesting irregular sanitation services in East Harlem and the absence of garbage cans on street corners in that neighborhood. They called attention to the problem by sweeping the streets and clearing empty lots and erecting traffic barriers at major intersections with the garbage they collected. Thus, they stopped traffic for blocks on end, attracted the attention of thousands of local residents, created a public town-hall meeting effect, and in the process captured the attention of local officials. Their demonstrations were covered heavily by the media in the summer of 1969 and contributed to making sanitation a major issue in the run-up to the mayoral election of November 1969. The group successfully exposed the city for not deeming Puerto Ricans and African Americans worthy of city services.[39]

A quieter and lesser-known campaign was their Lead Offensive. In the fall of 1969, the Young Lords launched a campaign to combat lead poisoning among children. In collaboration with medical residents, nurses, and hospital staff at Metropolitan Hospital in East Harlem, they launched a door-to-door testing drive and used press conferences to publish their results: 30 percent of the children they tested were lead positive. The Young Lords had launched their initiative after the nearly fatal case of Gregory Franklin, an African American boy who lived in a building with over one hundred housing violations. The militants held sit-ins at the Department of Health, leafleted in East Harlem, and used the media to expose government inaction. In 1974, the *Journal of Public Health* credited the Young Lords and their activism with the passage of anti-lead-poisoning legislation in the city. This was the first campaign in what became the Young Lords' crusade for medical rights for poor African American, Latino, and Asian city dwellers.[40]

In December 1969, the Young Lords took over the First Spanish Methodist Church in East Harlem and turned it into a social service sanctuary for the poor. They used everything at their disposal to illustrate their cause. At a press conference, a Young Lord explained: "People who claim to be Christian have forgotten that it was Jesus who walked among the poor, the most oppressed, the prostitutes, and drug addicts of his time. That it was Jesus who said that it was easier for a camel to pass through the eye of a needle than for a rich man to enter the kingdom of God."[41]

Then, in the summer of 1970, they did the unthinkable and occupied Lincoln Hospital, with the blessing of a radical flank of doctors. The Young Lords' efforts advanced swiftly from discreet one-on-one conversations with patients and employees concerning hospital conditions to a dramatic twelve-hour occupation of the Nurses Residence, a building that formed part of the Lincoln complex and had in an earlier era housed the first nursing school for African American women in the United States and had been a stop in the underground railroad. The Young Lords were also continuing the work of the BPP and various other activists who, in the winter of 1969, spearheaded a battle over control of the community mental health clinic affiliated with Lincoln. The Young Lords' occupation dramatized Lincoln's deplorable conditions, and the crisis at Lincoln Hospital became a major item in the city's political debates. The whirlwind of controversy was recorded in over one hundred mainstream and alternative news articles.[42] As a result, government officials were forced to find ways to improve care in the public hospitals. The Young Lords were among the first activists to challenge the advent of draconian reductions in social spending on public hospitals and privatization policies in the public sector. Their actions eventually led to the creation of one of the principle acupuncture drug treatment centers in the Western world at Lincoln.[43] At their best, the Young Lords demonstrated a willingness and keen ability to read the pulse of local communities, identify issues significant to them, and adapt their work and campaigns accordingly. They were also especially successful at building coalitions with health professionals in East Harlem and the Bronx. Their ability to link local concerns with international causes was effective and allowed them to tap into the broader concerns of the period. Their creative tactics and brilliant use of the media was also critical to their success and popularity.

They were also courageous in taking the best ideas of the Black Power and women's movements to expose and challenge gender inequality, homophobia, and color prejudice among Latinos. The group's commitment to the struggle against racism and their insistence that poor African Americans and Latinos shared common political and economic interests was core to their work. Although Puerto Ricans as a group did not necessarily identify with African Americans, upon their arrival on the U.S. mainland many Puerto Ricans encountered many of the same racial barriers as did African American southerners migrating to northern cities in the postwar years. The convergence of Puerto Rican migration with the rise of the civil rights movements had a profound impact on the racial consciousness of the children of Puerto Rican migrants. For example, numerous members of the Young Lords considered joining or were members of African American protest groups prior to the Young Lords' emergence. As suggested earlier, the group played a crucial role in identifying and challenging the unconscious racism embedded in Latino culture, language, and values.

The history of the Young Lords suggests that even though the story of the 1960s is told in black and white, by the mid-1960s, the movements and its members reflected the multiracial and multiethnic character of American cities. Most importantly, the history of the Young Lords challenges mainstream assumptions about the civil rights and Black Power movements. When we think about the black or brown radicals of this period, we immediately think about the struggle for racial equality. However, the group's campaigns demonstrate that while movements of the 1960s were impelled by issues of race, the objectives and the character of protest were integrally tied to issues of social and economic import. Increasingly, movement activists were concerned with finding solutions to problems as pedestrian as garbage collection, the removal of lead paint from tenement walls, the crisis of health care and its delivery, social welfare programs, and urban renewal, among other issues. Essentially, movement activists were concerned with issues pertaining to a social-democratic polity.

Conclusion

By the 1960s, postwar deindustrialization, white flight, and residential tax-base erosion in the cities had produced unprecedented levels of racial segregation, permanent unemployment, and all the attendant problems of urban decay: poor education, health, and housing; a disfigured physical landscape; and explosive tensions between the community and the police. It was against this backdrop that the northern civil rights movement emerged. The Young Lords' militant activism and the group's insurgent politics were rooted in a deep social disenchantment at worsening objective conditions, a disenchantment that only deepened when the hopes raised by the civil rights movement did not materialize in the North.

For their part, the Young Lords repudiated the dominant liberal Puerto Rican organizations of the time on the basis that their strategy of addressing racial and economic inequality within established legal and governmental institutions was tantamount to negotiating the terms on which poverty would be brokered rather than attacking the problem at its root. They captured the political imagination of a growing number of Puerto Ricans in New York by articulating the experiences and grievances of second-generation Puerto Rican youths, who were reared in a racially and economically segregated urban setting that was radically different from that of their island-born parents. In the late 1960s, the Young Lords became a magnet for disaffected urban youths. Spawned by postwar urban conditions, the Young Lords represented a new and bold development in the Puerto Rican community, which articulated the uniquely American identity of mainland-born Puerto Ricans and gave organizational expression and direction to their urban discontent.

In East Harlem, the fantastic growth of the Young Lords Party was a manifestation of the leftward ideological shift in the Puerto Rican community and the growing dissatisfaction with mainstream solutions to that community's mounting social problems. The leadership of this radical group satisfied the desire of many Puerto Ricans for a radical critique of society, one that addressed the domestic and international issues affecting their lives—from the persistence of poverty in the United States and the rationale for American intervention in Vietnam to the increasingly popular issue of Puerto Rican independence. Because of the success of the organization in appealing to large numbers of people in East Harlem and the city at large, the rise of the Young Lords represents the most observable political development within the Puerto Rican community following the riots of 1967. Through protests, grassroots organizing, and political education, the Young Lords consciously established an alternative to what they perceived as the failure of the social service–oriented antipoverty strategy adopted by the Puerto Rican reformers since the 1950s. The Young Lords enjoyed tremendous popularity in New York, in part because they tapped into these sentiments. They were also the first group to originate in the mainland United States whose main purpose was to achieve Puerto Rican independence and foster a sense of pride in being Puerto Rican through a political understanding of Puerto Rico's history of resistance against U.S. domination.[44]

As we have witnessed recently in New Orleans, the urban disrepair against which organizations like the Young Lords and Black Panthers fought, and its racialized character, is still with us today. There is a lot that can be concluded about this age of great dreams during which ordinary people took the reins of history in their own hands. One of the most important contributions of radicals was that they helped alter the terms of the political debate in America. The conservative ideas that have become dominant in the movement's aftermath for almost four generations have upheld that government is not charged with the task of solving social problems, that the invisible hand of the market will redistribute wealth and address all manner of crises, and that success is determined by individual virtue and poverty is the result of inherent character flaws.

In the 1960s however, radicals won the argument that poverty was brought about by circumstances beyond the control of the poor and that these circumstances had long historical roots and that they were tied to the organization of society. They won the argument that racial oppression was a natural outgrowth of a society divided by class; that urban renewal in the form of gentrification and business-sponsored development would not solve the profound problems of urban deindustrialization and disrepair; and finally, they argued that imperialist war was not acceptable in a democratic society. All of these ideas merit reconsideration in American society today.

8

"Brooklyn College Belongs to Us": Black Students and the Transformation of Public Higher Education in New York City

MARTHA BIONDI

lack student activism exploded in the spring of 1969. These students followed in the footsteps of the Student Nonviolent Coordinating Committee and were deeply influenced by its radical and Black Nationalist organizers, many of whom had left the South and were active on college campuses across the country. Coinciding with the grassroots community control of schools movement, African American college students in New York City aimed to redefine the relationship between educational institutions and urban black communities. In the spring of 1969, students at every single division of the City University of New York rose up in protest. The two-week occupation of City College in Harlem precipitated a political crisis in the city and ushered in a major shift in public policy; as a result, it received extensive local and national media attention, but strikingly, it has garnered little attention from historians. Similarly, the struggle at Brooklyn College has been virtually forgotten, even though it was crucial in reshaping the admissions policy, the university's relationship to communities of color, and the curriculum. As one observer has rightly noted, "The integration of CUNY has been the most significant civil rights victory in higher education in the history of the United States."[1] Yet this story has been left out of most narratives of the black freedom struggle, an elision that is all the more striking in light of the fact that much of the post–civil rights backlash has focused on ending affirmative action in college admissions.[2] This chapter examines the black student movement in New York City, focusing on Brooklyn and City colleges, in order to show the enormous impact that this generation of student activists had on university policies, structures, and cultures. While not as iconic as the students in suits and ties at Greensboro lunch counters earlier in the decade, these students may have read *Quotations from Chairman Mao Tse-tung* and contemplated guerilla warfare, but they won reforms that transformed public higher education and paved the way for the expansion of the black middle class in the New York City region. While emphasizing the students' achievements, the chapter also examines opposition to the movement, shedding light on ideas and alliances that would grow much stronger as political conservatism gained ascendancy in the United States.

Additionally, this story complicates the widely held view that the ascendancy of Black Nationalist politics in the late 1960s blocked multiracial alliances, moved class issues off the activist radar, muted black women's voices, and alienated and drove away white allies. Rather, this generation had a flexible and dynamic conception of so-called identity politics: They forged alliances with Latino and Asian American activists, occasionally collaborated with radical white students, and kept socioeconomic issues front and center. African American female students, moreover, fought for black studies and affirmative action as much as their male peers, notwithstanding the rise of a macho political rhetoric. One key change, of course, was that black students also wanted to organize all-black formations, and be the leading force in shaping the tactics and goals of antiracist activism on campus. And this they achieved.

The students were not protesting racial segregation in college admissions but rather token desegregation, the terms of which had marginalized black and Puerto Rican students in the overwhelmingly white campus culture, labeled them culturally deprived, and expected them to be grateful. Students pushed back against these terms. Black and Puerto Rican students had long ago gained entry to tuition-free City, Brooklyn, Hunter, and other colleges under the prevailing admissions standards. Affirmative action, meaning programs and policies aimed at admitting "minority" students who did not meet the prevailing entrance criteria, began with the Search for Education, Elevation, and Knowledge (SEEK) program in 1966. Reflecting the new clout of a growing bloc of black and Puerto Rican legislators in Albany, SEEK provided promising graduates of city high schools a college education and the extra academic support, counseling, and remediation needed to succeed. It was by far the largest program of its kind in the country. These new admissions policies, culminating in 1970 with the launch of open admissions, were part of a social movement to redefine both the mission of public universities and the criteria to determine "merit." Black students, in particular, posed the question: Should public colleges be expected to offer opportunity to a broad range of taxpaying New Yorkers, or should they be permitted to adopt the exclusionary practices of private institutions and rely on test scores to determine admission? Moreover, students demanded a new answer to an old but critical question of the civil rights era: How should the United States correct the consequences of segregation—in this case, the unequal educational system that it had produced? The prevailing view had been that efforts should focus on improving primary and secondary schools in order to better prepare students for college. But in the late 1960s, African American youths argued that it was the college's responsibility to offer the appropriate remediation. They increasingly framed access to higher education as a right of postwar U.S. citizenship. Fortunately for them, the broader urban turmoil across the United States played a role in encouraging college officials to reevaluate admissions policies. After several summers of very serious and deadly urban unrest, white administrators feared black militancy and the prospect of riots at their gates. According to one scholar, CUNY's motive in authorizing open admissions was "to appease an explosive urban youth population."[3]

Black student activists at Brooklyn College launched their movement on a campus that, in the spring of 1968, was 96 percent white.[4] The campus tumult of the late 1960s reveals the stunning lack of preparation for desegregation on American campuses. For its part, Brooklyn College had appointed a committee in 1964 "to look into the need to create educational opportunities for students on the campus, or students who were not being admitted." In the words of acting president George A. Peck, it "worked sporadically at first" and finally came up with a plan to admit two hundred black and Puerto Rican students in a special program in 1968.[5] The students did not demand open admissions for all graduates of city high schools—a policy that the Board of Higher Education was in fact already preparing to launch in 1975—but rather, more specifically, they called for a sharp increase in the black and Puerto Rican student population.[6] For all the vaunted erudition and cosmopolitanism of the faculties at the City University of New York, Brooklyn College offered thirteen courses "with content related to American minority groups," the president's office reported in 1969, and all of them had begun in 1968! A big problem, the administration contended, was "finding faculty to teach them,"[7] a statement that points to the slow pace of the production of African American PhDs in the United States fourteen years after *Brown* and twenty years after President Harry S. Truman had appointed a committee to study minority access to higher education.

Among the small number of black students at Brooklyn College, a few key leaders emerged, notably Leroy (Askia) Davis and Orlando Pile. Both young men were involved in off-campus organizing and their efforts at Brooklyn College should be seen as part of the overall black freedom struggle. Pile was the student representative on the Ocean Hill–Brownsville community school board and was also involved in local welfare rights organizing. African American women were at the center of both these campaigns, a fact that balances the largely masculinist portrait of the Black Power era and illustrates a broader range of influences on a generation that venerated Malcolm X and Frantz Fanon. Askia Davis came up to New York from Georgia at age fifteen. He saw *The Battle of Algiers*, read *Black Skin, White Masks,* and joined the Black Panther Party. But Malcolm X had the most decisive and far-reaching influence on his life trajectory. All his life he had eagerly awaited the day he could join the military. "I always dreamed of going to the air force academy," and becoming a pilot, he said—in order to drop bombs. "That was my goal. I was a warrior." He might have gone to Vietnam like his brother if he hadn't encountered *The Autobiography of Malcolm X.* "Reading Malcolm X really changed me—really, like overnight."[8]

In 1968 Davis and Pile began to reach out to the small number of black students—approaching them in the library, Davis recalled—and soon organized BLAC, the Black League of Afro-American Collegians. In conjunction with the Puerto Rican Alliance, BLAC became a major force on campus, especially as the protests dramatically increased black enrollments. BLAC would present eighteen demands to the administration in the spring of 1969, but they also tried to change campus conditions through their own direct action. One tactic they used to overcome black students' sense of isolation in the classroom, especially in the face of offensive or insensitive racial remarks, was to get groups of black students to register for the same course. In 1969, five or six black student activists plus several more non-political black students enrolled in an introductory literature course taught by Robert Fitzhugh. The first day, Askia Davis recalled, Fitzhugh walked in and saw "this sea of black faces. He was shocked." Still, Davis remembered, "We were polite. We wanted to learn." One day Orlando Pile asked Fitzhugh why there were no black writers on the syllabus and even presented the professor with a list of important black writers. One imagines that James Baldwin and Richard Wright were probably on this list. Fitzhugh retorted that these writers were "social activists, not major novelists." A "personal confrontation" ensued. Fitzhugh asked Pile why he didn't leave the class if he didn't like it, and Pile said, "Why don't you?" "And then," said Pile, still incredulous many years later, "the professor walked out!" BLAC leaders arranged with the dean for the black students to withdraw from the course, and the activists did, but the others chose to remain. A couple of weeks later, the remaining students changed their minds and told Pile that Fitzhugh was grading all their work poorly and had "disrespected them" when they brought it up. Number eleven on the list of eighteen demands called for the dismissal "of all White professors who have demonstrated racist tendencies," specifically Robert Fitzhugh of the English department.[9]

The "18 Demands," interestingly a much longer list than the "Five Demands" at City College, are wide ranging and reveal much about the students' political sensibilities and vision. The list is striking for its boldness and scope. Yet at the same time, it is concrete and pragmatic, suggesting the students' dual sense of themselves as radical yet efficacious. The first demand called for the admission to Brooklyn College of all black and Puerto Rican applicants regardless of their scholastic record. The second demand called for "a free tutorial program" and "basic skills courses" to enable students "to fulfill their scholastic potential." While the first goal seems to reject all entrance criteria, the second one illustrates that the students still took academic success seriously. Even though students were challenging prevailing definitions of who was qualified to enter college, they were not rejecting academic culture or excellence. On the contrary, they wanted to benefit from it.[10] Most significantly, the demands show the students' desire for Brooklyn College to serve the educational needs of the population of Brooklyn, not only of those applicants whose test scores were the highest.

These college student activists also called for the establishment of Afro-American and Puerto Rican institutes to be "controlled by Black and Puerto Rican students with the help of the Black and Puerto Rican faculty and the community." The wording of this demand suggests both that the students had a nontraditional conception of ethnic studies and that they did not trust the college to set up the institutes and so claimed this role for students of color. At many campuses student activists had a "movement" conception of black studies—seeing it as a bridge between black students and black communities, in addition to its transformative intellectual potential. The thirteenth demand called for a special course that would give academic credit for field work in the community, reflecting this generation's desire to make their college educations "relevant" to community needs, and their desire not to wall themselves off in an ivory tower. Indeed, Brooklyn College set up an entirely new college—the School of Contemporary Studies—that incorporated many of these goals. Echoing a similar demand at City College, the fifteenth demand asserted that students majoring in education—future public school teachers—should be required to take courses in black and Puerto Rican studies. This reflected the students' sense of obligation to use their position inside the college to affect the education of Brooklyn youth of all ages. The students also demanded the hiring of black and Puerto Rican professors in all units of the college, showing their desire not to let the creation of the new Afro-American and Puerto Rican institutes create an excuse for the other departments not to diversify.[11]

By early 1969, student activists had engaged in extensive organizing on campus and had gained considerable support. The BLAC faculty advisor was Professor Craig Bell, but Orlando Pile felt that each of the small number of black professors on campus supported them, as did several white professors as well, "especially and very vocally" Bart Meyers, who later penned a useful history of the struggle for the campus newspaper. In keeping with the nationalist ethos of the time, it was important to black and Puerto Rican students to lead and direct their own organizations and movement. The largely white Students for a Democratic Society chapter on campus supported the citywide push for open enrollment, and they were engaged in a range of campus actions that spring. Pile said that their support was fine but "they could not be part of us."[12]

In mid-April, frustrated that the faculty had not yet considered the eighteen demands, a group of black and Puerto Rican students came to a faculty meeting, took over the microphone, and commanded faculty not to leave. "Militant" students disrupting normal campus procedures and making "demands" to a "frightened" faculty became the archetypical sequence of events at American campuses in 1969. "We want the 18 demands presented now," Askia Davis declared. "You will not shut your eyes any longer," he told the faculty. "Brooklyn College belongs to us, not you."[13] The president subsequently participated in a forum of two thousand people, but the administration, according to the student radicals, took a "rigid stance."[14] Davis felt the president was "dead set against African American studies and open admissions."[15] Students at City College encountered similar difficulties on these issues, especially admissions, and it would ultimately fall to the Board of Higher Education to enact a new admissions policy.

In March, April, and May student militancy increased, culminating in a mass demonstration in the president's office at the end of April. One hundred and fifty students from BLAC and the Puerto Rican Alliance and forty white students "squeezed into" the president's office in Boylan Hall, where a meeting among administrators and student representatives over black and Puerto Rican issues was in progress. They dramatically presented the eighteen demands but the president was actually out of the office. Some students reportedly engaged in minor vandalism and someone spray painted the words "power" and "revolution" on walls inside and outside the building. The students stayed for a couple of hours and left when they heard that the police had been called. In the meantime, some radical white students took over other campus buildings, while black students blocked the entrance to Boylan Hall, and unknown persons set small fires on the campus.[16] In early May, one hundred students led by SDS held a demonstration inside the dean's office, and acts of arson and vandalism continued, alongside daily and increasingly large rallies. On May 6, President Peck alleged that a hundred students, mostly black and Puerto Rican, blocked firefighters from entering the administration building to douse a small fire, reportedly the fifth small blaze of the day.

In contrast to City College, where the administration engaged in negotiation with black and Puerto Rican student activists, including the "militants," at Brooklyn the administration decided to turn to law enforcement to quell student protest. They sought an injunction barring students from "congregating in or near buildings, creating loud or excessive noise, or employing, inciting or encouraging force or violence." Students fought the injunction with attorneys from the Emergency Civil Liberties Committee and the New York Civil Liberties Union, who argued that it was an unconstitutional restraint on freedom of speech and assembly. It should be noted that there were many white students who had been advocating and engaging in aggressive forms of protest—and this was well known to campus authorities. Indeed, some Brooklyn College officials, like white administrators at many American colleges, saw radical whites, especially those in SDS, as more destructive than black student activists. Some even viewed white radicals as instigating black student revolt. Peck later testified to a Senate committee investigating campus riots. Montana senator Lee Metcalf asked him, "So you think that SDS in spite of the fact that they were not part of this black revolt, spurred it on and encouraged it, and, using your phrase, masterminded it?" To which Peck replied, "All they could." He added that he did not think SDS had the same emotional commitment to "the cause of blacks" but used it to advance general social destruction. Interestingly, though, this worldview did not prevent Peck from targeting black and Puerto Rican students—but no white students—for arrest that spring.[17]

Shortly before dawn on May 12, 1969, police officers across the city raided the homes of seventeen African American and Puerto Rican Brooklyn College students, including Orlando Pile and Askia Davis. They arrested the students and even arrested Pile's mother, Blanche Pile, for interference. Another two students were also indicted. As college students with no criminal records and strong family and community ties, the $15,000 bail was widely seen as excessive. The students spent four days at Rikers Island. They were each charged with eighteen felonies and five misdemeanors, including inciting riot and arson, which together carried a sentence of 228 years. The allegations had come from an undercover police informant who had infiltrated BLAC and befriended the students. "He looked the part," Askia Davis noted, with his big afro, dark skin, and beard. "He had the rhetoric, but he was really a cop." In Pile's view, the allegations by the police informant were a form of retaliation: They represented the administration's attempt to thwart the black student movement and block their demands to change Brooklyn College. The next day the prosecutor claimed to have found in various homes "a revolver, a sharp-edged spear, and clubs" as well as batteries and gasoline, which he termed "material used to manufacture firebombs."[18]

The eighteen-year-old Davis had been a member of the Black Panther Party and had actually been named on the original warrant for the New York "Panther 21" but was in California when the police made those arrests. "I was meant to be the Panther 22," he said, which likely explains the overwhelming force they used to arrest him that morning in May. He remembered his thoughts when he heard a knock on the door early that morning. "A young lady lived next door. I was basically trying to seduce her. She used to knock at my door; we used to tease and flirt, but nothing ever happened. So I get this knock at five o'clock in the morning and I said, 'Wow, she finally gave in.'" Nine police officers came to make the arrest. Three came through the door. "They threw me to the floor, put a gun to my head, and cocked the trigger." When the officer finally pulled the gun back and looked at the very youthful-looking Davis, he said, "God, you're nothing but a kid." They searched the house and found nothing unlawful. Rikers was a "rough experience" although it made him feel he could endure hardship and prevail. He believed that authorities were trying to punish and intimidate them for their activism.[19]

The media made much of the radical literature the police reportedly found in the students' homes and used this to promote an image of them as violent, subversive radicals, undeserving of support or sympathy. The *New York Post* highlighted that the students were in possession of "The Writings of Che Guevara," "Quotations from Mao Tse-tung," and a "typewritten document entitled 'Blueprint for Campus Revolt,'" which the district attorney said referred to the "strategy at San Francisco State College."[20] *New York Daily News* readers were given an over-the-top account that sought to stoke fears of Communism: "Brooklyn District Attorney Eugene Gold revealed that 122 detectives making pre-dawn arrests in four boroughs found inflammatory writings of Chinese and Cuban Communists."[21] This media frame exacerbated the already-powerful stigma of criminal prosecution in the eyes of the public. But in the eyes of the students, the arrests backfired and increased campus support for BLAC's agenda.

Moreover, the arrests sparked an outpouring of support among black New Yorkers. "The black community really got together" to support us, Davis said. Attorneys George Wade and Ray Williams argued before Brooklyn Supreme Court judge Dominic Rinaldi that the bail was puni- tive. Williams also pointed to the racial bias in the arrests, noting that "there were S.D.S. students involved but they were not brought in because they are white." Outraged at the assertion, the judge warned him against "using the courtroom as a vehicle for racist statements." But the Appellate Division ordered the bail reduced to $6,500. U.S. representative Shirley Chisholm, herself a Brooklyn College alum, raised the bail money. She convinced Dr. Thomas W. Matthew, the president of NEGRO, the National Economic Growth and Reconstruction Orga- nization, to put up his share of Interfaith Hospital, a drug treatment clinic in Queens, as collateral. And she got the Reverend William A. Jones of Bethany Baptist to put up his church.[22] As it turns out, the case never went anywhere—the state never produced any evidence, and after about a year of delays and negotiation, the attorneys and judge reached a deal in which the students accepted a short probationary period, and the charges were dismissed and the students' records ultimately expunged. The *Kingsman* editorialized that the probationary period "seems suspi- ciously like a move to repress dissent on campus, since the 19 are not guilty enough to be prosecuted."[23]

After the arrests and subsequent stationing of one hundred New York City police officers on campus, a large group of students and faculty went on strike. Their demands were: Drop the charges against "the BC 19," implement the eighteen demands, and get the police off campus. Askia Davis said he didn't realize how much support the black and Puerto Rican students had from the majority white campus until this point. The *Kingsman* editorialized in favor of the strike: "The 20 arrests on Tuesday morning were conducted in a manner that heaped disgrace on the American legal system and added to many students' hatred and distrust of the New York City Police." It demanded that the administration remove police from campus, reporting that an officer had arrested a student for spitting, which led to a bloody clash.[24] The relentless pressure finally induced the college to make concessions, and President Peck and the faculty went on record urging the Board of Higher Education, the governing body of CUNY colleges, to enact a new open-admissions policy. They passed a resolution urging the Board of Higher Education "to offer a college education to every high school graduate in the city, particularly needy Negroes and Puerto Ricans."[25] Clearly, the students' efforts to bring the black liberation movement to Brooklyn College had an effect; it had a similar effect across the river in Manhattan, but without the criminal prosecutions.

Student activists at the City College of New York (CCNY) had also engaged in a long series of escalating tactics before two hundred of them took over the buildings of south campus on April 22, 1969, and renamed it the "University of Harlem." As at most colleges, the assassination of Martin Luther King Jr. had precipitated a transformation in black student consciousness and sparked a new determination, even a sense of obligation, to step up the pace of change. "The movement really began in 1968," south campus occupier Sekou Sundiata recalled.[26] The struggle at City was led by the Black and Puerto Rican Student Community (BPRSC)—a name that richly signifies the politics of the era by emphasizing the collective over the individual and asserting a black/brown partnership in a Black Nationalist era that was moving toward third worldism. The left-wing W. E. B. Du Bois Club also contributed to the formulation of the "five demands," having presented President Buell Gallagher with a petition of 1,600 signatures to "End Racism at CCNY" in November 1968. This evidently motivated students of color to launch their own effort. "We were indignant," Sundiata said, "that the Du Bois Society was circulating those kinds of demands which really articulated our interests, and that we had not moved on them ourselves."[27]

City College, located in the heart of Harlem, was only 4 percent black and 5 percent Puerto Rican.[28] As a professor put it, "There City College sits, smack dab in the middle of the largest Black community in the country, and only 9 percent of its day time students are Black or Puerto Rican. And 5 percent of that 9 percent came through the SEEK program."[29] As at Brooklyn College, City's faculty and students were predominantly Jewish, a composition that reflected, in part, the legacy of anti-Semitic admissions and hiring practices at private universities. The students relied on research by CUNY economics professor Alfred Conrad to ascertain the racial composition of area high schools and, as a result, they called for a student body that was 43 percent black. This constituted an enormous jump and suggests that students had embraced a radical new conception of a public university's responsibility to its community. As the students put it, "We are committed to make this college more relevant to the community."[30] While this may have seemed radical in 1969, in many ways it was an approach steeped in the history of City College, which had been founded as a free college to serve the children of the poor and from 1900–1925 had required only a high school diploma for entrance. A minimum grade average was then introduced but open admissions returned for World War II veterans.[31]

The second most controversial BPRSC demand was for a school for black and Puerto Rican studies. According to the students, the curriculum at City College offered "virtually nothing" on Africa or African Americans. In the words of Toni Cade, author of the groundbreaking feminist text *The Black Woman: An Anthology*, and a highly regarded mentor to the protesting students, the English department clung to "the deeply entrenched notion that Anglo-Saxon literature is The Literature."[32] The leadership of SEEK professor Toni Cade is worth elaborating on, especially since activism from the late 1960s, including the black student/black studies movement, has been framed—and not inaccurately—as a quest to restore black manhood.[33] Still, black women played critical roles in these movements. Cade penned an open letter to students encouraging them to seize control of their educational destinies. Steeped in the vernacular of the era, it offered both guidance and solidarity and conveyed the humanism propelling radical activism. It bears quoting at length. "Dear Bloods," she wrote: "There are two traditions within our culture that are worth looking at, for they tell us a great deal about our responses. One, we have been conditioned to turn off, short out, be cool; two, we have often been pushed to make something from nothing. The first response is a negative one. We did it, or do it, to survive surely—but at great cost to ourselves. We've learned how to bottle up anger, put our minds in a jar, wear a mask. The second is a creative urge. It too comes out of the need to survive. . . . Out of which bag do you dip?" she asked. "Something out of nothing is so much better than blowing a fuse," she advised. "On the assumption that all of you mumblers, grumblers, malcontents, workers, designers, etc. are serious about what you've been saying ('A real education—blah, blah, blah'), the Afro-American-Hispanic Studies Center is/was set up. Until it is fully operating, *the responsibility of getting that education rests with you in large part.* Jumping up and down, foaming at the mouth, rattling coffee-cups and other weaponry don't get it. If you are serious, set up a counter course in the Experimental College. If you are serious, contact each other." And she closed, "Serious, Miss Cade."[34]

Cade was not only a key supporter of the students, but she formulated and publicized a model for a black and Hispanic studies center at City College. "At least 90 percent of the several hundred rebellions that have taken place on the American college campuses and in the American high schools in the last six years," she wrote in a campus newspaper, "were propelled by and revealed a gross dissatisfaction with the curriculum (its premises, its omissions, its presentations, its designers)." Contestations over knowledge and learning had moved to the forefront of black activism. This essay was composed before the takeover of south campus, but Cade saw it coming. "We can safely assume that an explosion is imminent," she declared. "The students have already indicated that they are weary of being lied to, tired of playing games, damned if they'll be indoctrinated, programmed, ripped off any longer." Cade proposed that the center be "a course-offering agency, a research agency, a buttress, a skills bank, [and] a conference center." Doubtless her most controversial idea was for the center to be "controlled by Black and Latin students and faculty who will have the power to hire using their own standards, and to design courses considering their own needs." Toni Cade appended a list of courses that the center might offer, including "American Justice and the Afro-American," "Negritude," "Revolution," and "Trends in Western Thought." Her eventual goal, which in light of the demographics of City College was very radical, was that "the Center would lead ultimately to a Black University."[35]

In February 1969, the college had hired Barbara Christian, the literary scholar who would produce pioneering scholarship on black women writers during her long career at Berkeley, and Wilfred Cartey, a Trinidadian-born literary scholar, to design a black studies program. Both were also affiliated with Columbia University at the time. According to Christian, the call for such a school was "a very controversial demand." Initially, she wrote, "the students were primarily concerned with their own culture—black, African, Afro-American, West Indian, Puerto Rican culture." But, she said, the involvement of Asian American students in the struggle at City College encouraged them to broaden their vision. "The students then took a look at how many courses were offered on Latin America, how many courses on Asia. And there were very few." This desire to address the needs of all "minority" groups on campus induced Christian and Cartey to propose a school of urban and third-world studies, but the faculty senate rejected their proposal late that spring.[36] As we shall see, the college administration resisted the proposals designed by black professors and moved instead to implement a very different vision.

Paradoxically, as the students were struggling to radically expand the size of CUNY colleges, the already-existing SEEK program was slated for drastic cuts, a development that foreshadowed worrisome things to come. In his February 1969 budget proposal, Governor Nelson A. Rockefeller slashed SEEK funding. This sparked a mass spring mobilization on New York campuses, which all sent busloads of students to Albany to save SEEK—CCNY alone sent thirty-five buses. Still, despite their staunch support for SEEK, the Black and Puerto Rican Student Community rejected paternalist aspects of its structure—such as rules prohibiting their election to student government. But most bothersome was that SEEK counselors were mostly white and were required to be clinical psychologists. The students felt that this stigmatized SEEK students as "psychologically flawed." The only counselor of color was Betty Rawls, who became a strong ally and mentor to the student activists and participated in the spring negotiations with administrators. Thus, the BPRSC demanded "a voice for SEEK students in setting guidelines for the SEEK Program, including the hiring and firing of all personnel." Like their counterparts in Brooklyn, the students occupying south campus also demanded that courses in Spanish language and black and Puerto Rican history be required for all education majors.[37]

The response to the five demands revealed a wide gap in perception between black and white New York communities. On the one hand, the students received an outpouring of support from black and Puerto Rican New Yorkers, who provided south campus with food, solidarity, and protection. They viewed the sit-in as part of the civil rights movement's quest for equal opportunity and inclusion. But the students also faced substantial criticism and, they felt, misunderstanding. They were accused of lowering standards in both admissions and curricular offerings, of supporting racial exclusion, and of generally pushing an agenda that was more political than academic. In response, they issued press releases offering careful elaboration of their positions. They explained that yes, white students could take courses in the school for black and Puerto Rican studies; it was not a "racial" project, but one meant to teach and research the history and culture of "80% of the world's population." Moreover, "the school is not a vehicle for political indoctrination." It "will not have a watered down degree," they emphasized. Students had to meet all the regular requirements to graduate. And the admissions demand—to offer graduates of area high schools a proportionate place at City—"will not lower the standards of the college. Students would be given supportive services on the model of SEEK and would not be allowed to move on through the college unless they fulfill the standards for graduation at CCNY."[38]

Students also sought guidance and solidarity from faculty, who organized two support groups: the Black and Puerto Rican Faculty Group and the integrated but predominately white Faculty for Action.[39] The students worked with both groups. As white SEEK professor Fran Geteles remembered, the student activists were savvy organizers who understood that both groups had something to offer. Some scholars of the civil rights movement, and especially of the Student Nonviolent Coordinating Committee, have lamented that the rise of Black Power politics led to an emphasis on slogans and speeches at the expense of grassroots organizing.[40] But Geteles's memory complicates this interpretation. She felt that "the students were very smart politically. They adopted Black Nationalist thought and rhetoric but didn't behave in an exclusionary way. They were shrewd organizers." A Brooklyn College professor had a similar recollection. Carlos Russell, an Afro-Panamanian educator and activist who directed SEEK before becoming dean of the School of Contemporary Studies at Brooklyn College, described black student activists there as committed and idealistic. To illustrate, he related how one cold winter day, a student gave his shoes away to a homeless man: "They were like SNCC," he said, referring not to the group's northern image but to its reputation for identification with ordinary folks in the South.[41]

In response to the seizure of south campus, CCNY president Buell G. Gallagher closed the college. This created an opportunity to negotiate an end to the crisis, and for two weeks negotiators from all sides worked eight to fourteen hours a day to reach a settlement. But Gallagher's decision also galvanized the opposition. It's important to appreciate that City

College alumni held influential positions in city government, media, and the courts, and many clamored for a police response. Mayor John Lindsay's policy was to bring in police only if requested to do so by the college president, and Gallagher did not want a police raid. At a key faculty meeting, Wilfred Cartey stirred his colleagues with moving arguments against calling the police to open south campus, advocating instead "conciliation with black students." Also influencing administrators was CCNY's location in Harlem, an African American neighborhood whose community leaders had aligned themselves with the students. Askia Davis thinks this was the main reason arrests were not made at City but were made at Brooklyn College, which is located in an area that was affluent and white.[42]

Gallagher's early public statements reinforced two common—though contradictory—views of black student activists of this era: first, that they embodied/portended violence, and second, that they were more pragmatic and serious about reforming higher education than white student radicals, who were typically portrayed as either more frivolous or more destructive. The occupation of south campus at City College occurred shortly after a photo had circulated around the world of black students at Cornell exiting a building heavily armed after the administration had agreed to several of their demands. In the eyes of some, Cornell became Munich—and denunciations of liberal "capitulation" to threats of armed violence proliferated. Gallagher took to the airwaves in New York City, declaring over WCBS radio, "Both incidents [CCNY and Cornell] illustrate graphically the failure of student extremists to understand what a university stands for." At this juncture, Gallagher revealed his distance from black students and a lack of understanding of their particular motives: "The student militants' rejection of personal accountability, regardless of whether their background is privileged or ghetto, stands at the heart of the campus revolution across the country. Tyranny, whether exercised by the majority, or a minority, is still tyranny." He also echoed a widely held view among college officials that student radicalism would strengthen conservatism. "With each forcible takeover, each ransacking of administration files, each disruption of classes for the majority of students, the hands of the ultraconservatives in the legislature are strengthened."[43] Yet, at the same time, as Gallagher began negotiations with the students, he came to respect their sincerity and the seriousness of their mission. A week later he was asked to defend his decision not to call the police when he had called them several months earlier to quell a largely white antiwar protest. "The circumstances are not the same," he explained. "They were causing extensive damage . . . smoking pot and fornicating in public," but the black and Puerto Rican students occupying south campus "are behaving in an orderly manner." And as he got to know black and Puerto Rican student activists that spring, this view solidified.[44]

The upcoming fall election turned the CCNY sit-in into a citywide political controversy and foreshadowed the way that racial backlash politics would dramatically shape electoral discourse in the ensuing decades. State senator John J. Marchi, who was opposing the liberal Lindsay for the Republican nomination, attacked the mayor "for not taking swift police action" at City and other CUNY campuses.[45] Actually, there was at least one police officer on south campus—an undercover agent, whom the students had discovered, interrogated, and released.[46] Another political aspirant took the matter to court. City Comptroller Mario Procaccino, who was seeking the Democratic nomination for mayor, obtained a Supreme Court injunction directing the college to open on May 5. This was precisely when students and administrators all believed they were making substantial progress in the negotiations. Police opened the campus and occupied it for rest of term as a wave of fires, vandalism, and violent attacks on black students followed. Gallagher, president for seventeen years, resigned on May 10.[47] He said that "politically motivated outside forces" had made it "impossible to carry on the process of reason and persuasion."[48] Indeed, that same day a *New York Daily News* editorial called for the House Internal Security Committee to probe charges that "Red Cuba and Red China are helping to finance some of the worst campus troublemakers." It called for a "Hayakawa for City College," referring to the authoritarian president of San Francisco State College, who was willingly doing the bidding of conservative California politicians, most notably Governor Ronald Reagan. Their wish seemed to come true with the selection of Joseph Copeland as acting president, whose commencement address equated the occupiers of south campus with the Ku Klux Klan, sparking a walkout by graduating black and Puerto Rican students.[49]

The Jewish Defense League (JDL), a right-wing vigilante organization led by Rabbi Meir Kahane, had also gone to court to open the college, but Procaccino had gotten there first. Formed in 1968 to combat alleged anti-Semitism by black New Yorkers, the JDL quickly became notorious for fanning the flames of black–Jewish division in the city. In 1969, Rabbi Maurice N. Eisendrath, president of the Union of American Hebrew Congregations, voiced the perspective of mainstream Jewry when he condemned the group: "The so-called Jewish Defense League violates every ethic and tradition of Judaism and every concept of civil liberties and democratic processes in American life."[50] The JDL's activities at Brooklyn College betrayed the strong-arm tactics of the organization and its lack of support among the college's large Jewish population. By 1971, black and Puerto Rican students had a greater visibility and presence at Brooklyn College and had begun to win seats in student government. Askia Davis believes this growing political clout inspired an attack by the JDL. One day that year, Kahane "brought in a huge group" to campus. Coincidentally, a few hundred black and Puerto Rican students were meeting at the student center that day, and the two groups converged. "It was really bad," Davis recalled. Several people went to the hospital. Yet Davis remembers this clash as an important turning point. "Every year we were subject to some kind of attack at Brooklyn College." But this time, "they attacked us and got beaten. . . . They took a heavy blow that day." He stressed that the students were defending themselves: "We had no interest in fighting Kahane or anybody else. We were just kids. He brought grown men out on the campus and they came out with all kinds of objects: bats, and other things." Moreover, Davis recalled, the skirmish with the JDL did not reflect black–Jewish relations on campus: "We had more support among the Jewish students than he did," he said. In fact, college authorities obtained an injunction barring the JDL from campus, and Kahane later consented to "refrain from disruptive activities at Brooklyn College." Looking back, Davis said, "Just that we ended up feeling safe was a big, big accomplishment."[51]

The student uprisings across the city in the spring of 1969 induced the Board of Higher Education to accelerate and broaden an open-admissions plan slated to begin in 1975. The original plan was to assign most high school graduates to community colleges, rather than four-year, or senior, colleges but student protest won a much larger number of slots at the senior colleges, and moved up its launch to 1970. Of course, the students had not led the call for open admissions. Allen Ballard, a black CCNY professor, director of SEEK, and scholar of black education, argued that "by moving from a quota arrangement specifically designed to serve the needs of Black and Puerto Rican students to a position of open admissions, the board both diverted the thrust of the Black and Puerto Rican demands and gained a white middle class constituency for the program." Ballard, it should be noted, was the first black director of SEEK, and he implemented the BPRSC demand to permit the hiring of social workers, rather than solely clinical psychologists, as SEEK counselors. Still, the impact of open admissions on black and Puerto Rican educational opportunity was nonetheless substantial. "I don't know, as of this writing," Ballard wrote in 1973, "whether open admissions will be a success or not. However, it has opened vistas for Black and Puerto Rican high school youths previously condemned to a life of poverty because their averages and SAT scores did meet the requirements of the City University of New York."[52] The impact of open admissions was dramatic: 35,000 freshmen entered CUNY campuses in 1970, a 75 percent increase from 1969. One-quarter of these entering students were black or Latino. After open admissions, 75 percent of New York City high school graduates attended college, a rate well ahead of the national average. According to the historian Conrad Dyer, two-thirds of these students would have been ineligible to attend college, even community college, under the old admissions standards. In 1975, five times as many black and Puerto Rican students were enrolled in the senior colleges as in 1969.[53]

The demand for curricular change, however, produced a much more equivocal outcome. Over the summer, the Board of Higher Education had rejected the demand to establish a separate school of third-world studies but authorized CUNY colleges to set up urban and ethnic studies departments. Without consulting the BPRSC or black and Puerto Rican professors, including the two—Christian and Cartey—City had hired to design such a program, acting CCNY president Joseph Copeland announced the creation of the new Department of Urban and Ethnic Studies and appointed Osborne E. Scott, a former army chaplain and current vice president of the American Leprosy Missions, as chair.[54] Wilfred Cartey called the two-course department "an insult not only to the black and Puerto Rican community, but to City College itself." This move by a college president to simultaneously grant a black studies program and then turn around and contain or undermine it was not unique to City College. Most colleges around the country failed to finance or build the kinds of innovative, large, and comprehensive African American studies units that black student activists and their faculty allies had envisioned. At City, this development was transparent, as Copeland had been hired as a revanchist president. His quest to put black folks in their place found blunt expression when he publicly called Professor Cartey "shiftless." Calling it an "insidious and malicious" remark, Cartey raised the prospect of a lawsuit and declared: "I'm not seeking an apology. I'm seeking redress for a group." For his part, Copeland did not deny using the word, saying, "I've never associated that word in my understanding with any racial group." But this supposed naïveté is contradicted by his evident awareness of the implication of the word in the offending quote. "He's too goddamn shiftless—and you can use that word in your story there—shiftless," he had said to a campus reporter.[55]

The tendency by many to credit—or blame—the City College protest with the onset of open admissions has, along with the legacy of the criminal prosecution, worked to suppress an acknowledgment of the significance of the struggle at Brooklyn College. But the students there achieved a great deal. "We were responsible for changing the climate of the campus," says Orlando Pile, now a physician.[56] After open admissions, the number of black and Puerto Rican students rose significantly, but as Davis underscored, "it wasn't just blacks and Latinos who benefited from open admissions—a lot of working-class whites had been shut out too." Other reforms included the establishment of an Afro-American Studies Institute and a Puerto Rican Studies Institute, which both became departments a year later, significant changes in required courses, and more counselors.[57] An important, though controversial, legacy of the protest was the creation in 1972 of the School of Contemporary Studies as a division of the college, whose mission was to be "present oriented, concerned primarily with the social problems that are engaging our contemporary world." Until its demise in 1976, the school was located in downtown Brooklyn and offered a unique field studies requirement where students did internships in legal services agencies, health service organizations, and penal institutions. As its dean, Carlos Russell, recalled, the program "brought the streets and classrooms together." An evaluating committee later reported that "some students appear to have been profoundly affected by their experience in field study." Nevertheless, the main campus faculty tended to regard the school's curriculum, faculty, and students as beneath the standards of Brooklyn College, and rifts developed internally between Russell and his faculty.[58]

These changes on New York campuses were part of a national trend, as many colleges and universities began to increase black enrollment and implement other reforms in the face of concerted black student protest. Having long ignored or postponed social change, universities suddenly had to act fast in the face of student revolt. Yet many commentators then and since have blamed student activists for "coercing" change or ushering in black studies programs of questionable quality, even though of course it was administrators who established the programs. But others saw inevitability to the confrontations. In May 1969 George Paster, the dean of students at City College, resigned in protest over what he viewed as the impermeability to change of academic institutions. "People who want to change such institutions," he said, "have to grab them by the scruff of the neck and yell: 'please listen to me' if they are ever to be heard. I honestly don't know anyway you can break through the rigidity of the institution other than the way the blacks and Puerto Ricans have done it." He felt that students used force "to be heard[,] not really to destroy." Moreover, in a point echoed by administrators at other campuses, Paster said that "once they had been heard, we sat down to some of the best and most productive discussions ever in the college—they have taught us so much."[59]

Still, open admissions always retained critics who argued that high admissions standards were more important than broad access to public higher education. "Only at CUNY," a SEEK professor wryly observed, "were those standards viewed as fixed, immutable and exempt from social and political realities."[60] Albert H. Bowker, the former chancellor of the City University of New York, thought racial resentment drove the attacks on open admissions. "There's been a lot of white flight from City College," he observed. "And most of the people who write about this are City College graduates who are mad."[61] In a fateful conjuncture, open admissions coincided with the New York City budget crisis of the 1970s, and the ensuing drop in funding seemed to make the discourse of failure shrouding open admissions a self-fulfilling prophecy. The severe budget cuts climaxed in the "retrenchment of 1976" when the state of New York took over the City University of New York, laid off many faculty, and imposed tuition for the first time.[62] The caseload of SEEK counselor Fran Geteles doubled from fifty to one hundred students. "Class sizes also grew sharply," she said, "which made it much harder to help students than before. Remedial classes had been no more than twenty; now some had forty students."[63]

A *New York Times* review of a 1984 play called *Open Admissions* reflected the skeptical view of open admissions, saying that it "shuffles its poor students through four years of overcrowded and under-taught classes—then pushes them out the door with a worthless diploma."[64] Still, those "worthless" diplomas brought thousands of black and Puerto Rican students to the middle class. But the attacks took their toll. By 1990, some of the creators and proponents of open admissions were lamenting that the college had made such a radical change with too little resources and planning. Allen Ballard thought CUNY should have implemented "a well articulated, gradually phased in, well funded operation aimed at a savable number of Black and Puerto Rican students in the high schools." Professor Leslie Berger felt similarly: "It was almost criminal to let them come in and let them fail because of the lack of service. We knew what we needed. It was no mystery."[65] In 1998, Republican Mayor Rudolph Giuliani declared that "open enrollment is a failure" and the CUNY Board of Trustees replaced it with standardized tests for admissions and eliminated all remedial courses from the senior colleges. As a City College student wrote, "the avenue for education for many NY high school students has been closed."[66]

This discourse of failure obscures the fact that a generation of lawyers, civil servants, teachers, artists, and social workers in New York City got their start through open admissions, notwithstanding its severe underfunding and other flaws. CUNY colleges today are both more competitive and more expensive, reflecting and reinforcing the widening socioeconomic divisions in the United States. Black and Puerto Rican college students in the late 1960s rejected market-driven approaches to higher education. They insisted upon the right of working-class African Americans and Puerto Ricans to receive the benefits of public higher education in New York City. Their tax dollars, after all, were paying for it. As Barbara Christian put it in 1969, a "much over-looked factor is that City College is supported by taxes. And Black and Puerto Rican people pay taxes just like everybody else. Yet they are not in any way represented in the ethnic make-up of the College."[67] Inspiring this generation was the conviction that seniors at poorly funded and poorly performing public high schools should not be punished for society's failure to provide high-quality secondary education for all but rather should be rewarded for their determination and desire to gain a college education. These student activists understood that college was critical to class mobility, especially since workers of color in New York City had been the first and hardest hit by deindustrialization and automation.[68] It's important to appreciate that the struggle for affirmative action, open admissions, and black and third-world studies was centered at public universities as much as, if not more than, at private ones. This is a story not of elites but of the children of migrants and immigrants. Like their counterparts in the South, they were tired of waiting for someone to enforce Supreme Court rulings; they understood that to achieve more far-reaching social change, they had to put their bodies on the line—and so they did.

9

Racial Events, Diplomacy, and Dinkins's Image

WILBUR C. RICH

N ew York City is a political environment replete with socially isolated ethnic groups. Groups usually come into contact with each
other in the commercial realm, and retail sales has been the theater for
this encounter. This is how the Chinese met whites and how Jews met
blacks. Usually the buyer and seller enjoy a limited and peaceful transac-
tion, but occasionally there is a misunderstanding that leads to conflict.
An incident may start as an individual conflict then escalate into a confrontation of imagined and real competing group interests. When that
happens, a simple misunderstanding or conflict can take on a larger
meaning and may require a third party (presumably a neutral individual)
to resolve it.

The premise of David Dinkins's mayoral campaign was that the city
needed a mayor who could resolve these recurrent racial/ethnic conflicts. The Bensonhurst and Howard Beach incidents had convinced
many New Yorkers that the racial situation was getting out of hand.
Dinkins portrayed himself as the man who could create a political environment in which such conflicts would be unlikely and as a man who
could anticipate these racial incidents before they occurred and resolve
them once they did.

The test of Mayor David N. Dinkins's ability as a healer and a conciliator came early in his administration. Ironically, the test was not a black–
white conflict but a black–Korean one. The conflict started at Bong Jae

Jang's Red Apple, a produce store in Flatbush, Brooklyn. On January 18, 1990, shortly after Dinkins's inauguration, Giselaine Fetissainte, a Haitian immigrant, accused Mr. Jang and two of his employees of assaulting her for allegedly stealing. They denied the charge and claimed that she became angry when asked to pay for some produce.[1]

There are different versions of what happened, but the incident sparked a boycott by Flatbush residents against Red Apple, led by Sonny Carson, the activist whose connection to the Dinkins campaign had been so controversial.[2] The boycott also included the Korean-owned grocery store across the street, Church Fruits. The protesters wanted the employees of Red Apple to be arrested and prosecuted for assault. Furthermore, protesters also wanted both stores (since the owners were closely tied to each other) to be put out of business.

Howard Kurtz of the *Washington Post* claimed that the incident was a minor altercation that escalated. Then, strangely, the *New York Post* began covering the boycott and openly criticized the rest of the press for ignoring it. Slowly, the other news organizations descended on Church Avenue. The television crews showed up, giving Carson and his followers an audience of thousands. Suddenly Dinkins was being denounced for failing to end the boycott. But the Minicams never pulled back far enough to show that there were only a few dozen chanting protestors or that some blacks in the neighborhood thought the boycott was unfair.[3]

A week after the boycott started, Brooklyn police commanders attempted to arrange a meeting with community leaders, which turned out to be unproductive. The protesters and their leaders were not ready to negotiate. The New York City Commission on Human Rights tried "quiet diplomacy" with the groups involved,[4] but this also failed, creating pressure for direct involvement by Mayor Dinkins.

The leader of the Korean Produce Association, Bo Young Jung, stated in a March 1 letter to the mayor, "You are looked upon by many New Yorkers as a healer. It was under [that] premise that you were elected to lead our great city. What better opportunity to show your strength and ability."[5] This invoking of Dinkins's preferred image was designed to force the mayor to get more personally involved in setting the dispute. Meanwhile, the media started with its racial-conflict frame.

Claire Kim's *Bitter Fruit* presents the press narrative as a scapegoating story in which the blacks lashed out against the hardworking and thrifty Koreans whose success shows up black failures.[6] She saw the unfolding of events as an example of racial ordering, locating Asians above blacks but below whites. For her, the Red Apple coverage used all the stereotypes of Asian Americans to undermine the community-control aspirations of blacks. A Russell Baker article in the *Christian Science Monitor* supported this view. He observed, "Of 200,000 businesses in New York City, Latinos own a whopping 40,000. Combined, other recent immigrant groups—chiefly Koreans, Arabs and Indians—own about 18,000 businesses. By the year 2000, that should top 30,000. Blacks, however, may own as few as 1,500 enterprises."[7] The article went on to discuss high unemployment among blacks and their lack of capital to start businesses, but the point was that blacks were clearly at the bottom rung, lagging behind immigrants.

Kim asserted that "the quieting of Black collective action against Korean merchants ritualistically affirms the American racial order: Blacks are confirmed as the pathological underclass; Korean merchants as the hardworking model minority; Whites as neutral enforcers of colorblind justice."[8] However, when one adds a black mayor who aspires to be a deracialized one, perceptions become more complicated.

The presence of Robert "Sonny" Carson, one of the leaders of the boycott, made settling the controversy even more difficult. Carson had been identified by the media as a former Dinkins campaign worker and convicted kidnapper. They quoted him as declaring himself "antiwhite."[9] Carson wanted to frame the boycott as the result of a racial affront to the black community and to expand the boycott to other boroughs. Carson was a self-styled grassroots leader who had been banished from the Dinkins campaign and was now resurfacing in this crisis. He reportedly said, "In the future, there'll be funerals, not boycotts."[10] A May 8, 1990, *New York Times* editorial reported this statement and attacked the so-called quiet negotiation tactics used by Deputy Mayor Bill Lynch. The editorial ended, "Is that all Mayor Dinkins can think of to do? Racist fires are alight."[11] The mayor's office tried to get more involved in April after Lynch met with Korean leaders. The mayor's office formed a "fact-finding" committee of Koreans and blacks to continue to engage in quiet negotiations. But progress was slow, and the situation was not helped by comments made by former mayor Ed Koch in a *New York Post* column. The essence of the Koch comments was that civic and religious leaders should condemn racist remarks by demonstrators. He reasoned that black leaders should be on the side of the storeowners. Koch wrote, "If I were mayor and I was dealing with an extortionist . . . a thug like Sonny Carson . . . I would go out there myself and I'd cross the picket line and I would buy all the fruits and vegetables Gracie Mansion needed for that week."[12] Dinkins responded that he would "go today or tomorrow if I thought a trip at this time would solve the problem." Sam Roberts responded with an article in the *New York Times* titled: "Which Mayor Knows Best on the Boycott?" Roberts agreed that bigots, regardless of color, should be denounced. Although Roberts criticized Koch as a less-than-ideal messenger, he pointed out that "at some point [Dinkins's] failed diplomacy may be perceived as weakness."[13]

Dinkins criticized protesters, saying, "A large mountain has been made out of a very small molehill," and argued that the protesters' demands "have expanded this beyond reasonableness." More important, he sought to explain why he did not criticize Sonny Carson by name.

> I have in the past spoken out, sometimes pretty much alone, and sometimes expressed myself in disagreement with those who are African-American. Now it seems to me that either I have some credibility [on such subjects] or I don't. Now people can disagree with my methods and that's fine; I think that's fair game. People can say, "Dave, if you were to go out there and stand on your head, it would resolve it." They're entitled to those views. But I don't want to exacerbate the situation. I don't want those who are there picketing to figure that I'm telling them that they have no right to express dissent.[14]

On May 10, 1990, state supreme court justice Gerald Held urged both sides to negotiate and ordered the boycotters to stay at least fifty feet from each of the two grocery stores. However, police officials appealed and refused to enforce the fifty-foot rule because it would force demonstrators to gather across the street in front of a church, which might cause more violent confrontations.[15] Judge Held also said that he "regrets the failure of the Mayor of the City of New York to personally intervene and use the prestige of his office and his high standing in the community to convince the parties to bring a suitable end to this dispute.[16] In reaction to the judge's criticism, Dinkins said, "One, I'm pleased that the judge feels that I have a high standing in the community. That's nice. Two, to personally intervene, without knowing what his definition of personal intervention is, let me hasten to say that I have personally intervened. . . . If the time comes when it appears that would be helpful, I'm certainly happy to do."[17] Dinkins had said earlier that "whether it

would be resolved by me appearing on Church Avenue is highly prob-
lematical. I may have an adverse impact.''[18]
    The city also argued that police officers were not obligated to enforce
court orders in civil cases between private parties and that they had
exclusive discretion in law enforcement. On June 26, 1990, the judge
held that the police department was not enforcing his order and ordered
them to do so. Eight months later, a unanimous appellate court ruled
that the NYPD had to enforce the court order.
    Mayor Dinkins claimed that the parties were close to settling the dis-
pute but that the media attention had exacerbated the demonstration.
The mayor's initial tactic was to use quiet negotiations with his aides.[19]
Some reporters expected more from the mayor because of his reputation
for building a ''gorgeous mosaic'' and because he was New York's first
black mayor. Sales and Bush concluded that, in practice, the mosaic
''meant a continuation of clubhouse loyalties and an unwarranted concern for the sensibilities and agendas of powerful white ethnics, while
muting the demands of his poor Black and Latino supporters.''[20] Mayor
Dinkins responded, ''Some people think that confrontation is superior
to conciliation. I disagree.''[21] Some considered the mayor's use of conciliation an excuse for inaction. Others believed that Dinkins was working
hard, only behind the scenes.
    In response to accusations that he was not being vocal enough, Din-
kins gave a speech on May 11, 1990, at City Hall, saying, ''We gather
tonight, here at the seat of the government, to reaffirm our commitment
to renew out mission and to reassert a simple truth: All of us want to live
our lives in peace and dignity, free to walk any street and shop in any
store, at any time, in any neighborhood, without fear of force or violence.''[22] In his speech, Dinkins also said he would stiffen penalties for
hate, foster tolerance, teach merchants about consumer rights, and help
small businesses. Dinkins also said, ''My administration will never lead
by dividing. At the same time, and in the same spirit, we will never allow
any group or any person to turn to violence . . . no matter how legitimate
their anger or frustration may be.''[23] The *New York Times* editorial praised
the speech and read it as evidence of ''leadership.''[24] The Reverend Al
Sharpton felt the speech did not address the substantive issues: ''It was
more like a James Brown record—talk loud and saying nothing.''[25]
    Todd Purdum's first article in the *New York Times* about the speech
proved important for its references. The article stated that speechwriter
John Siegel drafted the Dinkins speech, with contributions from Andrew
Cuomo, Norman Steisel, and Ken Sunshine. Four television networks

carried the twenty-five-minute speech live, and it got the biggest applause when the mayor asked the media to join in the effort to foster race tolerance. Purdum also suggested that the speech was delivered in anticipation of the Bensonhurst case verdict. The article also quoted Dinkins as saying, "This was a crime committed by individuals. All of Bensonhurst did not commit this crime; rather, a few people committed this crime in Bensonhurst. We must absolutely, categorically reject the notion of group guilt. We abhor those who preach it, and we must be mindful that predictions of violence and anger tend to self-fulfilling. But whatever the outcome, as we have so many times over so many years, we must repress our rage, channel our energies and come together to make this tragedy transforming."[26]

Purdum characterized the speech as "Surreal Air at City Hall" and quoted the "we must repress our rage" statement. Dinkins condemned the boycott of Red Apple and asserted, "I oppose any boycott based on race."[27] He called the boycott inappropriate and offered himself as a mediator, even though earlier he had stated that picketing was "as American as apple pie."[28] Purdum ended the article with supporting quotes from politicians, blacks, and labor leaders. Reporter Jim Sleeper offered another view of Dinkins behavior: "What accounted for Dinkins's bizarre indulgence of Carson and his crowd? The answer may lie, paradoxically, in the mayor's determination to transcend the politics of race without transcending the politics of the establishment. It may be that his embrace of the permanent government's fiscal-crisis politics left him feeling morally vulnerable to the militants' attack."[29]

Korean Americans understood the lesson of the boycott, which was their relative marginality in New York politics. Just giving money to political campaigns was not enough. The boycott caused them to attempt to mobilize for integration into city politics. Thousands of Koreans rallied outside City Hall in September 1990, promoting racial harmony. The crowd booed during comments made by Mayor Dinkins, expressing disappointment at how he had handled the boycott. A couple of days after the rally, Dinkins showed his support for the merchants by going to the Red Apple and purchasing ten dollars' worth of fruits and vegetables. This gesture may have taken the oxygen out of the protest, but it did little to rebuild Dinkins image as a mediator.

The boycott did spur Korean Americans to form the Korean American Civil Rights Committee of the Korean Association of New York. The association intended to advocate Korean American interests in matters related to business, discrimination, and voter registration.

Sung Soo Kim, a Korean American business owner and the founder of the Korean American Small Business Service Center in New York, said, "Before they can have a real impact on the city's political scene and begin electing their own candidates, Korean-Americans will have to broaden the issues that concern them."[30] On May 30, 1990, Bong Jae Jang announced that he was selling his store. Dinkins expressed his regrets. In August, *New York Times* reporter Don Terry's article questioned Dinkins's quiet tactics, and he observed: "That dispute appears no closer to resolution today than when it started in January, 1990. The city's inability to settle the Church Avenue conflict has been politically embarrassing for Mr. Dinkins. And as it has dragged on his critics have attacked what they say is his slow and overly cautious style."[31] A committee of black and Korean leaders appointed by Dinkins criticized Brooklyn district attorney Charles Hynes for moving too slowly in prosecuting in the Church Avenue case.

Two years after the incident, the U.S. Civil Rights Commission issued a report criticizing the way Mayor Dinkins had handled the boycott. The report constituted a small section of the federal agency's two-hundred-page study of increasing acts of bigotry against Asian Americans throughout the United States. Mayor Dinkins stated in 1992 that "the reason Church Avenue did not get resolved more quickly is because there were people involved who did not want it to be resolved."[32] Dinkins's response to the report was that it was Monday morning quarterbacking.

Given time, the mayor's office did help improve communication between blacks and Koreans. In 1990 and 1991, the city helped organize goodwill missions to Korea. Only black ministers participated in the first mission, but the second included a cross section of community leaders. The missions also led to the formation of the Ethnic Committee for Racial Harmony and Outreach, which promotes dialogue between blacks and Koreans. The boycott also mobilized and politicized the Korean community in New York. Pyong Gap Min, a sociology professor at Queens College, suggested, "This is the beginning. They [Koreans] do it, and in the future they will stand upon that collective mobilization more often."[33] Min was one of the founders of the Korean American Civil Rights Committee of the Korean Association of New York.

The Red Apple incident allowed the media to challenge Dinkins's public image as a mediator in race-related disputes. The media saw the case as a test of Dinkins's mediating skills. Larry Simonberg, a press aide to former mayor Ed Koch, wrote a full-page opinion, admonishing Dinkins not to oversimplify racial tensions. Simonberg asserted that Dinkins's statement during the campaign that "the climate is set at City Hall" led people to believe that he could wipe out deep-seated causes of racism. "You are now expected by many to be able to end the boycott of Korean stores in Flatbush by simple fiat. The lack of progress damaged your reputation as a conciliator." Simonberg concluded by saying, "Don't play weatherman again and don't let others issue such a glib forecast."[34]

The Red Apple conflict faded away once the protest limits were enforced. The sight of a black mayor crossing the picket line to buy produce robbed the protesters of some of their racial claims. Because Korean Americans were a small minority group with no political organization, the Red Apple incident represented an opportunity for Dinkins to show his conciliatory skills. If he stumbled in this situation, then a future racial incident could sink his image. The incident in Crown Heights did precisely that, triggering the unraveling of Dinkins's prevailing image.

The Crown Heights Incident

August 19, 1991, will live (to borrow a phrase) in infamy. At about 8:21 P.M., a car driven by a Hasidic man of the Lubavitcher sect named Yosef Lifish ran a red light to keep up with his colleagues, swerved, and jumped a curb, striking two black children, Gavin and Angela Cato, cousins. Gavin was killed, and Angela was badly injured. Lifish was part of a three-car convoy led by an unmarked police vehicle that served as an escort for the Lubavitcher Rebbe Menachem Mendel Schneerson. Police escorts for the rabbi had been policy since the Koch administration. There were two immediate questions. Did the car actually run a red light? Second, did the Hatzolah ambulance ignore the injured children and instead take the Hasidic driver away?

Rumors spread that a Hatzolah ambulance immediately tended to the slightly injured men, instead of the grievously injured black children. A crowd began shouting, "Kill the Jew." Police commissioner Lee Brown told the press that the Hatzolah ambulance and the emergency service ambulance arrived "almost simultaneously." Police asked the Hatzolah ambulance to remove the driver of the station wagon "in the interest of preserving the peace as the crowd was becoming increasingly violent."[35] Dinkins stated that the rumor that the Hatzolah paramedics had ignored the children was false. He stated, "That's just inaccurate because I spoke to the father [of one of the children]."[36]

In the evening, blacks assembled and pelted Jewish homes with stones in the Crown Heights section of Brooklyn. Later that same evening, at approximately 11:15 P.M., a gang that allegedly included Lemrick Nelson Jr. stabbed Yankel Rosenbaum, an Australian rabbinic student. (Nelson was later tried for the murder.) *Daily News* reporter Dean Chang described police as saying that a "separate band of black youths roamed Crown Heights seeking revenge."[37] Pictures of blacks turning over a car and rampaging teens supported a *New York Post* article by Mike McAlary. McAlary tried to be evenhanded in the assignment of blame for the riots, and he cited name-calling by both sides. In addition, McAlary worked the names of Sonny Carson and Leonard Jeffries into the piece: "They have their audience, and moved hateful groups to the street."[38] Dinkins's slow reaction to the chain of events seemed to have made the situation worse and further damaged his image.

Just as he did during the Red Apple incident, he assigned the management of the crisis to Bill Lynch. Lynch established a City Hall presence in Public School 167, where he attempted to bring together Jewish and black leaders to defuse the situation. A two-and-half-hour meeting with sixty leaders and police brought about no progress. There was too much anger and too many rumors for them to come up with a resolution.

Dinkins went to the Crown Heights neighborhood and also visited the victim in Kings County Hospital, where, Dinkins recalled, "I visited him [Rosenbaum] in the hospital. We were told he would be OK, but the doctors overlooked the wound, even though the ambulance attendant had indicated to them that there was more than one wound. So he died."[39] The death of Rosenbaum further eroded trust in the competence of Dinkins, but not of the hospital.

The mayor became embroiled in an endless explanatory and social accounting fiasco as reporters kept seeking information. Dinkins was quoted as saying "There's an awful lot to suggest he [Lifish] did go through the red light. We are in a tense situation. We've had a tragedy. There are at least two deaths, and it's painful. We ought not to have further injury."[40] Dinkins attempted to frame the incident as an accident, the subtext of which was that the lead police car was responsible. He suggested that the police cruiser heading the convoys was responsible for keeping it together. Dinkins then proffered a story: "Part of what I did in the Marine Corps was to drive convoys. What you do if folks get ahead, you've got two options. The one behind to speed up or the one ahead to recognize it and slow down."⁴¹ Obviously, this framing did not work.

For reporters and the general public, the Jewish-black tension story offered more possibilities. The rioting lasted for several hours. Blacks appeared at the Lubavitcher synagogue, chanting, "No Justice, no peace." One headline stated, "Anarchy Grips Crown Heights."⁴² Jimmy Breslin, a famous columnist for the *Daily News*, was actually pulled out of a cab and robbed.

During the disturbance, Dinkins used a bullhorn, declaring, "I care about you. I care about you very desperately. I too want justice, and we will get justice but we will not get it with violence." However, Dinkins was greeted with boos and soon became a target for flying rocks and bottles as he tried to enter a building on President Street. Dinkins recalled, "I was personally in Crown Heights ducking bricks and bottles. Not the behavior of someone that needed to be sheltered and hiding some damn where."⁴³ Again, Dinkins had put his skill as a race mediator on the line and was attacked. Dinkins claimed the media distorted the situation: "The media stated that Crown Heights was a situation of rioting for several days culminating in the death of Yankel Rosenbaum. That is just factually inaccurate . . . The accusation was that I had held back the cops. That was not true. [And] that we [Dinkins's office] had permitted blacks to attack Jews. That was not true. In fact, for several days we had rioting, [but] not continuously every minute of every day."⁴⁴

Bill Lynch also agreed that the press "missed the boat on the coverage. You would think there [were] weeks of riots. It only happened two days."⁴⁵ Yet many people criticized Mayor Dinkins's handling of the black rioters. The press asked Dinkins why he did not take a walking tour, as John Lindsay had done in the 1960s to calm down Harlem. Dinkins did walk through the neighborhood, but to no avail. Dinkins's press secretary, Leland Jones, responded by saying "We'll be very careful in choosing when the mayor goes there."⁴⁶ Bill Lynch commented, "We're not sitting here wringing our hands. It's not easy where there are people who are hell-bent on confrontation, the thing is quote-unquote out of control."⁴⁷ Dinkins's "increase the peace" theme was ignored, and he was called a traitor. The angry crowd shouted, "The Mayor is not safe."⁴⁸ It was reported that Dinkins aborted the walking tour.

The press began framing this most recent disturbance as the result of long-standing and growing tension between the two groups. *Daily News* reporter Don Singleton asserted that from the outside, the neighborhood looked like a melting pot, but "bubbling just beneath the surface is a long history of conflicts and uneasiness between the area's Hasidic Jews and blacks."[49]

By the next day this incident had pushed a story about a coup in Russia and President Mikhail Gorbachev off the front page. The *Daily News* headline read, "Streets of Rage."[50] However, each group saw the latest incident differently. The Hasidic Jews saw it as a continuation of anti-Semitic persecution. For some of them, the riots evoked memories of Czarist pogroms and the Nazi Holocaust. They saw their black neighbors as intent upon destroying them as Jews. Blacks saw the incident as yet another example of the arrogance of the Lubavitcher community. They also feared the violence caused by the Hasidic vigilante patrols.

Bob Herbert, a respected black reporter, wrote a *Daily News* column titled "Blood Feud in Crown Heights," in which he compared the Hasidim to the Hatfields and the African Americans to the McCoys. "The African Americans felt that the Hasidim got preferential treatment. The Hasidim get too much in the way of police protection. Some African Americans believed their own community is being denied police protection that could be directed at drug dealers.[51] The editorial page of the *Daily News* called for a permanent neighborhood council to facilitate communication between the two groups.[52]

The events surrounding the Crown Heights incident may remain in dispute. The week after the riots and before the trial of Lemrick Nelson was a time of hyperbolic rhetoric. Earl Campbell of the *New York Daily News* characterized the black youths as being out of control and with no values. "That was the future Dinkins got a glimpse of when he visited Crown Heights. He was starting at the fire next time. Not even a police bodyguard will protect him from those flames."[53]

Dinkins's problem worsened as the Reverend Al Sharpton and Alton Maddox, an activist lawyer, organized a march in the Crown Heights neighborhood days after the incident. Maddox threatened to make a citizen's arrest of Lifish, the driver of the car that hit the Cato children. Dinkins tried to dissuade people from marching but failed, and the march went on the next day. An estimated two thousand people peacefully participated in the demonstration. Dinkins himself participated and laid a wreath at both Gavin Cato's and Yankel Rosenbaum's death sites.

In a related effort to repair his image, Dinkins gave a speech at the First Baptist Church of Crown Heights to a mainly black audience. The speech went well. Dinkins asserted, "Today our mosaic stands badly incomplete. Now two of its brightest and most vibrant tiles have been lost. We can never bring Gavin and Yankel back, but we can let their deaths serve as the catalyst for meaningful changes that will prevent other deaths."[54] The next day reporters felt it newsworthy to report that Dinkins had decided to watch the U.S. Open in Flushing Meadow in Corona Park.[55] It was a small article, but it brought the readers back to the tennis competition. In addition, the *Daily News* editorial stated that the crisis was not over yet.[56]

Several months later a jury found Nelson not guilty, prompting a *New York Post* editorial writer, Eric Breindel, to use the pogrom references to attack the way the Dinkins administration handled the incident and the trial. In a *Wall Street Journal* editorial, Breindel claimed that the Nelson supporters signaled "a sense of triumph," and the police were relieved at Nelson's acquittal. He even suggested that Dinkins tried to mislead the public by focusing on the few City Hall marchers with signs that said: "Wanted for Murder: David Dinkins." This rambling essay successfully managed to link the Korean boycott, black anti-Semitism, and white middle-class flight. For the latter, he claimed that the "message was plain: New York no longer welcomes them."[57]

New Yorker writer David Remnick called the language used by the Hasidic community and its supporters consistent with the Hasidic sect's apocalyptic culture and "tragically overblown rhetoric." Remnick asked, "Who really believes David Dinkins is a 'Jew hater'? Is New York in 1992 really worse than Nazi Germany?"[58]

Orthodox Jews created the Jewish Action Alliance to stop anti-Semitism. They attacked a WLIB radio talk show because the callers were using anti-Jewish rhetoric. They also attacked Lee Brown, Dinkins's police commissioner. Some people believed that Dinkins had ordered the police to go easy on rioters. Several journalists made a connection between Dinkins's handling of Crown Heights and his chances for reelection.

The Crown Heights incident incorporated all the features that a reporter needed: a race riot that could be compared to others, a city with its first black mayor, and a conflict between Jews and blacks that left the police baffled. Every move that Dinkins made could be analyzed and second-guessed. Dinkins was aware of this situation when he told a reporter that "for me, it's a lose-lose. You're damned if you do and damned if you don't."[59] Dinkins outlined the dilemma he was in: "Some would like to say, I hereby denounce Sonny Carson, I hereby denounce Al Sharpton, I hereby denounce Al Maddox and on and on. And the same reporters put to me the question. 'But are you doing all you can Mr. Mayor. Are you reaching out to these people? Have you sought them out?' And I would like to know, do you want me to denounce them just before or just after I sit down and meet them."[60]

This exchange with a reporter is both interesting and revealing. Dinkins saw himself in a bind with reporters and actors in the Crown Heights incident. The entire Crown Heights incident was particularly frustrating for the mayor because it involved two groups that he had been closely associated with, blacks and Jews. Now both groups were criticizing his handling of the situation.

Village Voice reporter Wayne Barrett suggested that Dinkins passed up an opportunity to transcend the death of Yankel Rosenbaum and the Lemrick Nelson acquittal. Barrett suggested that Dinkins should have been more enthusiastic about a federal probe and waited too long to support the Justice Department investigation. Barrett also said that the statement issued by Dinkins after the Nelson verdict read like "an endorsement for the flawed outcome."[61] Barrett suggested that the "mayor could've found language that put perceptible distance between himself and the acquittal, questioning it without denouncing it; he has instead very consciously chosen not to—an invitation to anger."[62] Furthermore, Barrett suggested that the mayor should have appointed a commission that would have preempted the state's investigation, which he predicted would be critical of the mayor's reactions to the events in Crown Heights.

Governor Mario Cuomo created a special investigation group to review the accusations and allegations surrounding Crown Heights. It was a classic example of state encroachment into a local matter. Richard Girgenti, state director of the Criminal Division, held hearings and produced a two-volume report. The four-hundred-page Girgenti report did not directly criticize the mayor's handling of the situation, but the implications were clear. However, the report did target the breakdown in the police leadership hierarchy.

On July 21, 1993, the *New York Times* headlined "Crown Heights Study Finds Dinkins and Police at Fault in Letting Unrest Escalate."[63] Dinkins's press secretary, Leland Jones, recalled, "We got no advance copy of it as it was being handed in. We got no tip from Cuomo."[64] The lack of a strong rebuttal to the report further racialized the incident and supported the press's characterization of Mayor Dinkins as "incompetent." In response to the report, *New York Amsterdam News* reporter Herb Boyd published an article titled "Crown Heights Report Exonerates Mayor Dinkins from Any Blame."[65] An editorial written by Wilbert Tatum, the publisher, attacked the report as being biased in favor of the

Jews and redundant and as "following the lead of a White press corps in New York City that had already made it clear that Blacks were the culprits in the drama and that they would brook no interference with their interpretations and conclusions about events, no matter what information to the contrary was unearthed and presented by those who would share credit or blame for the 'Report.' "[66]

For some in the press, Dinkins's performance in the Crown Heights incident was further evidence that his skills as a racial conciliator were lacking. The report also pointed out that a "leadership vacuum existed at the highest level."[67] This was clearly a reference to Commissioner Brown and Mayor Dinkins. The effort to repair Dinkins's image was doomed. Bill Lynch was correct when he stated that "this is not like Bensonhurst."[68] In the end, this situation got out of control.

The Rosenbaum murder turned the issue into more of a racial one, and the Lemrick Nelson acquittal brought outrage from the Jewish community. Dinkins's speech in response was titled "Reason, Respect and Reconciliation in New York," and apparently he thought it an act of "social accounting" that would calm down the situation. The *New York Amsterdam News* ran the entire speech as an op-ed page. During the speech, the mayor returned to his themes of reason and racial unity while asserting that he was not responsible for the verdict in the Nelson case:

> Astonishingly, a few people even sought to blame me for the verdict reached by the jury in the Rosenbaum case, even though I had nothing to do with his prosecution or his defense. The mayor has nothing to do with the operation of any district attorney office.
>   . . . I'm proud to be accountable because the buck does stop here at this desk. That's why there are more cops on the beat. That's why crime is down across the board for the first time in almost 40 years.
>   . . . I have never nor will I ever pander or cater to one group to gain an advantage over another group.
>   . . . Unlike some before me, I will never use code words and subliminal message to create mistrust between groups.
>   . . . If we trust in the truth and in each other, then the cement that binds our gorgeous mosaic will remain seamless and strong.[69]

The language in his speech was intended to repair his public image. However, emotions in the city were running too high, and the speech could not reframe the events or make an effective "social accounting."

Village Voice reporter Michael Tomasky compared Dinkins's speech to the inadequate response President George H.W. Bush made after the Rodney King verdict. Tomasky thought the mayor was not reacting from the "gut."[70] *New York Times* reporter Sam Roberts talked about his frustration when covering stories involving Dinkins. Roberts asserted, "He spoke these convoluted sentences. He didn't speak declarative sentences. He never said anything directly. He had this ambiguous way of talking."[71] In other words, Dinkins lacked the communicative skill necessary to reframe the Crown Heights incident.

Media coverage of the Crown Heights affair contributed to the transformation of an accident and a murder into a black-Jewish conflict. The framing is critical to understanding this particular incident. Carol Conaway, a political scientist, faulted the reporters for framing the Crown Heights event as purely a racial incident. She suggested that if the media divided the participants into African Americans, Caribbean Americans, and Lubavitch Hasidim, the incident would have been properly framed as a conflict of both culture and religion. In other words, the reporters were framing it as a racial incident, while the antagonists characterized it as an anti-Semitic incident. Conaway saw the incident in anti-Semitic terms.[72] She argued that all incidents between whites and blacks do not have to be framed as racial ones.

The reaction to the Crown Heights incident would not go away. In November 1992, the *CBS Evening News* reported that tensions remained in Crown Heights even after Dinkins denounced race baiting in Crown Heights. The *Evening News* showed a clip of Dinkins commenting, "I will never, nor will I ever, tolerate or sanction or allow disorder or lawlessness by any group toward any other. By the same token, I cannot allow a quiet riot of words and epithets to poison our citizenry."[73] CBS reporter Jacqueline Adams, an African American, responded, "Not surprisingly, few in Crown Heights were impressed." The clip also showed a statement by a resident of Crown Heights. Adams ended the piece with: "Hyperbole and high drama are the norm in this city. What mayor could permanently put an end to racism? Still, unless David Dinkins came up with a bold program to bridge the city's racial divide, many activists believe the tension between blacks and Jews would only worsen."[74] This news clip haunted Dinkins's remaining time in office and was used as a major factor against him in the mayor's reelection bid. In fact, it would take many years to close the book on this incident, since the Nelson case dragged on.

As is the case in most racial disturbances, rumors played a big role in making the settling of the incident more difficult and lengthy. It has been said that nothing is more inviting to the media than one racial group claiming another racial group has done something wrong. Proclaiming innocence is a natural refuge for both races. The question is, Why? Is it a matter of framing or a difference in crisis management style?

Summary

Were the Red Apple and Crown Heights incidents caused by a failure to communicate? Or was the latter a case of a middle-aged politician trying to persuade and assuage West Indian youths? Were the so-called Black Nationalists leading the disturbances, or were they appropriating it to get attention from the city leaders and the media? There were certainly a lot of things said and done, none of which seem to have improved the situation. There were a variety of messages in both incidents. As mayor, Dinkins needed to trump all other attempts to frame the circumstances surrounding the events and to impose his own criteria for success. In other words, he had to communicate well at every opportunity that became available. This was particularly true in the media. In many instances what one says is enhanced by how well one uses language. Albert Scardino, Dinkins's first secretary, agreed with Sam Roberts's assessment of Dinkins's speaking style:

> He didn't have the best media presence in the world. Because he unfortunately spoke in a sort of rich nineteenth-century Victorian stylized manner in which he used what he thought[,] and what he had grown up with, was appropriate and proper English. But he used a lot of "One would have thought that" kind of expression[s] instead of being more blunt and direct the way Ed Koch had been. It was very difficult to convey what he was trying to communicate.
>
> He was often misinterpreted by the media because he was not particularly comfortable with television. His language and the depth of his feeling and philosophy was a very very poor match for TV and for tabloid journalism. I think as a result he was not able [to] communicate himself and his message [as] effectively as others might have.[75]

The two racially charged incidents illustrate how important it is for the mayor to win the contest of words that follow controversial events.

If one has difficulty communicating, then one runs the risk of being misunderstood and possibly alienating both groups. In each situation, quick and coherent social accounting is critical to assuage the combatants. Social accounting should attempt to convert a faulty anticipatory response into a socially acceptable or corrective one.

On the national television show *The MacNeil/Lehrer NewsHour*, Dinkins complimented the media coverage of his speech on race regarding the Red Apple incident:

> Let me say the media has been enormously helpful and the electronics media, especially by giving the time they gave on Friday. We had no way of knowing whether [or] not that would be forthcoming. The decision to do the speech on Friday was made on Thursday. We figured we could do it on WNYC, the public radio, the city station, and hopefully some of the other stations would carry some of it. We assumed the print people would cover it, but there's a big difference to have that live on television in prime time, so that was very useful.[76]

A supportive press can help convince the public that the mayor did the right thing or that he intended to do the right thing. If the mayor is to be successful in selling his version of political events, he needs a sympathetic press. Dinkins did not get that support and his prevailing image collapsed.

The Red Apple and Crown Heights incidents had a profound effect on the image of Mayor Dinkins. The Red Apple boycott was a classic framing struggle, with Carson's group defining it as a discourse about racial injustice, the Korean merchants and activists vying to make it a conflict between a hardworking minority (Koreans) and its nonworking, whining minority counterparts (blacks), and Mayor Dinkins attempting to contain the conflict as the simple boycott of a retailer. Russell Baker's article in the *Christian Science Monitor* supported this construction.[77] The media accepted some of the merchants' framing but also were intrigued by Dinkins's bungling of what they viewed as his first opportunity to show off his mediating skills.

Political scientist Claire Kim interpreted the overall Red Apple conflict in a broader context. After interviews with several participants, she concluded that the conflict was part of a racial ordering that pitted minorities against each other in the service of preserving the notion of race. She believed that the rhetoric of "colorblind justice" was a tool to promote cleavage between the two groups and reproduce the racial order.

There is no evidence that Dinkins saw the conflicts in those terms. He contended that these were easily solved disputes that were confounded by the personalities involved, and he seemed comfortable with assigning his expert, Bill Lynch, to manage them.[78] Dinkins's Red Apple speech reflected his views. Despite Todd Purdum's point that the speech was written by his white aides, the speech followed Dinkins's overall civility themes. The text included the sentence "I oppose any boycott based on race," but few picked up on the meaning of that statement. The black response might have been, "I can't believe he said that." The entire Montgomery Bus Boycott was based on race. Was the mayor engaging in some "gratuitous endearing"?

Dinkins claims that initially he thought the Red Apple incident was similar to two others in Queens and Brooklyn involving a Korean merchant and a black consumer. They were solved in two days. He asserted that they were "solved by the same people who worked on the Red Apple, Bill Lynch. In the Red Apple, we had some folks that did not want it to be resolved. Some blacks that didn't want it resolved."[79]

There is no evidence that Dinkins had any relationship with the Korean community prior to the incident. Furthermore, the Korean community had little, if any, political profile. Dinkins should have been able to impose his frame on events. Why? Claire Kim concludes: "Of course, as both the direct beneficiary of and supposed antidote to the resurgent Black Power movement, David Dinkins was between a rock and a hard place from the moment he was elected. The ambiguity of his 'gorgeous mosaic' campaign had helped him to walk the tightwire between Black and White expectations into Gracie Mansion. But the Red Apple Boycott brought his balancing act to an abrupt halt."[80]

The attempt at quiet negotiations failed, and Dinkins was forced to renounce his "erstwhile allies in the name of colorblindness."[81] Apparently, he did not regard it as a test of his image. He could not have predicted this would become a national story. The CBS program *48 Hours* did a story about the boycott with reporter Bernard Goldberg interviewing people on the picket line. Goldberg wanted to know what the mayor thought of blacks calling Koreans "yellow monkeys." He asked the mayor if he had been called a "nigger." The mayor admitted that he had been called the " 'n' word many times" but responded philosophically to name-calling: "I don't think that you ought to burn the flag, but our Supreme Courts of the United States says that's freedom of speech. Because I don't agree with what one says doesn't mean that I don't feel they have a right to say it."[82] This was vintage Dinkins, making what he thought was an appropriate response but losing the opportunity to use the moment.

In retrospect, Dinkins's decision to delegate the mediation was a mistake. Although Bill Lynch tried to take the blame for the Red Apple debacle, he acknowledged that the incident tarnished the mayor's image. He stated, "Yes my soul is bleeding, for the Mayor and this trying year. When there's a mistake or a miscue, if we don't do something, it ends up at his [Dinkins's] feet."[83]

Dinkins's image as a race mediator was seriously damaged by the Red Apple incident, and his prevailing image was so weak that he had little to draw on in the Crown Heights incident. Even the small *News India-Times* carried an editorial that scolded the Indian community for its silence on these two events and condemned Dinkins's reaction to them.[84] The events of Crown Heights took on a life on their own, and there was limited room for intuitive intervention. Although it was not a national issue in the beginning, Benjamin Hooks of the NAACP said, "Crown Heights is being politicized by the minute. And that means that the chance that this will spill over grows by the minute."[85] Simmering turf issues between blacks and Jews complicated Dinkins's strategy of careful reengineering of civility. Although Dinkins had been a member of Black Americans in Support of Israel Committee and had traveled to Israel, his preferred self-image of evenhandedness was forgotten during the Crown Heights controversy. Dinkins misread and seriously misjudged the volatility of the situation. In our interview, Dinkins repeated his statement about his obituary. "When my obituary is written, they already have a boilerplate. In the first paragraph, it will read, 'The first black mayor of New York City,' and the next sentence will be about Crown Heights."[86]

Dinkins's prediction may come true, but he also admitted that the Girgenti report was "one of the reasons we did not succeed."[87] Martin Gottlieb called the Girgenti report "a scathing portrait of ineptitude and miscommunication" on the part of the Dinkins administration. The choice of the word "ineptitude"[88] reminded readers of the subtext of Dinkins's competence as a crisis manager. This report was released at the beginning of the Dinkins campaign for reelection. Wayne Barrett of the *Village Voice* suggested that Governor Cuomo was the ghostwriter for the report:

> The best evidence of the governor's hand is what is not in the generally thorough report. As telling as much of what Girgenti

found out about the mayor's miscalculations and indecisiveness is, not all of the hard facts surrounding these horrid events were allowed to fall where they might. The Cuomo Report is so focused on David Dinkins as to resemble another assassination analysis. Substituting a single culprit theory for a single-bullet fantasy.[89]

An alternative explanation for the reactions to the incident was that Dinkins tried to be neutral in the story. If Dinkins had supported the Jewish version of the story, he would have lost all credibility in the black community. If he had supported the black version, he would have lost credibility in the Jewish community. Dinkins may have thought that race neutrality was a possible safe compromise, but it was not. Obviously, some blacks did not realize the unfolding of events would end up destroying Dinkins's image. For many of them, the situation offered an opportunity to vent their anger toward vigilantism and arrogance on the part of the Hasidim. It is doubtful whether the curious history of the Lubavitchers was known.

However, it was assumed that Dinkins had some credit with the Jews. He did, but only with the liberal and secular Jewish activist community. Unlike Koch, who provided police protection for the Rebbe, Dinkins had never "tipped his hat" to the Hasidic community. Reporters played up the racial angle and framed the story as a lack of leadership, which led to a misjudgment by the mayor. Former *New York Times* reporter Paul Delaney reminds us that editors tell the reporter how to pitch the story. "The editor's ideas are planted. You start from a premise. The mayor blew it on Crown Heights. Tell us how he blew it."[90] David Dinkins seemed to be aware of this when he observed: "Too often reporters will make a judgment what they think is the case and then they will try to substantiate it. As opposed to analyzing, investigating, and reporting their findings. They start out with a conclusion and try to justify it. I can't say all reporters do that. I think too many do. I think we are afraid to complain because to complain is to blame the media for your failures. That is a lot of damn nonsense. It really is."[91]

The Crown Heights event was a turning point in the history of the Dinkins administration. During the crisis Dinkins attempted to take a centrist position, which won him little support from either group. Dinkins even made an appeal to the General Assembly of the Council of Jewish Federations. He asserted that "no member of the African-American community has spoken out more forcefully and consistently against anti-Semitism than I."[92] Yet his "social accounting" of the situation was not effective. The *New York Amsterdam News* blamed Rabbi Avi Weiss for the escalation of the Crown Heights situation and printed letters from Jews supporting Dinkins.[93] David Saperstein of the Jewish Telegraphic Agency wrote an editorial that asserted:

> Media coverage, obsessively fixed on the negative aspects of our relationship, feeds the suspicion and mistrust, which often plague our communities. When, in the very early days of the Crown Heights crisis, black leaders first gathered at City Hall to condemn the violence, there was virtually no coverage—leaving Jews to feel a sense of betrayal by the silence of old friends. When, recently Rev. Calvin Butts and Jesse Jackson raised serious concerns about the justice system in the wake of Lemrick Nelson's acquittal, there was no virtually no coverage.[94]

Although the New York Board of Rabbis joined the African American clergy in commending Dinkins for his effort to bring peace to the area, doubts about the mayor's actions were carried over into the reelection campaign. Crown Heights became a subtext of Dinkins's 1993 reelection bid.

Herbert Daughtry, a minister and social activist in Brooklyn, suggested that the Crown Heights incident caused the defeat of Dinkins:

> The 1993 defeat of David Dinkins for a second term as New York's first Black mayor was one devastating result of the Crown Heights episode. Dinkins was blamed for the continued violence and rioting in Crown Heights, specifically for not applying greater police action. In fact, the Mayor was accused of restraining the police in the community.
>
> There were two coded messages communicated in the accusation: Dinkins deliberately handcuffed the police because the rioters were Black. Therefore, this Black mayor must be removed.
>
> One of the reasons Dinkins had been elected in the first place was to keep Blacks in check; to ease the racial tensions which had reached the boiling point. . . . If Dinkins could not keep things cool, he was of no use.[95]

There is no denying that race played a role in the reporting on Crown Heights. Mike McAlary saw it as Dinkins's story. Just as Bensonhurst had sealed Koch's fate, Crown Heights would do the same for Dinkins.

McAlary asserted that Yusuf Hawkins (the African American youth killed in Bensonhurst) and the "divisive politicians hit the payment dead together" and concluded, "In that moment, with the city's racial sensibilities hot to the touch, a peacemaker dared to stand up. David Dinkins declared himself the candidate of healing. He was elected with the sole charge of soothing racial passions. No one hired him to fill potholes. He was hired, instead, to fill a vacuum of sensitivity."[96]

10

"One City, One Standard": The Struggle for Equality in Rudolph Giuliani's New York

JERALD PODAIR

ne City, One Standard." Rudolph Giuliani, New York's mayor from 1994 to 2001, defined his administration, and himself, through these words. They were more than a campaign slogan, although they served him well as such during his successful 1993 bid for City Hall. They were also an articulation of his understanding of "equality," a word that, along with "freedom," comes closer to capturing the essence of the American national experience than any other. Americans have argued over the meaning of this elusive word—sometimes violently—for centuries. Contexts and circumstances change, but the questions remain the same. What is equality? Is it merely equal treatment under the law? Or does it have a more substantive meaning? Does it include equal economic rights? How different do life outcomes have to be before they become evidence of inequality? And can treating Americans equally nonetheless render them unequal?

These questions animated the civil rights movement in New York City during Giuliani's two terms in office. They were, however, hardly new. "One City, One Standard" represented only the latest attempt to win an argument over the meaning of equality in the city that had been raging since the 1960s. The heated battles between Giuliani and his critics in New York's black community over issues related to crime, "quality of life" policing, workfare, privatization, social service cuts, and City University academic standards during the 1990s were proxies for deeper disagreements about the nature of equality and the future of civil rights in the city of the twenty-first century.

The historian Martha Biondi has shown how black activists worked in New York during the years following World War II for what she terms "full equality."[1] Their struggle was for much more than equality under the law. They sought a substantive form of justice that was avowedly "race conscious" and identity based. They demanded fair housing practices, an end to lending discrimination, curbs on police behavior, an emphasis on black culture in the public educational system, and, generally, the reallocation and equalization of resources in the city.[2] This vision of equality as substantive—that is, as an outcome and a result—came of age in New York in the late 1960s and early 1970s during the administration of Mayor John Lindsay (1966–1973). Lindsay's mayoralty coalesced the city's black community and Manhattan-based white professional, business, intellectual, and political elites around an ambitious program of expanded city social services; civilian oversight of the police force; redistribution of income through more generous grants of public assistance and tax increases; community control of the public schools in black neighborhoods; and the use of race as a consideration in hiring, contracting, and university admissions decisions.

But Italian, Irish, and Jewish "ethnics" in the white middle- and working-class enclaves of the city's outer boroughs had a different vision for the city, one constructed around a much narrower definition of equality. The Civil Rights Act of 1964's proscription against discrimination in public accommodations and the Voting Rights Act of 1965's guarantee of the franchise to all citizens delimited their understanding of the term. Equality, to them, was race neutral. It was procedural in nature, offering legal protections but no promises of equal levels of achievement or life outcomes. Fearful of the black poor, and suspicious of Manhattan liberals, outer-borough whites employed attacks on welfare-benefit increases, government spending, high taxes, restraints on the police, local school control, and affirmative action—as well as on the patrician Lindsay himself—to express this more limited view of equality in city life. Mario Procaccino, Lindsay's unsuccessful opponent in the 1969 mayoral election, gave voice to the outer-borough, white, middle-class conception of equality: "One standard for everybody. There'll be no double standards."[3] Three decades later, Rudolph Giuliani, proud son of New York's outer boroughs, had become this view's most powerful champion in the battle to define equality in the city.

Rudolph Giuliani was the perfect embodiment of New York's white ethnic culture. Born in Brooklyn in 1944, son of a bartender, he attended Bishop Loughlin Memorial High School in that borough and Manhattan College (which, despite its name, was located in the Bronx) before graduating from New York University School of Law in 1968. Until his young adulthood, his world had been that of white Catholic New York, a regimented culture that stressed obedience, faith, family, and loyalty.

There was, of course, much to recommend this culture. Giuliani's father taught him the value of hard work and the rewards of self-reliance. Catholicism gave him strength and discipline. His Italian heritage offered a sense of pride and identity. But there were also aspects of the culture that were less attractive. Its assumption that anyone who truly wished to rise in American society could do so regardless of race, and that the nation provided an equal opportunity to all, gave it more than a passing resemblance to the Protestant ethic, especially its nineteenth-century offshoot, free-labor ideology. A major influence on the antislavery movement in the years preceding the Civil War, the free-labor idea envisioned an America where, in the words of its most famous proponent, Abraham Lincoln, "the man who labored for another last year, this year labors for himself, and next year he will hire others to labor for him."[4] But free-labor culture, like Giuliani's, viewed those who were less advanced in the race of life with veiled contempt, as lacking the drive necessary for upward mobility in American society. In Giuliani's world, this view often carried racialized connotations.

Reinforcing these attitudes was the insularity of Giuliani's culture. The residentially segregated neighborhoods in which he grew up contained few African Americans. Giuliani's schooling, with the exception of law school, was similarly white dominated. His culture thus drew him inward, denying him the diverse racial experiences that might have smoothed the rougher edges of his public persona during his mayoral career. After serving in the Reagan Justice Department in the early 1980s, Giuliani became a crusading United States attorney in New York, prosecuting corrupt politicians with headline-grabbing gusto. In 1989, he ran for mayor, losing narrowly to African American David Dinkins. Four years later he tried again and in another close election—in which he received only 5 percent of the African American vote—unseated the city's first black mayor.[5] Giuliani arrived at City Hall in January 1994 with his white outer-borough system of values intact, ready to make "One City, One Standard" a reality.

The black community that Giuliani faced as his administration began was still smarting from the defeat of David Dinkins. To an extent, any white politician who had run against an African American mayor twice and wrested the office from him would have aroused its ire. But Giuliani's world and that of black New Yorkers had been on a collision course for decades. Even before Dinkins's 1989 election, African Americans had wielded significant political power in New York. Much of it centered around four Harlem Democratic party figures who emerged during the 1960s and 1970s—Congressman Charles Rangel, Manhattan borough president Percy Sutton, state senator Basil Paterson, and Dinkins, who had served as a state assemblyman, New York City clerk, and Manhattan borough president and was a respected mediator and behind-the-scenes negotiator between the city's black and white communities.

Together, the four men created an African American power brokerage in the city in the 1970s and 1980s, with influence that radiated beyond their Harlem base. If they could not send one of their own to City Hall during this time—mayors Abraham Beame (1974–1977) and Edward Koch (1978–1989) relied primarily on white electoral support—no white politician could act without factoring in the expectations of these Harlem leaders. After Dinkins assumed office in 1990, they moved to the center of New York's political universe, controlling votes, jobs, and influence.

Black political power in New York derived in large part from the city's "public sector," which included social service and antipoverty agencies, the public education and City University systems, municipal hospitals, the housing administration, and the hundreds of thousands of employees who staffed them. By the early 1990s, New York had the highest per capita number of public workers in the nation, with the exception of Washington, D.C.[6] A large percentage of these were members of minority groups. African Americans in particular had used public-sector jobs, as many white ethnics had before them, as escalators into the city's middle class.

Public employee unions, including District Council 37 of the American Federation of State, County, and Municipal Employees (AFSCME) and Local 1199 of the Drug, Hospital, and Health Care Employees Union used the city's labor-friendly environment and tradition of municipal service generosity to negotiate wage and benefit packages for their members that were among the highest in the country. In the process, the unions became political powers in their own right. They allied with the African American community and its leaders, influencing local elections through candidate endorsements, campaign contributions, and vote-pulling operations. Poorer African Americans, who relied on the services offered by the public sector, also became integral parts of this alliance. By the early 1990s, a partnership of social service providers, public employee unions, and African American political officials had given black New Yorkers an unprecedented degree of control over the direction of their city.

Also affecting that direction, albeit from a less conventional position, was the street preacher and activist Al Sharpton. The rotund, stiletto-tongued Sharpton embodied the frustrations and resentments of the average black New Yorker, much as Marcus Garvey and Malcolm X had in their day. Hailing from outside the established political system, Sharpton was free to articulate publicly what African Americans would only say in private.[7] The sources of Sharpton's power were shadowy and ill defined—his National Action Network was not a mass organization—but his ability to bring protesters into the streets was unmatched. He had played a major role in electing Dinkins in 1989 when, shortly before the Democratic mayoral primary with incumbent Edward Koch, a black teenager named Yusuf Hawkins was killed by a white mob in the largely Italian Brooklyn community of Bensonhurst. Sharpton organized protest marches through the neighborhood, and after he was stabbed during one of them, even New Yorkers who regarded him as a demagogue were outraged. Dinkins defeated Koch decisively in the Democratic primary and went on to win the mayoralty in November.

While Dinkins viewed Sharpton as an untrustworthy street hustler and racial divider, he felt he could not ignore him, and he sought to satisfy his demands. Sharpton's rise thus also contributed to the black community's growing sense of empowerment during the Dinkins years. African Americans had become the core constituency of a powerful impulse toward activist government, generous municipal services, and a view of equality in the city that was redistributionist, results oriented, and race conscious.

Dinkins's mayoralty can only be described as star crossed. A recession caused immediate budget problems, forcing service cutbacks that angered his electoral base. The flagging economy caused the loss of hundreds of thousands of private-sector jobs. While the crime rate decreased during Dinkins's last three years in office, it had already spiked so high—in 1990, his first year as mayor, the number of murders in the city reached a record 2,245, which dropped to 1,946 by 1993—that this was barely acknowledged by a citizenry numb from fear and the effects of panhandlers, vandals, and the homeless on the quality of their everyday lives.[8]

Dinkins's reputation as an intergroup conciliator was severely damaged, at least among whites, by his actions during two racially charged Brooklyn controversies—one involving an African American–led boycott of a Korean-operated grocery whose owner allegedly assaulted a black patron, and the other a violent outbreak in the Crown Heights neighborhood after a black child was killed by a Jewish motorist—when his weak responses were viewed as evidence of a racial double standard. These controversies, along with the state of the economy and the perceived decline in the "livability" of the city, created an opening for Giuliani not only to reverse the outcome of the 1989 mayoral race but also to impose his own vision of an "equal" New York City.

Giuliani entered office believing that "America is built on equal treatment," and that "society expects a certain standard of behavior from all its members, all the time."[9] Early in his administration, he declared: "I don't have a special message for any group. People in this city don't need special things. They need more general things—safety, jobs, education."[10] He gave these ideas immediate practical application. During his first month, he abolished a Dinkins-sponsored affirmative action program for minority firms seeking city contracts. Giuliani also dissolved a series of offices created by Dinkins to serve as liaisons to racial and ethnic groups in the city, arguing that offering services to "African Americans" or "European Americans" on a separate basis encouraged divisiveness and promoted inequality.

The most tangible evidence of Giuliani's different conception of an equal New York, however, came in the area of law enforcement. In the years preceding his successful mayoral run, Giuliani had steeped himself in what was popularly known as the "broken windows" theory of crime prevention. The broken windows theory, originally propounded in 1982 by criminologists George Kelling and James Q. Wilson in the pages of the *Atlantic Monthly*, linked serious crimes, including murder, armed robbery, and rape, to "quality of life" offenses such as subway-turnstile jumping, panhandling, petty vandalism, and graffiti writing. These lesser transgressions, if widespread, would demoralize law-abiding citizens and drive them out of cities, eroding both the civic culture and the tax base. In addition, minor miscreants might be parole violators or fugitives from justice or might be carrying illegal weapons. Arresting them would remove truly dangerous criminals from the streets, which would in turn allow cities to attract and retain industrious, productive, and "decent" people, along with private businesses and the jobs that came with them. The broken windows theory also fit Giuliani's view of equality as "one standard" for all citizens. What Dinkins and his allies had ignored, or minimized, Giuliani would prosecute with vigor.

During the 1993 mayoral campaign, Dinkins questioned the racial implications of the broken windows theory, wondering whether the burden of strict "equal" law enforcement at the grassroots level would fall unequally on African Americans. Giuliani dismissed these concerns, however, and once inaugurated on January 1, 1994, moved decisively to realize "One City, One Standard" on the streets of New York. In this he would be aided immeasurably by a windfall of thousands of new police officers hired under a program begun by Dinkins, but not actually deployed until his term had ended. Giuliani's new police commissioner was William Bratton, a former chief of New York City Transit and the Boston police, and another broken windows disciple. He sought to set a new tone by immediately arresting the so-called squeegee men, a predominantly minority group of panhandlers who cleaned the windshields of intimidated motorists at street corners and highway ramps for spare change. True to the broken windows philosophy, the arrests were for relatively trivial offenses, such as jaywalking and blocking traffic, which would not have elicited a police response during the Dinkins administration. But Giuliani and Bratton intended the arrests to communicate a shift in values for the city, and their import was not lost on New York's African American population.

Just eight days after his inauguration, Giuliani further underscored this change in atmosphere through his words and actions in the wake of a police raid on a mosque operated by the Nation of Islam in Harlem. Responding to a false report of a crime in progress at the mosque, officers scuffled with black Muslims, who accused them of desecrating their house of worship. The patrolmen were thrown down a flight of stairs and police department property was taken. Giuliani backed his officers unhesitatingly and even insisted that they reenter the mosque to retrieve their property. Giuliani and Bratton met with black officials and Harlem residents to mediate, but not with Sharpton. The mayor also insisted that the activist be excluded from a scheduled conference between the police commissioner and Nation of Islam representatives. Giuliani would refuse to meet with Sharpton—and, indeed, did not even mention his name—for years afterward.[11] When Congressman Rangel and other black elected officials criticized his handling of the mosque episode, Giuliani went on the attack. Black leaders, he said, would "have to learn how to discipline themselves in the way in which they speak."[12]

The racial overtones of the new mayor's words, along with his banishment of Sharpton and unquestioning support of the actions of white policemen at the Nation of Islam mosque, poisoned Giuliani's relationship with New York's black community. Goodwill toward him in that community, never substantial, evaporated. Speaking invitations from black churches and community organizations were rescinded. The small number of black clergy who sought to maintain a working relationship with the mayor were ostracized. At Giuliani's first major appearance before an African American audience following his "discipline" remark, he was taunted and heckled as he addressed a Martin Luther King Jr. commemoration in Brooklyn. Resentful and embarrassed, he spent much of his time in office avoiding black groups and neighborhoods. Rangel, while occasionally willing to negotiate with Giuliani in private, attacked him relentlessly in public. For all intents and purposes, the mayor and black New Yorkers resided in different perceptual universes.

The racial bitterness that marked the beginning of his first mayoral term, however, served a purpose for Giuliani. The Harlem mosque controversy allowed him to put his "one standard" view of equality into practice and distance himself from the ideas of past administrations. African Americans, he wanted it known, would be treated exactly the same as whites in all matters. But was "the same" treatment "equal" treatment? Giuliani's crime prevention policies, implemented to national acclaim between 1994 and 2001, brought this troubling question to light.

Giuliani and Bratton coupled their broken windows approach to policing with a novel computerized crime-tracking system known as Compstat, which permitted authorities to discern patterns of criminal activity throughout the city and shift resources accordingly. During Giuliani's mayoralty, New York experienced the largest percentage-wise reduction in crime of any major American city.[13] Murders fell almost 70 percent and overall crime 57 percent between 1993, Dinkins's last year in office, and the end of Giuliani's tenure in 2001.[14] Giuliani pointed with pride to the fact that approximately 1,500 more New Yorkers were murdered during the four Dinkins years than in all eight of his own, and that by his last year in office, Chicago, with roughly one-third of New York's population, had twenty more murders.[15] He also noted that the largest drops in crime occurred in minority neighborhoods. In Harlem, the number of murders was reduced from thirty-five in 1993 to five in

2001, and there were substantial drop-offs in Bedford-Stuyvesant and the South Bronx.[16]

When asked by a reporter in 1997 how he had helped minorities, Giuliani snapped, "They are alive, how about we start with that?"[17] On one level, he was correct. There were 1,946 murders in New York in 1993.[18] Had this rate continued during the Giuliani years, thousands of lives—and many minority lives—would have been lost. But Giuliani's flippancy obscured the high price of this accomplishment. His aggressive policing policies targeted young black men, who were stopped and frisked at a rate disproportionately higher than whites.[19] In one year, 1998, there were 27,000 police frisks in the city, only 5,000 of which resulted in arrests. This meant that 22,000 New Yorkers, a significant portion of whom were African American, were detained by police without cause.[20] Even those few African Americans who were close to Giuliani were not immune. On two occasions, Rudy Washington, a black deputy mayor, was stopped in his car and harassed by overzealous officers. Floyd Flake, an African American congressman and Giuliani supporter, suffered a similar fate.[21]

This use of racial profiling infuriated the black community. A particular target of its wrath was the special Street Crime Unit, the shock troops of the Giuliani anticrime initiative. African Americans made up only 3 percent of the unit, whose self-proclaimed motto was "We Own the Night."[22] The Street Crime Unit operated under the most minimal of constraints. The Compstat system demanded statistically measurable results, analogous in some respects to the body counts of the war in Vietnam. The pressure to perform led to instances of horrific overreaction, from street crime and regular police units alike. In 1997, Abner Louima, an immigrant from Haiti, was sodomized by a policeman after his arrest outside a Brooklyn nightclub. While Giuliani immediately denounced the assault, and the officer received a thirty-year prison term, the incident inflamed the black community, especially after Louima claimed that the policeman had shouted, "This is Giuliani time. It is not Dinkins time," as he injured him. While Louima later confessed that this had never occurred, the phrase "Giuliani time" nonetheless took hold among black New Yorkers as a symbol of the mayor's estrangement from them.

In a second controversial incident, Patrick Dorismond, another Haitian, was fatally shot during an argument with undercover narcotics agents in 2000 after they failed to entrap him into buying drugs. Giuliani sought to impugn Dorismond's reputation after his death, releasing his confidential court records and characterizing him as habitually violent. Once again, the city's black population seethed. Almost unanimously—by a margin of 94 to 1 percent, according to the Quinnipiac College Polling Institute, a longtime bellwether of city opinion—African Americans condemned Giuliani's response to the shooting.[23]

But the event that defined Giuliani's anticrime program, and his relationship with minorities in the city, came on the night of February 4, 1999, when officers from the Street Crime Unit came upon a black man in the vestibule of a Bronx apartment house. The man, Amadou Diallo, was a native of Guinea who was residing in the United States illegally. When the police ordered him to step out of the building, a confused Diallo, perhaps fearing discovery and deportation, instead put his hand into a pocket. The police, equally confused, began firing wildly, killing Diallo. When they reached his body, they discovered he was unarmed. The four officers had fired a total of forty-one shots in a matter of seconds, and this number joined "Giuliani time" as shorthand expressions of black New York's frustration with a mayor whose values seemed alien and foreign.

True to those values, Giuliani defended the conduct of "his" police in the Diallo shooting. But his reaction only served to unite blacks across virtually the entire ideological spectrum—from the Nation of Islam and Al Sharpton to David Dinkins. A Quinnipiac College poll conducted in the immediate aftermath of the Diallo incident showed that 89 percent of black New Yorkers were critical of Giuliani's response, compared with 52 percent of whites.[24] Demonstrations and sit-ins at police headquarters in Lower Manhattan during the succeeding weeks attracted national attention, especially after the dignified Dinkins was arrested for refusing to leave the scene.[25]

The Diallo tragedy illustrated the vast perceptual gulf between Giuliani and black New Yorkers, and indeed between white and black New Yorkers. Giuliani was willing to tolerate a certain number of police excesses and deadly mistakes in exchange for a lowered crime rate. Black New Yorkers, who largely bore the brunt of these excesses and mistakes, were much less willing to do so. In the Quinnipiac poll taken in the wake of the Diallo tragedy, blacks and whites were asked if they thought "a safer New York City [was] worth the cost of losing some rights and freedoms." Only 17 percent of black New Yorkers, opposed to 33 percent of whites, answered yes; 72 percent of the African Americans polled maintained that a drop in crime could not justify a curtailment of liberties.[26] Giuliani believed that aggressive law enforcement employing the same standard for all epitomized an "equal" city. Black citizens, noting the racially unbalanced results of this brand of law enforcement, felt otherwise.[27]

Louima, Dorismond, and Diallo, along with thousands of other black males, had been the victims of racial profiling, a profoundly unequal practice that mocked Giuliani's professions of "One City, One Standard." Statistics showed black New Yorkers were safer than they had been in years, but they were also afraid of what might happen to them at the hands of the police. In a 1999 Quinnipiac poll, 62 percent of black respondents expressed concern that they might be the victims of police brutality. In contrast, white citizens extolled Giuliani's successes. To them, all that mattered was that the days of "coddling" criminals and "special treatment" of minorities were over; only 15 percent of whites in the 1999 Quinnipiac poll feared police brutality.[28] Late in Giuliani's mayoralty, a leading pollster remarked that "in perception of the police, New York is two separate cities."[29] Giuliani's anticrime measures had divided the city over specific policies and first principles alike.

Other Giuliani initiatives exposed similar fault lines. The city he inherited in 1994 boasted a tradition of providing the most generous array of social services in the nation. While many in the ranks of government service, organized labor, and the Democratic Party celebrated this legacy, Giuliani did not. He was determined to change the culture of what one observer described as "a union-driven social democratic city of civil servants" and bring municipal spending under control.[30] The agencies Giuliani selected for budgetary discipline, however, were those upon which poorer African Americans relied heavily and in which African Americans were a major employee presence, including the Human Resources Administration, the Health and Hospitals Corporation, Youth Services, and the City University system.[31]

Giuliani employed the race-neutral language of economy and individual initiative to justify his attempts to impose budgetary restraints on social service providers.[32] He decried the fact that 1.2 million New Yorkers were on public assistance when he took office, and that approximately 20 percent of the city's workforce were in government jobs.[33] But in a city where one-third of African American employment was government related, and in which the white-dominated police and fire departments were largely immune to funding cuts, Giuliani's arguments and actions had clear racial implications.[34] As they had about his crime policies, blacks and whites in New York disagreed sharply over Giuliani's budget cuts. A 1997 Quinnipiac poll showed 53 percent of whites but only 25 percent of blacks approved of the mayor's handling of the budget. The percentages were even more skewed—61 percent of whites and 28 percent of blacks approved—in a poll conducted the next year.[35] Giuliani's budgetary measures were not explicitly designed to take power from African Americans, but reducing the city payroll, cutting welfare benefits, downsizing city-owned hospitals, and privatizing city services had this effect nonetheless.

Nor, for that matter, did Giuliani intend for most of the 485,000 new private-sector jobs created during his administration to go primarily to whites, but this is what occurred.[36] The city's service industry–centered economy, with its steep educational and technological entry requirements that structurally impeded African American advancement, had been in place long before Giuliani arrived on the scene. Still, the changes in the private-sector employment market that he set in motion benefited whites and disadvantaged blacks. They combined with the mayor's public-sector cuts to create an inhospitable economic environment for African Americans between 1994 and 2001. Once again, race-neutral policy decisions led to race-skewed results, providing another venue for arguments over the nature of equality in city life that had divided black and white New Yorkers for decades.

The centerpiece of Giuliani's campaign to redefine New York's culture, along with his broken windows policing initiative, was his "workfare" program, launched in 1995. He resolved to take advantage of the more conservative atmosphere in the city to remake the entire welfare system. Giuliani's program imposed strict eligibility checks, fingerprinting of recipients, a requirement that those whose federal benefits expired reapply for city "safety net" assistance, and most controversially, workfare itself, under which aid recipients performed maintenance services in exchange for continued support. Giuliani also retooled welfare offices as "job centers," which emphasized private-sector employment and used workfare only as a last resort. Giuliani secured the cooperation of municipal unions, including the largest, District Council 37, AFSCME, by promising that workfare participants would not displace permanent employees, as well as by threatening to contract unionized services to private firms.

As he had with his anticrime and budget-reduction programs, Giuliani sought to avoid casting workfare in racial terms, stressing instead the more generally applicable virtues of honest labor, self-reliance, and upward mobility. He also used the rhetoric of equality of treatment, arguing that welfare recipients, regardless of race, would benefit if held to the same standards of personal responsibility as other citizens. He lashed out at those who criticized workfare as "apostles of dependency," defenders of an untenable ethos of special treatment.[37] This angered African American leaders, who viewed his arguments for welfare reform as racially coded. They pointed to the uneven impact of his program on minorities, and blacks in particular. Giuliani and supporters of workfare, in contrast, wondered out loud how holding every New Yorker to a single, consistent standard could be construed as evidence of inequality and racism.

White and black views of Giuliani's welfare policies reflected familiar racial patterns. In 1998, 56 percent of whites polled approved of the way the mayor was handling welfare, while 29 percent disapproved. The corresponding percentages for African Americans were 36 and 55. When asked in 2000 whether Giuliani was sympathetic to the problems of the impoverished, 37 percent of white New Yorkers answered yes, contrasted with 4 percent of blacks. The African American community was almost unanimous (94 percent) in its belief that the mayor was hostile to the city's poor.[38] The controversy over workfare was yet another manifestation of the deep divisions over practice and principle that separated Giuliani and black New Yorkers.

If Giuliani's sole purpose was to reduce the public assistance rolls through his welfare and workfare policies, he succeeded. Between 1994 and 2001, the city's caseload dropped by over 600,000, a 60 percent decrease.[39] Beyond these numbers, the record is less clear. While there is some evidence of success in job placement—workforce participation by single mothers rose during the Giuliani years—this may have been as much a function of the city's improving economy as administration policy.[40] What was clear, however, was that Rudolph Giuliani and his adversaries held different visions for the city and different understandings of the principles that would govern it.

These differences, moreover, played out across a sharply defined black-white axis. Giuliani's relations with New York's Latino population were often tense, but they did not rise to the level of animosity that characterized his relations with African Americans. As fellow Catholics, they may have been drawn to the mayor's cultural conservatism, and he made an effort to reach out to Hispanics with appointments and a more conciliatory approach to their political leadership. The number of Latinos in city employment rose by 1.8 percent during Giuliani's mayoralty, about the same percentage by which black employment fell.[41] In addition, Herman Badillo, a former congressman and Bronx borough president and the first Hispanic political figure to rise to prominence in New
.

York, was a strong Giuliani supporter and ran on his mayoral ticket in 1993. Increased Hispanic electoral support, in fact, may have been the decisive factor in Giuliani's victory that year, and he received 43 percent of the Latino vote in his 1997 reelection campaign.[42]

While there is no question that Latinos, Asians, gays, women, and Manhattan-based whites made up a significant portion of the anti-Giuliani constituency, its ideological and emotional core lay within the city's black community. From the 1960s on, African Americans gave voice to a vision of city life in which government played the major ameliorative role and in which "equality" meant judging citizens according to their needs, not by an arbitrary standard. This vision united David Dinkins and Al Sharpton, linking them across time to the black activists and leaders who nourished similar dreams in the 1960s and 1970s. They, in turn, recalled the New Deal city of the 1930s and 1940s, which had established the principle that government was responsible for the well-being of its people and defined "equality" in terms of substance and result.

Rudolph Giuliani rejected this vision and spent his mayoralty seeking to impose one of his own, which drew on a set of markedly different assumptions. It called up another past, one rooted in the outer-borough neighborhoods of the city and the white middle-class ethnics who lived in them. During the 1960s, these New Yorkers, buffeted by the racial upheavals of the decade, began to lose faith in a city government structure that, in its effort to achieve "full equality" in the city, seemed to have lost faith in them. They responded by constructing an alternative civic culture that viewed government with suspicion, relied on conceptions of individual merit and personal responsibility, and endorsed a raceblind "equality of treatment" that applied an identical set of rules to all. Giuliani was this culture's heir and representative, and "One City, One Standard" was its late twentieth-century embodiment.

Rudolph Giuliani's two mayoral terms were a victory for his culture and vision of an "equal" New York, but not necessarily a final one. New York's tradition of active, compassionate government is of long standing, and not easily brushed aside. And while "One City, One Standard" provided a blueprint for governing, it did not offer a definition of "equality" that could unite the city. Giuliani left office in 2001 no closer to achieving that goal than he had been when he arrived in 1994. His legacy was a city with a significantly lower crime rate and substantially reduced welfare rolls, but also one with a foreshortened understanding of equality that alienated and marginalized its black population.[43] His successors will continue to face the task of reconciling the competing visions of the city

Giuliani and his adversaries in the black community fought over so bitterly between 1994 and 2001. They will need to ask themselves what government can do to break down the structural barriers that still prevent black New Yorkers from achieving "full equality" in city life. They will also need to ask themselves once again whether "equal treatment" is truly "equal" if it results in disproportionate hardship for one group of New Yorkers. "One City, One Standard," Rudolph Giuliani's answer to this question in the late twentieth century may not be the answer in the twenty-first.

Notes

Introduction: Civil Rights in New York City

Clarence Taylor

1. Thomas Sugrue, *Sweet Land of Liberty: The Forgotten Struggle for Civil Rights in the North* (New York: Random House, 2008), xv–xvi.

2. Clarence Taylor, *The Black Churches of Brooklyn* (New York: Columbia University Press, 1994); *Knocking at Our Own Door: Milton A. Galamison and the Struggle to Integrate New York City Schools* (New York: Columbia University Press, 1997); Jonathan Birnbaum and Clarence Taylor, eds., *Civil Rights since 1787: A Reader on the Black Struggle* (New York: New York University Press, 2000).

3. Some works are James R. Ralph Jr., *Northern Protest: Martin Luther King, Jr., Chicago, and the Civil Rights Movement* (Cambridge, Mass.: Harvard University Press, 1993); Martha Biondi, *To Stand and Fight: The Struggle for Civil Rights in Postwar New York City* (Cambridge, Mass.: Harvard University Press, 2003); Randal Maurice Jelks, *African Americans in the Furniture City: The Struggle for Civil Rights in Grand Rapids* (Urbana: University of Illinois Press, 2006); Jeanne F. Theoharis and Komozi Woodard, *Freedom North: Black Freedom Struggles outside the South* (New York: Palgrave Macmillan, 2003); Jeanne Theoharis and Komozi Woodard, *Groundwork: Local Black Freedom Movements in America* (New York: New York University Press, 2005); Gretchen Cassel, *Dissent in Wichita: The Civil Rights Movement in the Midwest* (Urbana: University of Illinois Press, 2001); Mathew Countryman, *Up South: Civil Rights and Black Power in Philadelphia* (Philadelphia: University of Pennsylvania Press, 2005); Adina Back, "Up South in New York: The 1950s School Desegregation Struggles" (PhD diss., New York University, 1997); Jeanne F. Theoharis, "'We Saved the City': Black Struggles for Educational Equality in Boston," *Radical History Review* 81 (2001): 61–93; Gerald Horne, *The Fire This Time: The Watts Uprising and the 1960s* (Charlottesville: University Press of Virginia, 1995); Thomas Sugrue, *Origins of*

the Urban Crisis (Princeton, N.J.: Princeton University Press, 1996); Taylor, *Knocking at Our Own Door.*

4. Birnbaum and Taylor, *Civil Rights since 1787,* 388–93, 539–47.

5. Lizabeth Cohn, *Making a New Deal: Industrial Workers in Chicago, 1919–1939* (Cambridge: Cambridge University Press, 1990); Biondi, *To Stand and Fight,* 16; Mark Naison, *Communists in Harlem during the Depression* (Urbana: University of Illinois Press, 1983), 50–51; Peter Levy, "Gloria Richardson and the Civil Rights Movement in Cambridge, Maryland," in Theoharis and Woodard, *Groundwork,* 97–115; Taylor, *Knocking at Our Own Door,* 158–60.

6. "Identify the Enemy," *New York Teacher News* editorial, February 26, 1944.

7. Edward B. Fiske, "New York Growth Is Linked to Immigration," *New York Times,* February 22, 1991; Cao O, "Providing Leadership to Asian Agencies: Asian American Federation of New York," http://www.naswnyc.org/CSPP/Asian/providingLeadership.html.

1. To Be a Good American: The New York Teachers Union and Race during the Second World War

Clarence Taylor

1. Martha Biondi, *To Stand and Fight: The Struggle for Civil Rights in Postwar New York City* (Cambridge, Mass.: Harvard University Press, 2003), 243–44; Joshua B. Freeman, *Working-Class New York: Life and Labor since World War II* (New York: Free Press, 2000), 72–74; New York Teacher News, October 9, 1943.

2. Freeman, *Working-Class New York,* 73; *New York Teacher News,* October 9, 1943, and October 16, 1943.

3. Celia Lewis Zitron, *The New York City Teachers Union, 1916–1964* (New York: Humanities Press, 1968), 15–27; New York Teachers Union Membership List of 1940, Rapp-Coudert Papers, State Library of New York, Albany.

4. Michael Denning, *The Cultural Front* (London: Verso, 1997), 4–9.

5. New York Teachers Union Membership List of 1940; Heinrich W. Guggenheimer and Eva H. Guggenheimer, *Jewish Family Names and Their Origins: An Etymological Dictionary* (Newark, N.J.: KTAV, 2007). There is no way of determining the exact number of Jewish teachers in the union. I have not found any information on the religious, racial, or ethnic makeup of its membership. Therefore, I have relied on surnames that appear in the 1940 membership list. To be sure, there are some problems with this method. Some non-Jewish members may have been married to Jews and used their spouses' names. On the other hand, there may have been Jews who were married to non-Jewish members and used their spouses' last names. Many Jews changed their last names to more Anglicized names. Moreover, some surnames are shared by Jews and non-Jews. Although an examination of surnames is far from perfect, such an approach gives

us some idea of the makeup of the TU. Leonard Dinnerstein, *Antisemitism in America* (New York: Oxford University Press, 1994), 128–29.

6. Ruth Jacknow Markowitz, *My Daughter, the Teacher: Jewish Teachers in the New York City Schools* (New Brunswick, N.J.: Rutgers University Press, 1993), p. 163.

7. *New York Teacher News*, October 16, 1943.

8. *New York Teacher News*, October 9, 1943.

9. *New York Teacher News*, October 2, 1943; Road to Victory, *New York Teacher News*, February 19, 1944.

10. "Road to Victory," *New York Teacher News*, November 13, 1943; "Road to Victory," *New York Teacher News*, November 20, 1943.

11. "Hysteria-Fascist Pattern," *New York Teacher News*, November 20, 1943

12. "Road to Victory," *New York Teacher News*, November 20, 1943.

13. *New York Teacher News*, January 8, 1944.

14. Ibid.; "Road to Victory," *New York Teacher News*, November 13, 1944.

15. "Road to Victory," *New York Teacher News*, February 26, 1944.

16. "Road to Victory," *New York Teacher News*, January 8, 1944.

17. "Road to Victory," *New York Teacher News*, January 22, 1944.

18. Ibid.; "No Diploma for Anti-Semites," *New York Teacher News*, February 26, 1944.

19. Robert Harris, "Teachers and Blacks: The New York City Teachers Union and the Negro, 1916–1964" (master's thesis, 1971), 70; *New York Teacher News*, June 30, 1945; Teachers Union, "Schools for Victory," 1942, Charles James Hendley Papers, Tamiment Library, New York University.

20. *New York Teacher News*, January 22, 1944.

21. Teachers Union, "Policy for the Teachers Union, 1941–1942," Charles James Hendley Papers, Tamiment Library, New York University.

22. Ibid.

23. Teachers Union, "Teachers' Part in Victory for Democracy," Charles James Hendley Papers, Tamiment Library, New York University; Teachers Union, "Education and National Defense," n.d., Charles James Hendley Papers, Tamiment Library, New York University.

24. Teachers Union, "Education for Victory in 1943," Seventh Annual Educational Conference, Charles James Hendley Papers, Tamiment Library, New York University.

25. Ibid.

26. *New York Teacher News*, January 15, 1944.

27. *New York Teacher News*, January 8, 1944, and January 29, 1944.

28. *New York Teacher News*, January 29, 1944.

29. Ibid.

30. Rachel Davis DuBois, *All This and Something More: Pioneering in Intercultural Education, an Autobiography* (Bryn Mawr, Pa.: Dorrance, 1984), 3–18.

31. Ibid., 30–34.

32. Ibid., 37.

33. Ibid., 34–47.

34. Ibid., 47–52.

35. Ibid., 52–55.

36. Ibid., 88.

37. *New York Teacher* 3, no. 9 (June 1938); "Road to Victory," *New York Teacher News,* February 26, 1944.

38. Barbara Diane Savage, *Broadcasting Freedom: Radio, War, and the Politics of Race, 1938–1948* (Chapel Hill: University of North Carolina Press, 1999), 24–25.

39. Marion Milstein and Jenny L. Mayer, "Schools for Tolerance II," *New York Teacher* 4, no. 4 (January 1939): 10–11.

40. Ibid., 4.

41. Harris, "Teachers and Blacks," 72–73.

42. *New York Teacher News,* April 8, 1944.

43. *New York Teacher News,* June 30, 1945.

44. *New York Teacher News,* September 15, 1945.

45. *New York Teacher News,* April 1, 1944.

46. Harris, "Teachers and Blacks," 75.

47. Margaret M. Caffrey, *Ruth Benedict: Stranger in This Land* (Austin: University of Texas Press, 1984), 282–84.

48. Ibid., 284–86; Judith Schachter Modell, *Ruth Benedict: Patterns of Life* (Philadelphia: University of Pennsylvania, 1983), 247–48.

49. Harris, "Teachers and Blacks," 77; Ute Gacs, Aisha Khan, Jerrie McIntyre, and Ruth Weinberg, *Women Anthropologists: A Biographical Dictionary* (New York: Greenwood Press, 1988), 376.

50. *New York Teacher News,* November 20, 1943.

51. Road to Victory, *New York Teacher News,* January 15, 1944.

52. Gac, Khan, McIntyre, and Weinberg, *Women Anthropologists,* 376.

53. Ruth Benedict and Gene Weltfish, "The Races of Mankind," in Benedict, *Race: Science and Politics* (New York: Viking, 1945), 169–71.

54. Ibid., 177–86.

55. Ibid., 187–88.

56. Harris, "Teachers and Blacks," 73; *New York Teacher News,* December 18, 1943.

57. *New York Teacher* 3, no. 9 (June 1938): 33–34.

58. "Road to Peace," *New York Teacher News,* February 16, 1946.

59. Ibid.

2. Cops, Schools, and Communism: Local Politics and Global Ideologies—New York City in the 1950s

Barbara Ransby

1. On Baker's involvement in the New York City NAACP branch, see NAACP Papers, group II, series C, B127, branch file, New York, Library of Congress.

2. Ella Baker to "Dear Sir," n.d., Ella Baker Papers (cites the 1950 call for the Emergency Mobilization); Gerald Horne, *Black and Red: W. E. B. DuBois and the Afro-American Response to the Cold War, 1944–1963* (Albany: State University of New York Press, 1986); Gloster Current, memo to Thurgood Marshall, Nov. 7, 1952, NAACP Papers, group II, box A128, folder: Committee on Political Domination. Current's memo, which outlines the NAACP's stance on the exclusion of Communists, reads: "The 41st Annual Convention in Boston adopted an anti-communist resolution on June 23, 1950." That resolution (which was attached to the memo) empowered the board of directors "to take the necessary action to eradicate such infiltration [by Communists] and if necessary to suspend and reorganize or lift the charter and expel any unit, which . . . comes under Communist or other political control or domination." Current goes on to cite a January 2, 1951, recommendation from the board of the NAACP that required branch officials to report "communistic or other political infiltration or domination." Similar resolutions were passed in 1956 at the San Francisco annual convention.

3. Baker acknowledged that Communists and socialists of various stripes had been some of the most militant fighters against racial discrimination and economic injustice.

4. Baker, interview by *Urban Review* editors, 10. For information on Bea Levison, see Gerald E. Markowitz and David Rosner, *Children, Race and Power: Kenneth and Mamie Clark's Northside Center* (Charlottesville: University Press of Virginia, 1996),46, 111, 147

5. See Clarence Taylor, *Knocking at Our Own Door: Milton A. Galamison and the Struggle to Integrate New York City Schools* (New York: Columbia University Press, 1997). In Baker, interview by Hayden and Thrasher, 59, mention is made of Galamison and Stein.

6. Ella Baker to Mamie and Kenneth Clark, July 28, 1952, Kenneth B. Clark Papers, box 60, folder 7, Library of Congress, Washington, D.C.; Kenneth Clark to "Dear Friend," ca. 1953, letter on Intergroup Committee on New York Public Schools letterhead (Ella Baker is listed on the letterhead as a member of the steering committee), Clark Papers, box 56, folder 2.

7. Markowitz and Rosner, *Children, Race and Power,* 24, 27, 32–33.

8. Ibid., 18.

9. "Harlem Students Learn Inferiority," *Amsterdam News*, May 1, 1954, I; "Dear Friends" letter from Kenneth Clark, June 14, 1954; press release regarding "Children Apart" conference, Apr. 23, 1954, Clark Papers, box 56, folder 2. Ella Baker to Kenneth Clark, July 18, 1953, Clark Papers, box 93, folder 10.

10. Ellen Cantarow with Susan Gushee O'Malley and Sharon Hartman Stone, "Ella Baker," in *Moving the Mountain: Women Working for Social Change* (Old Westbury, N.Y.: Feminist Press, 1980), 68.

11. See Daisy Bates, *The Long Shadow of Little Rock* (Fayetteville: University of Arkansas Press, 2007), for a vivid first-person account.

12. Taylor, *Knocking at Our Own Door,* 67–69.

13. Ibid., 70.

14. Sara Black, "Don't Forget N.Y. Has Its Own School Problem," *Amsterdam News*, Sept. 28, 1957, I.

15. Ibid.

16. See Markowitz and Rosner, *Children, Race and Power*; Martha Biondi, *To Stand and Fight: The Struggle for Civil Rights in Postwar New York City* (Cambridge, Mass.: Harvard University Press, 2003).

17. Ella Baker to Ruth Moore, Feb. 25, 1957, on In Friendship letterhead, Amzie Moore Papers, box 2, folder: Correspondence, 2, State Historical Society of Wisconsin, Madison.

18. NAACP Papers, group II, box A456. folder: New York City Police Brutality, 1953–54; "Law Which Police Flaunted," *Amsterdam News*, Feb 21, 1953, 2.

19. "Resignation Urged of 2 Top Officials," *Amsterdam News,* Feb. 21, 1953, 2.

20. "Two Public Protests Set for Sunday," *Amsterdam News*, Feb. 28, 1953, 3. See Feb. 19, 1953, press release from NAACP national office, "Civic groups demand action against secret rights pact," NAACP Papers, group II, box A456 folder: New York City Police Brutality.

21. Telegram to Mayor Vincent R. Impellitteri from Ella Baker, Feb. 16, 1953, NAACP Papers, group II, box A456, New York City Police Brutality, 1953–54

22. NAACP Papers, group II, box A456, folder: New York City Police Brutality, 1953–54.

23. Telegram to Mayor Vincent R. Impellitteri from Ella Baker, Feb 26,1953, NAACP Papers, group II, box A456, folder: New York City Police Brutality, 1953–54; "Two Public Protests Set for Sunday," *Amsterdam News*, Feb. 28, 1953, 3.

24. "Two Public Protests Set for Sunday."

25. "A 'Red' Plot Says Police Assn.—NAACP Leaders Answer Charges," *Amsterdam News,* March 21, 1953, 2.

26. "Monaghan Starts Anti-bias Training," *Amsterdam News,* March 28, 1953.

27. "Ella Baker Liberal Party Candidate" (flyer), Baker Papers, 1950s files, folder: Liberal Party or New York Politics.

28. By 1951 Baker had known Robinson for at least three years. She had proposed working with him to garner support for the Morningside Community Center, but these plans did not materialize. Ella Baker to James Robinson, Jan. 26, 1948, Baker Papers.

29. For information on Baker's city council candidacy, see "Ella Baker Resigns to Run for Council," *Amsterdam News,* Sept 12, 1953.

30. Pauli Murray to Ella Baker, Nov. 2, 1953, Baker Papers.

31. See also Murray, *Pauli Murray: The Autobiography of a Black Activist, Feminist, Lawyer, Priest and Poet* (Nashville: University of Tennessee Press, 1989), and

Pauli Murray Papers, "Liberal Party," box 73h73h, Schlesinger Library, Radcliffe College, Cambridge, Mass.

32. Yevette Richards, *Maida Springer: Pan-Africanist and International Labor Leader* (Pittsburgh: University of Pittsburgh Press, 2000), 71.

33. Mark Naison, *Communists in Harlem during the Depression* (Urbana: University of Illinois Press, 2004), 232–47; Richards, *Maida Springer,* 71.

34. The House Un-American Activities Committee became a permanent standing committee of the U.S. House of Representatives in 1946 after two previous incarnations. The committee then zealously took up the task of ferreting out alleged spies and enemies of the government. The committee's hearings, held around the country, put dissidents of all sorts on trial, forcing them to prove they were not Communists. Many were blacklisted, careers were destroyed, and several people went to jail for refusing on principal to cooperate with such an undemocratic body.

35. For more on anti-Communism and the American left, including African American progressives and organized labor, see Carol Polsgrove, *Divided Minds: Intellectuals and the Civil Rights Movement* (New York: Norton, 2001), and Mary L. Dudziak, *Cold War Civil Rights: Race and the Image of American Democracy* (Princeton, N.J.: Princeton University Pres, 2002).

36. "Lovestonites," in *Encyclopedia of the American Left,* ed. Mari Jo Buhle, Paul Buhle, and Dan Georgakas 436.

37. FBI report, Ella Baker files, New York. There are numerous unsigned reports throughout Baker's file. My conclusions are drawn from information from nearly a dozen short, unsigned reports.

38. NAACP Papers, group II, box A128, folder: Committee on Political Domination, 1952.

39. "Report of the New York Branch of the NAACP, Internal Security Committee, Oct. 14, 1957, submitted by Aloncita J. Flood; James Robinson to Roy Wilkins, letter with committee report attached, Nov. 18, 19578, NAACP Papers, group III, box C102, folder: Internal Security Committee.

40. Russell Crawford to Benjamin J. Davis Jr., Nov. 9, 1957, NAACP Papers, group III, box C102, folder: Internal Security Committee.

41. Joanne Grant, *Ella Baker: Freedom Bound* (New York: Wiley, 1999), 99.

42. A. Philip Randolph to "Dear Friends," Feb. 17, 1956, A. Philip Randolph Papers, box 23, folder: In Friendship, 1956, Library of Congress, Washington D.C.

43. A. Philip Randolph to In Friendship, Feb. 17, 1956, Norman Thomas Papers (microfilm), reel 30, folder: General Correspondence, New York Public Library.

44. B Norman Thomas to A. Philip Randolph, March 8, 1956, Randolph Papers, box 23, folder: In Friendship, 1956.

45. J. Oscar Lee to Norman Thomas, Jan. 30, 1956 (outlines other activities under way); Fay Bennett to Norman Thomas, Jan. 19, 1956, Norma Thomas Papers (microfilm) 30.

46. Minutes of the executive committee of In Friendship, June 20, 1956, New York City, A. Philip Randolph Papers, box 23, folder: In Friendship, 1956, 2, Library of Congress, Washington, D.C.

47. Baker, interview by Walker 7.

48. Ella J. Baker, memo to executive committee of In Friendship, July 26, 1956, NAACP Papers, group III, box A177.

49. Ella Baker to Rev. Kilgore, Feb. 26, 1956, Baker Papers.

3. "Taxation without Sanitation Is Tyranny": Civil Rights Struggles over Garbage Collection in Brooklyn, New York, during the Fall of 1962
Brian Purnell

The author is especially grateful to Professor Monroe Fordham, the editors at *Afro-Americans in New York Life and History*, and those who read and commented on earlier drafts of this work: Martha Biondi, Angela Dillard, Peter Eisenstadt, Adam Green, Mark Naison, Jeffrey Sammons, Clarence Taylor, Jeanne Theoharis, Craig Wilder, and Fordham University Press's anonymous readers. My debt to former members of Brooklyn CORE and their families is also evident throughout the notes.

1. On early efforts to address trash problems in Bedford-Stuyvesant through neighborhood cleanups, see "Our Job," *Amsterdam News*, January 9, 1960, 8.

2. Community Council of Greater New York, *Brooklyn Communities Population Characteristics and Neighborhood Social Resources*, 2 vols. (New York: Research Department, Bureau of Community Statistical Services, September 1959), ix–xliv; Craig Steven Wilder, *A Covenant with Color: Race and Social Power in Brooklyn* (New York: Columbia University Press, 2000); Harold X. Connolly, *A Ghetto Grows in Brooklyn* (New York: New York University Press, 1977); Harold X. Connolly, "The Future? Look over Your City and Weep for It Is Dying," in *Brooklyn USA: The Fourth Largest City in America*, ed. Rita Miller (New York: Brooklyn College Press, 1979), 349–62, and "Bedford-Stuyvesant: A Brief Note," in Miller, *Brooklyn USA*, 227. See also David Ment, *The Shaping of a City: A Brief History of Brooklyn* (New York: Brooklyn Educational and Cultural Alliance, 1979), 87–98; David Ment and Mary S. Donovan, *The People of Brooklyn: A History of Two Neighborhoods—Bedford-Stuyvesant and Sunset Park* (New York: Brooklyn Educational and Cultural Alliance, 1980), 32–47.

3. Wilder, *A Covenant with Color*, 181–97.

4. Brian Purnell, "A Movement Grows in Brooklyn: The Brooklyn Chapter of the Congress of Racial Equality (CORE) and the Northern Civil Rights Movement during the Early 1960s" (PhD diss., New York University, 2006).

5. Matthew Lassiter, "De Jure/De Facto Segregation: The Long Shadow of a National Myth," in *The Myth of Southern Exceptionalism,* ed. Matthew D. Lassiter and Joseph Crespino (New York: Oxford University Press, 2009), 25–48; Jeanne Theoharis, introduction to *Freedom North: Black Freedom Struggles outside*

the *South, 1940–1980,* ed. Jeanne Theoharis and Komozi Woodard (New York: Palgrave Macmillan, 2003), 1–16.

6. In addition to chapters in this volume, see Thomas Sugrue, *Sweet Land of Liberty: The Forgotten Struggle for Civil Rights in the North* (New York: Random House, 2008); Thomas Sugrue, *Origins of the Urban Crisis: Race and Inequality in Postwar Detroit* (Princeton, N.J.: Princeton University Press, 1996); Thomas Sugrue, "Crabgrass-Roots Politics: Race, Rights, and Reaction against Liberalism in the Urban North, 1940–1964," *Journal of American History* 82 (1995): 551–78; Arnold Hirsch, "Massive Resistance in the Urban North: Trumbull Park, Chicago, 1953–1966," *Journal of American History* 82 (1995): 522–50; Charles M. Payne, *I've Got the Light of Freedom: The Organizing Tradition and the Mississippi Freedom Struggle* (Berkeley: University of California Press, 1995); John Dittmer, *Local People: The Struggle for Civil Rights in Mississippi* (Urbana: University of Illinois Press, 1994); Timothy B. Tyson, *Radio Free Dixie: Robert F. Williams and the Roots of Black Power* (Chapel Hill: University of North Carolina Press, 1999); Komozi Woodard, *A Nation within a Nation: Amiri Baraka (LeRoi Jones) and Black Power Politics* (Chapel Hill: University of North Carolina Press, 1999); Lance Hill, *The Deacons for Defense: Armed Resistance and the Civil Rights Movement* (Chapel Hill: University of North Carolina Press, 2004); Jeanne Theoharis and Komozi Woodard, eds., *Freedom North,* and *Groundwork: Local Black Freedom Movements in America* (New York: New York University Press, 2005); Matthew Countryman, *Up South: Civil Rights and Black Power in Philadelphia* (Philadelphia: University of Pennsylvania Press, 2006); James Ralph, *Northern Protest: Martin Luther King, Jr., Chicago and the Civil Rights Movement* (Cambridge, Mass.: Harvard University Press, 1993); Martha Biondi, *To Stand and Fight: The Struggle for Civil Rights in Postwar New York* (Cambridge, Mass.: Harvard University Press, 2003); Robert Self, *American Babylon: Race and the Struggle for Postwar Oakland* (Princeton, N.J.: Princeton University Press, 2003); Nancy MacLean, *Freedom Is Not Enough: The Opening of the American Workplace* (Cambridge, Mass.: Harvard University Press, 2006); Barbara Ransby, *Ella Baker and the Black Freedom Movement: A Radical Democratic Vision* (Chapel Hill: University of North Carolina Press, 2003); Clarence Taylor, *Knocking at Our Own Door: Milton Galamison and the Struggle to Integrate New York City Schools* (Lanham, Md.: Lexington Books, 2001); Harvard Sitkoff, *A New Deal for Blacks: The Emergence of Civil Rights as a National Issue—the Depression Decade* (New York: Oxford University Press, 2008); Van Gosse, *Rethinking the New Left: An Interpretive History* (New York: Palgrave, 2005); Jacquelyn Dowd Hall, "The Long Civil Rights Movement and the Political Uses of the Past," *Journal of American History* 91, no. 4 (2005): 1233–63; Peniel E. Joseph, "Reconceptualizing the Heroic Period of the Civil Rights Movement. 1954–1965," *Souls* 2, no. 2 (2000): 6–17, and *Waiting 'til the Midnight Hour: A Narrative History of Black Power in America* (New York: Henry Holt, 2006); Robert Korstad and Nelson Lichtenstein, "Opportunities Found and Lost: Labor Radicals, and the Early Civil Rights Movement,"

Journal of American History 75, no. 3 (1988): 786–811; Steven Lawson, "Freedom Then, Freedom Now: The Historiography of the Civil Rights Movement," *American Historical Review* 96, no. 2 (1991): 456–71. For a critique of some the approaches in this scholarship, see Sundiata K. Cha-Jua and Clarence Lang, "The 'Long Movement' as Vampire: Temporal and Spatial Fallacies in Recent Black Freedom Studies," *Journal of African American History* 92, no. 2 (2007): 265–88.

7. Hall, "The Long Civil Rights Movement."

8. Harold X. Connolly, "Blacks in Brooklyn from 1900–1960" (PhD diss., New York University, 1973), 145–80. See also Wilder, *A Covenant with Color.*

9. Oliver Leeds, interview with Dianne Esses, December 15, 1988 (in the author's possession).

10. *Stuyford Leader* 1, no. 5 (1950), in State Historical Society of Wisconsin (hereafter SHSW), box 1, folder 5.

11. Arnold Goldwag, interview with the author, October 13, 2000, Brooklyn Collection, Grand Army Plaza Branch, Brooklyn Public Library, NY (hereafter, material found in the Brooklyn Public Library's Brooklyn Collection will be cited as Brooklyn Collection).

12. "Brooklyn Sanitation Problem," SHSW, box 1, folder 5.

13. Paul and Rita Heinegg, interview with author, January 5, 2004, Brooklyn Collection. Rita met her future husband, Paul Heinegg, when they both joined Brooklyn CORE in 1963.

14. Arnold Goldwag, interview with author, October 13, 2000, Brooklyn Collection.

15. Oliver Leeds, interview with Dianne Esses, December 15, 1988.

16. Ibid.

17. Memo to Miss Hortense Gabel, assistant to the mayor, Rent and Rehabilitation Administration, SHSW, box 1, folder 5.

18. Ibid.

19. Marjorie Leeds's handwritten notes, August 24, 1962, SHSW, box 1, folder 5.

20. "Memo to Kings County and New York City Authorities regarding the unsanitary and dilapidated condition of the sidewalks, building, and garbage collection on Gates Avenue, between Broadway and Bedford Avenues in the borough of Brooklyn," SHSW, box 1, folders 2 and 5.

21. Marjorie Leeds's handwritten notes, August 24, 1962, SHSW, box 1, folder 5.

22. Ibid.

23. *North Star* 1, no. 1 (n.d.), in Brooklyn Historical Society, Arnold Goldwag Brooklyn Congress of Racial Equality Collection, 2009.007, Box 4, Folder, "1962—Garbage." On the fear of informants, see Robert Law, interview with the author, April 14, 2004, Brooklyn Collection.

24. Oliver Leeds to Abe Stark, September 7, 1962, SHSW, box 1, folder 2.

25. Henry Liebman to Brooklyn CORE, September 13, 1962, SHSW, box 1, folder 2.

26. Gilbert Banks, interview with the author, April 1–2, 2000, Brooklyn Collection.

27. Msemaji and Nandi Weusi (Maurice and Winnie Fredericks), interview with the author, March 9, 2001, and Mary Ellen Phifer Kirton, interview with the author, February 23, 2004, both in Brooklyn Collection.

28. On the "CORE way," see Martin Oppenheimer, *A Manual for Direct Action* (Chicago: Quadrangle Books, 1965).

29. "Plan Garbage Dump at Official's Door," unknown newspaper, September 15, 1962, file clippings, Rioghan Kirchner Papers, Brooklyn Collection.

30. Msemaji and Nandi Weusi (Maurice and Winnie Fredericks), interview with author, March 9, 2001.

31. Oliver Leeds, interview with Dianne Esses, December 15, 1988.

32. Robert Law, interview with author, April 14, 2004.

33. Msemaji and Nandi Weusi (Maurice and Winnie Fredericks), interview with author, March 9, 2001, and Robert Law, interview with the author, April 14, 2004, both in Brooklyn Collection; "Brooklyn Group Flaunts Debris," *New York Times*, September 16, 1962.

34. Oliver Leeds, interview with Dianne Esses, December 15, 1988.

35. Oliver Leeds, interview with Dianne Esses, December 15, 1988; "B'klyn Rebels Slop Boro Hall with Garbage," unknown newspaper, September 16, 1962, file clippings, Rioghan Kirchner Papers, Brooklyn Collection; Summons #K295101, Leeds Family Personal Papers (document in author's possession).

36. *North Star* 1, no. 2 (1962): 1, in Arnold Goldwag Papers; Robert Law, interview with the author, April 14, 2004; Oliver Leeds, interview with Dianne Esses, December 15, 1988; "Neighborhood Action Report" and "Stark to Seek End to Garbage Mess," file clippings, Rioghan Kirchner Papers, Brooklyn Collection; National CORE seemed to have no problem with Brooklyn CORE's antagonistic demonstration or its seeming impatience with negotiation and leafleting. The assistant community relations director for National CORE, Robert Brookins Gore, expressed strong support for Operation Clean Sweep. In a letter to William Fetherston of Brooklyn, New York, Gore wrote, "A great deal of work needs to be done in order to make all of us more aware of our responsibility to society as well as the responsibility society has for us. . . . Programs such as 'Operation Clean Sweep' do provide this very function. It causes the city to be more concerned and it awakens members of the community to the fact that there are many ways to alleviate problems; through personal action and through governmental action." SHSW, box 1, folder 5.

37. "Stark to Seek End to Garbage Mess"; "Stark Asks Daily Garbage Pickup"; "Stark to Take Birns on Tour of Housing," file clippings, Rioghan Kirchner Papers, Brooklyn Collection. In subsequent weeks, Stark took shots at

the court system, which only issued fines to landlords for slum conditions. Since housing conditions worsened and negligent landlords did not seem to mind paying summonses, Stark thought imprisonment would be a more suitable punishment. See "'Jail All Slumlords; They Don't Mind Paying $$': Abe Stark Appeals to Courts," file clippings, Rioghan Kirchner Papers, Brooklyn Collection.

38. "'Jail All Slumlords; They Don't Mind Paying $$': Abe Stark Appeals to Courts," file clippings, Rioghan Kirchner Papers, Brooklyn Collection.

39. "CORE Gets 2 Promises on Garbage: Summonses Sure; 5 day Pick-Up Depends on Budget," unknown newspaper, in file clippings, Rioghan Kirchner Papers, Brooklyn, Collection.

40. Ibid.

41. For historical analysis of the urban "underclass," and the culture of poverty, see Michael B. Katz, ed., *The "Underclass" Debate: Views from History,* (Princeton, N.J.: Princeton University Press, 1993), especially Joe William Trotter Jr., "Blacks in the Urban North: The 'Underclass Question' in Historical Perspective," 55–81.

42. *North Star* 1, no. 2 (1962): 1, in Arnold Goldwag Papers; Frank J. Lucia to Oliver Leeds, December 3, 1962, SHSW, box 1, folder 5. Beginning around September 1962, Brooklyn CORE titled its monthly newsletter the *North Star,* after Frederick Douglass's nineteenth-century antislavery newspaper. See Brooklyn Historical Society, Arnold Goldwag Brooklyn Congress of Racial Equality Collection, 2009.007, box 2, folder: CORE Literature + Reports, 1956–1966.

43. Frank J. Lucia to Oliver Leeds, December 3, 1962, SHSW, box 1, folder 5.

44. Ibid.

45. Ibid.; Oliver Leeds and Robert Law to Mayor Wagner and Frank J. Lucia, SHSW, box 1, folder 5.

46. Thomas Jones to Oliver Leeds, January 22, 1963; Frank Lucia to Oliver Leeds, January 24, 1963; Henry Liebman to Oliver Leeds, February 1, 1963, all in SHSW, box 1, folder 5. On black ministers in Brooklyn, see Clarence Taylor, *Black Churches of Brooklyn* (New York: Columbia University Press, 1996), and *Knocking at Our Own Door.* On Thomas Russell Jones, see Jeffrey Gerson, "Building the Brooklyn Machine: Jewish and Black Succession in the Brooklyn Democratic Party Organization, 1919–1964" (PhD diss., CUNY Graduate Center, 1990).

47. Mickey Melendez, *We Took the Streets: Fighting for Latino Rights with the Young Lords* (New York: St. Martin's Press, 2003), 101–11; Johanna Fernandez, "Between Social Service Reform and Revolutionary Politics: The Young Lords, Late Sixties Radicalism, and Community Organizing in New York City," in Theoharis and Woodard, *Freedom North,* 264–69. On Brownsville, see Wendell Pritchett, *Brownsville, Brooklyn: Blacks, Jews, and the Changing Face of the Ghetto* (Chicago: University of Chicago Press, 2002), 239–240. On the sanitation workers' strike, see Vincent J. Cannato, *The Ungovernable City: John Lindsay and His Struggle to Save New York* (New York: Basic Books, 2002), 196–204.

48. James Baldwin famously used this lyric as the title of his 1963 book. In it, Baldwin made an eloquent and prescient argument that racial conflagration would certainly follow if citizens and leaders did not amend the racial strife that had characterized U.S. politics and culture since the country's inception. See James Baldwin, *The Fire Next Time* (New York: Dial Press, 1963).

4. Rochdale Village and the Rise and Fall of Integrated Housing in New York City

Peter Eisenstadt

Earlier versions of this chapter were presented to the Rochester United States Historians and the Columbia University Seminar on the City, and I am grateful for their incisive suggestions, and for the comments of Rob Snyder and Clarence Taylor on the manuscript. Clarence deserves further thanks for being the animating force and tutelary spirit behind this volume of essays. An earlier version of this article appeared as "Rochdale Village and the Rise and Fall of Integrated Housing in New York City," *Afro-Americans in New York Life and History* 31, no. 2 (July 2007). A more comprehensive account of all the issues discussed here can be found in Peter Eisenstadt, *Rochdale Village: Robert Moses, 6,000 Families, and New York City's Great Experiment in Interracial Housing* (forthcoming from Cornell University Press). This article is dedicated to the memory of my beloved brother, Freddy.

1. United Housing Federation, *Rochdale Village: A New Concept in Community Living* (New York, 1967).

2. Joshua B. Freeman, *Working-Class New York: Life and Labor since World War II* (New York: New Press, 2000), 119.

3. A good review of integrated housing projects and developments in the United States from the 1950s through the mid-1970s is Morris Milgram, *Good Neighborhood: The Challenge of Open Housing* (New York: Norton, 1977).

4. South Jamaica lacks a good history, but see Pearl Renfroe Grissom, *Some Factors Affecting the Lives of Negroes in South Jamaica* (New York: Family Welfare Society of Queens, 1932); James M. Rose, *A Study in Triumph: African Americans in Queens Co, NY, 1683–1993* (New York: Store Front Museum/Paul Robeson Theatre, 1986); Edward Carpenter and Jacquelyn Peterson, *South Jamaica: A Community Study* (New York: Queens College Children and Parents Center, 1966).

5. There are no hard figures on the black-white percentages in Rochdale when it opened, but a UHF advertisement claimed there were 4,700 white families in Rochdale, roughly 80 percent of the population. "Rochdale Village, a Self-Help Community," *New York Times* (hereafter *NYT*), April 8, 1964. Abraham Kazan, the president of the UHF, gave a figure of 20 percent African American in his oral history, *Reminiscences of Abraham H. Kazan* (1969), 512–13, Columbia Oral History Collection. Harvey Swados, in "When Black and White

Live Together," *New York Times Magazine*, November 13, 1966, gives a figure of 15 percent African American. Some contemporary observers gave a lower percentage of African Americans in Rochdale. Myron Becker in "City Housing Project Plan Stirs up Rochdale Village," *Long Island Press*, April 11, 1965, cites a figure of 8 percent. Rev. William Mowat, who conducted a survey of race and religion in Rochdale, is cited as claiming in 1965 that the African American population was "far fewer" than 20 percent, but he didn't offer his own figures, Jerome Zukosky, "Rochdale Village: A Test of Race and Religion," *New York Herald Tribune*, March 14, 1965. In the absence of conclusive evidence, the UHF figures should be taken as authoritative.

The one extant study of religious affiliation in Rochdale, from 1965, concluded (with an unspecified methodology) that there were about 4,000 Jewish households in Rochdale, which means that of the 4,700 white families in Rochdale, about 85 percent of them would have been Jewish. Protestant Council of the City of New York [William R. Mowat], *An Experimental Ministry to a High-Rise Middle-Income Housing Complex* (New York, 1967), 3. For anyone who lived there in the mid-1960s, this religious percentage seems intuitively correct.

6. Freeman, *Working-Class New York*, 119.

7. Swados, "When Black and White Live Together."

8. One author who has described the late 1950s through the early 1960s as an "era of integration" is Vincent J. Cannato; see his *The Ungovernable City: John Lindsay and His Struggle to Save New York* (New York: Basic Books, 2001), 268–71.

9. Morton Deutsch and Mary Evans Collins, *Interracial Housing: A Psycholosocial Evaluation of a Social Experiment* (Minneapolis: University of Minnesota Press, 1951), 126. The Deutsch and Collins study was sponsored by Marshall Field Foundation, which worked extensively with city officials, including Robert Moses, in unsuccessful efforts to build private interracial housing in Greenwich Village in the early 1950s; see Joel Schwartz, *The New York Approach: Robert Moses, Urban Liberals, and the Redevelopment of the Inner City* (Columbus: Ohio University Press, 1993), 139–42, 179–83.

10. For antidiscrimination law in New York City and state, see Paul Moreno, "Division of Human Rights," in *The Encyclopedia of New York State*, ed. Peter Eisenstadt (Syracuse, N.Y.: Syracuse University Press, 2005), 749; Tod M. Ottman, "Government That Has Both a Heart and a Head: The Growth of New York State Government during the World War II Era, 1930–1950" (PhD diss., SUNY Albany, 2001), 188–89; Stephen Grant Meyer, *As Long as They Don't Move Next Door: Segregation and Racial Conflict in American Neighborhoods* (Lanham, Md.: Rowman and Littlefield, 2000), 158–61.

11. Perhaps the emblematic figure in the liberal campaign for open housing at the time was Charles Abrams, the author of *Forbidden Neighbors: A Study of Prejudice in Housing* (New York: Harper, 1955), the best-known study of its subject. In 1955 he was named chairman of the State Commission against Discrimination, and he worked for several years to increase its jurisdiction and

enforcement powers. He resigned in 1959 after a clash with newly elected Governor Nelson Rockefeller. Abrams recognized both the promise and the problems with state enforcement of civil rights legislation in New York State. For Abrams, see A. Scott Henderson, *Housing and the Democratic Ideal: The Life and Thought of Charles Abrams* (New York: Columbia University Press, 2000), esp. 157–66.

12. Freeman, *Working-Class New York*, 93–95; Martha Biondi, *To Stand and Fight: The Struggle for Civil Rights in Postwar New York City* (Cambridge, Mass.: Harvard University Press, 2003).

13. Doxey Wilkerson, "Freedom—Through Victory in War and Peace," in Rayford W. Logan, *What the Negro Wants*, ed. Kenneth R. Janken (1944; South Bend, Ind.: University of Notre Dame Press, 2001), 193–216. Wilkerson, a professor of education at Howard University, joined the Communist Party in 1943. In 1946, as a party member, he criticized the revival of the Communist Party's far-fetched scheme for self-determination within a black homeland in the South, arguing that progress for black Americans was possible without the overthrow of capitalism. See Joseph R. Starobin, *American Communism in Crisis, 1943–1957* (Berkeley: University of California Press, 1972), 132–33.

14. Doxey A. Wilkerson, "Teacher Institute of Individualizing Instruction for Classroom Integration at P.S. 30 and P.S 80, Queens, New York City: 1965–66," 1966, in author's possession. See also Edmund Gordon and Doxey Wilkerson, *Compensatory Education for the Disadvantaged: Programs and Practices: Preschool through College* (New York: College Entrance Examination Board, 1966); Herbert Plever, interview, September 2004. Wilkerson collaborated with another former Communist, Annie Stein, in preparing the educational park proposal for Rochdale; Jack and Sue Raskin, interview, September 2004. For Annie Stein's role as an advisor to Milton Galamison in his campaign to integrate New York City's public schools (with its major demonstration in February 1964, a few months after the opening of Rochdale), see Clarence Taylor in *Knocking at Our Own Door: Milton A. Galamison and the Struggle to Integrate New York City Schools* (New York: Columbia University Press, 1997), 55–63, 141.

15. For social democracy and housing in postwar New York City, see Freeman, *Working-Class New York*, 105–24, and Hilary Botein, " 'Solid Testimony of Labor's Present Status': Unions and Housing and Postwar New York City" (PhD diss., Columbia University, 2005).

16. For Kazan's early contacts with anarchism in the years around World War I, see Kazan, *Reminiscences*, 26–27, Columbia Oral History Collection; for Kazan's anarchist roots and the influence of the anti-Communist theorist Rudolph Rocker, see Harold Ostroff, interview, September 2004. For Jewish anarchism in New York City, see Paul Avrich, *Anarchist Portraits* (Princeton, N.J.: Princeton University Press, 1988), 176–99, and Tony Michels, *A Fire in Their Hearts: Yiddish Socialists in New York* (Cambridge, Mass.: Harvard University Press, 2005).

17. For background on Kazan, early cooperative activity in New York City, and the UHF, see Kenneth G. Wray, "Abraham E. Kazan: The Story of the Amalgamated Houses and the United Housing Foundation" (master's thesis, Columbia University, 1991); Andrew Hazelton, "Garden Courts to Tower Blocks: The Architecture and Social History of the Labor Cooperative Housing Movement in New York, 1913–1950," paper in possession of the author; Tony Schuman, "Labor and Housing in New York City: Architect Herman Jessor and the Cooperative Housing Movement," paper in possession of the author; Hilary Ann Botein, " 'Solid Testimony of Labor's Present Status': Unions and Housing in Post-war New York City" (PhD diss., Columbia University, 2005), 70–101; *Radicals in the Bronx*, video, produced by Michal Goldman, co-produced by Ellen Brodsky and Andrew Hazelton, 2004; Amalgamated Housing Cooperative, *Story of a Co-op Community: The First 75 Years* (New York, 2002); Richard Plunz, *A History of Housing in New York City: Dwelling Type and Social Change in the American Metropolis* (New York: Columbia University Press, 1990), 151–59.

18. The UHF saw the cooperative movement as a "third way" between capitalism and Communism. See, for instance, Norman Thomas, "People's Capitalism," *Co-op Contact* 1, no, 8 (April 1956). As late as 1964, the UHF reprinted excerpts from Robert Owen's classic socialist tract, "A New System of Society," in their journal, *Co-op Contact* 6, no. 2 (March 1964).

19. "Abraham E. Kazan Dies at 82; Master Co-op Housing Builder," *NYT*, December 22, 1971.

20. Kazan, *Reminiscences*, 504; "Land Acquired for Rochdale Village," *Co-op Contact*, 4, no. 5 (June–July 1960).

21. Joel Schwartz, *The New York Approach: Robert Moses, Urban Liberals, and Redevelopment of the Inner City* (Columbus: Ohio University Press, 1993), 135.

22. Harold Ostroff, interview, September 2004.

23. Kazan, *Reminiscences*, 493.

24. For sports attendance figures, see Arthur Daley, "What's That, John?" *NYT*, December 20, 1953; Stanley Levey, "Racing Now Virtual King of Sports, Topping Baseball in Gate Appeal," *NYT*, April 30, 1953; John Thorn et al., *Total Baseball* (New York: Sportclassic Books, 1999), 107–8.

25. For a sample of the coverage of the sale of the plot of the Jamaica Race Track to the UHF, see Stanley Levey, "Racing Now Virtual King of Sports, Topping Baseball in Gate Appeal," *NYT*, April 30, 1953; Daley, "What's That, John?" *NYT*, December 20, 1953; Alexander Feinberg, "New Racing Plant for City Mapped." *NYT*, January 16, 1954; "Jockey Club Plans Gives $100 Million Plan for State Tracks," *NYT*, September 1, 1954; Leo Egan, "Strong Opposition to 'Dream' Race Track Here," *NYT*, March 26, 1955; Joseph C. Nichols, "Two Long Island Courses Will Be Rebuilt," *NYT*, October 28, 1955; Homer Bigart, "Moses Plans Deals on Jamaica Race Track," *NYT*, October 5, 1956; Charles Grutzner, "Slum Work Urged to Spur Economy," *NYT*, April 18, 1958; "Jamaica Project Pleases Moses," *NYT*, May 18, 1959; Charles Grutzner,

"Jamaica Track Open to Housing if Aqueduct Gets Idlewild Plot," *NYT,* January 24, 1959; "Huge Co-op Plan Favored by Moses," *NYT,* August 20, 1959; editorial, "Great Housing Opportunity," *NYT,* December 4, 1959; press release, State of New York, Executive Chamber, Albany, February 18, 1960, UHF Clipping File, UHF Papers, Kheel Center, ILR School, Cornell University; Charles G. Bennett, "Jamaica Housing Meets Opposition," *NYT,* April 14, 1960; "Riverside Houses Voted as Revised," *NYT,* April 29, 1960; "Racetrack Housing Approved by City," *Long Island Press,* April 29, 1960; Kazan, *Reminiscences,* 493–504. Although it possibly entered into private discussions, I have found nothing to indicate that the racial mix in South Jamaica was a factor in the decision to close Jamaica Race Track.

26. Robert Moses to John Cashmore, August 26, 1955, Correspondence—1955 folder B, Robert Moses Papers, New York Public Library (all Moses correspondence from this source, unless otherwise noted); Robert Moses to F. M. Flynn, August 22, 1955 Correspondence—1955 C, 1955, folder W, Robert Moses Papers; Robert Moses to Robert F. Wagner, July 6, 1955, Correspondence—1955 folder W, 1955, Robert Moses Papers; Homer Bigart, "Moses Plans Deals on Jamaica Race Track," *NYT,* October 5, 1956. The text of Moses's speech proposing the development of the Jamaica Race Track is reprinted in Robert Moses, "The Role of Housing Cooperatives in Urban Redevelopment," *Co-op Contact* 1, no. 11 (November 1956).

27. Charles Grutzner, "Moses Is Annoyed by a 'Slow' Track," *NYT,* October 18, 1957.

28. "Jamaica Project Pleases Moses," *NYT,* May 18, 1959.

29. Kazan, *Reminiscences,* 493. For the increased hostility of the press toward Moses in the summer and fall of 1959, see Robert Caro, *The Power Broker: Robert Moses and the Fall of New York* (New York: Vintage Books, 1974), 961–1025.

30. For black fears of declining real estate values, see Swados, "When Black and White Live Together."

31. Harold Ostroff, speech at Princeton University, April 18, 1968, text in possession of author. Donald Martin, one of Kazan's closest aides, is quoted as arguing that the lesson of Rochdale Village is that "people can put up with a lot of integration when they can get good housing at an attractive price"; Kenneth G. Wray, "Abraham E. Kazan: The Story of the Amalgamated Houses and the United Housing Foundation" (master's thesis, Columbia University School of Architecture and Planning, 1991), 50. See also "Rochdale Tenants: New Home Is Okay," *Long Island Press* February 26, 1964; Anne Estock, "Big Boosters for Largest Co-op," *Long Island Press,* March 29, 1964.

32. UHF minutes, April 8, 1960, UHF Papers, Kheel Center, ILR School, Cornell University.

33. For the extreme paucity of private interracial developments in the 1950s, see Eunice and George Grier, *Privately Developed Interracial Housing: An Analysis of Experience* (Berkeley: University of California Press, 1960).

34. Henry Lee Moon, the NAACP director of publicity, and the author of the important study *The Balance of Power: The Negro Vote* (Garden City, N.Y.: Doubleday, 1948), lived in the Queensview cooperative and served on the board of directors of Rochdale Village from 1963 to 1966 and two terms as a director for the UHF; see Bea and Jack Moss, "One of Queensview's Most Distinguished Families," *Co-op Contact* 1, no. 5 (March 1956); United Housing Federation, *Rochdale Village: A New Concept in Community Living* (New York, 1967), 24, on Henry Lee and Mollie Moon.

35. Eleanor Roosevelt, "Housing for Everyone" *Co-op Contact* 1, no. 7 (May 1956). See also Donald D. Martin, "Open Membership," *Co-op Contact* 2, no. 8 (October 1957). On Little Rock and open housing, see "Civil Rights and Housing," *Co-op Contact* 4, no. 3 (February–March 1960).

36. For Moses's opposition to civil rights legislation, see his article in the *New York Times, Magazine*, August 1, 1943 (I am grateful to Martha Biondi for this reference), and for Moses on the Ives-Quinn law, see the *New York Journal-American*, February 21, 1945, cited in Martha Biondi, *To Stand and Fight*, 19. For his role at Stuyvesant Town, see Biondi, *To Stand and Fight*, 121–36, and Schwartz, *The New York Approach*, 84–107.

37. *New York Post*, July 1, 1956; Robert Moses to James Felt, August 20, 1956, folder F, Robert Moses Papers. To his close friend Herbert Bayard Swope, he wrote in early 1956 that civil rights legislation, if vigorously enforced "will turn the clock a quarter of a century." Moses to Swope, Correspondence—1956, Robert Moses Papers.

38. *New York Post*, July 1, 1956. In Robert Moses, *Public Work: A Dangerous Trade* (New York: McGraw-Hill, 1970), 431–33, Moses quotes a letter he wrote in the late 1940s privately criticizing the president of Met Life for his conservatism and "poor advisers" on racial matters. For other examples of interracial housing projects backed by Moses, see Schwartz, *The New York Approach*, 136–43; Lawrence Kaplan and Carol Kaplan, *Between Ocean and City: The Transformation of Rockaway, New York* (New York: Columbia University Press, 2003), 88–89.

39. Robert Moses to Elmer Carter, March 13, 1959, folder C, Robert Moses Papers. This is not the place for a full-scale discussion of the legacy of Robert Moses, but it is clear that Robert Caro's *The Power Broker: Robert Moses and the Fall of New York* (New York: Random House, 1974) steers clear of many subjects that might complicate his indictment of Moses as a heartless racist indifferent to the aspirations of average New Yorkers. Caro's *The Power Broker* speaks of many aspects of Moses's career but has nary a mention of the UHF, Abraham Kazan, or Rochdale Village.

40. Kazan, *Reminiscences*, 504. Robert Moses to Nelson Rockefeller, September 30, 1959, Rockefeller Subject Files, 1959–1962, Housing, New York State Archives. The reluctance of union officials to provide funds for Rochdale was confirmed by Nicholas Gyory, former president of the Millinery Workers International Union; Nicholas Gyory, interview, November 2005.

41. Robert Moses to J. Anthony Panuch, November 30, 1959, Correspondence—1959, Robert Moses Papers.

42. Robert Moses, "Rochdale: Master Planner Moses Views a Master Housing Plan," *Long Island Press*, December 1, 1963; Moses, *Public Work*, 466; Robert Moses, "Rochdale Village: A Model for the Future," *Newsday*, February 3, 1968.

43. Swados, "When Black and White Live Together."

44. Zukovsky, "Rochdale Village."

45. Reprinted in *Inside Rochdale*, January 27, 1965.

46. Zukovsky, "Rochdale Village"; Anita Starr, interview, November 2004. According to Swados, "thousands" of white families changed their minds about moving to Rochdale, many after already making their down payments.

47. A rumor reported in the *Long Island Press* that Rochdale was planned to be 60 percent white, 40 percent black, was vigorously denied; see Abraham Kazan to Florence Goodman, June 7, 1961, UHF Papers, Kheel Center, ILR School, Cornell University. Harold Ostoff gave me a similar unambiguous denial about quotas in Rochdale when I interviewed him, and I see no evidence to challenge his account. Ostoff, interview, September 2004.

48. "Enjoy Country Living in Rochdale Village," advertisement in *NYT*, January 8, 1961. There was a notice about Rochdale at the same time in the *New Pittsburgh Courier*, a well-known black paper that had a national edition: Pat Patterson, "Long Island Sounds," *New Pittsburgh Courier*, January 7, 1961.

49. Eddie Abramson, interview, November 2004; Joseph Raskin, interview, March 2006.

50. See "One of Last 5 Wooden Schools in City to Be Closed Tomorrow," *NYT*, April 9, 1964, on the closing of P.S. 16; Rochdale Village Committee for Public Schools, "Letter to Dr. Ryan, Werner, and Members of the Board," December 5, 1963, letter in possession of the author; Jack and Sue Raskin, interview, September 2004; Herb and Sylvia Plever, interview, September 2004; Adele Goret, interview, September 2004. See also the important account provided by an anonymous informant from the committee, which maintained the Board of Education was intending to use of one of Rochdale's elementary schools primarily for whites, the other primarily for blacks, in David Rogers, *110 Livingston Street: Politics and Bureaucracy in the New York City Schools* (New York: Random House, 1968), 509–11; this is disputed by those I interviewed, who argued the problem was the remarkable torpor of the Board of Education, which they challenged in a number of imaginative ways, including tying up the Board of Education's switchboard with incessant phone calls.

51. *Inside Rochdale*, November 14, 1965.

52. Alan Truscott, "Bridge: Woman Student Is Winner at Integrated Event in Queens," *NYT* July 13, 1967. For another integrated bridge tournament at Rochdale, see the bridge column in the *New York Times* for January 31, 1968.

53. For Rochdale Village Community Singers, see *Inside Rochdale*, February 11, 1966, and March 3, 1966, as well as the programs of Rochdale Village Community Chorus (in possession of the author).

54. Bernard Seeman, "Rochdale Village Must Set an Example," *Inside Rochdale*, November 26, 1966. The paper editorialized in 1968 that, because of the urban crisis, "We Need More Rochdale Villages," *Inside Rochdale*, February 12, 1968.

55. Swados, "When Black and White Live Together."

56. Jack and Sue Raskin, interview, September 2004.

57. Eddie Abramson, interview, December 2004; Juanita Watkins, interview, January 2005.

58. Numbers on the white exodus need to be pieced together from many sources. In 1970, 447 families, representing about 7.6 percent of the apartments, left Rochdale: Leonard Bridges to Rochdale Village Board of Directors, December 15, 1970, UHF Papers, Kheel Center, ILR School, Cornell University. By 1973, 1,800 families, or about 31 percent of the families, are reported as having moved out over the previous three years: "Cooperation Means Responsibility," *Rochdale Village Bulletin*, May 1973. Estimates of the black population of Rochdale include 50 percent in 1974 ("Rochdale Village Preparing for 10th Anniversary Dinner," *Long Island Press,* January 6, 1974), 70 percent in 1977 (Murray Schumach, "If It Really Takes All Kinds, Queens Certainly Takes All Kinds," *NYT,* March 2, 1977), and 85 percent in 1979 ("A Vision of Utopia Fading at Rochdale," *NYT,* June 8, 1979). The white population continued to decline, and by the early 1990s, Rochdale Village was 98 percent nonwhite (Diana Shaman, "Queens Co-op Working out Problems," *NYT,* March 12, 1993).

59. For negative comments by blacks on their Jewish neighbors, see Swados, "When Black and White Live Together"; Zukovsky, "Rochdale Village"; Donna Rodriguez, conversation with the author, December 2004. For racialized comments on crime by black "outsiders," see Helen Katz, "When Will the Madness End?" *Inside Rochdale,* November 26, 1966; *Inside Rochdale,* December 11, 1966; "Crime Plagues Local Stores," *Inside Rochdale,* January 1970.

60. For the sad story of the swimming pool, see "Hearing on Addition for Lincoln Center to Be Held June 19," *NYT,* June 6, 1963; "Rochdale Pool Starts Protests Swirling," *Long Island Press,* May 1, 1963; "Residents Oppose Rochdale Pool Site," *Long Island Press,* May 4, 1963; *Proposed Department of Parks Recreation Center at New York Blvd and 134th Street* (New York, 1963); Queens borough president Mario J. Cariello to commissioner of parks Newbold Morris, May 4, 1964, Department of Parks and Recreation, Rochdale Village, 1964, Municipal Archives.

61. *Inside Rochdale*, April 15, 1965. This was in opposition to the plan to build low-income housing adjacent to Rochdale, a plan opposed by both Rochdale and South Jamaica community groups.

62. For the demonstrations at the Rochdale construction site, see William Booth, "Inside Story of the Rochdale Fight," *New York Amsterdam News,* August 3, 1963; Peter Kihss, "143 More Seized in Protests Here," *NYT,* July 24, 1963; Hal Shapiro, "Why They Picket at Rochdale," *Long Island Press,* August 8, 1963;

Martin Arnold, "Rights Protests Cost $15,000 a Day in Police Overtime," *NYT*, August 6, 1963; "Rockefeller Bars Negro Job Quota; Hails Union Plan," *NYT*, July 26, 1963; Will Lissner, "Pickets Chain Themselves to Cranes," *NYT*, September 6, 1963; Homer Bigart, "Wagner's Panel on Hiring Negroes Notes Progress," *NYT*, August 3, 1963; Simon Anekwe, "Rochdale Defendants Freed in Queens Picketing Trial," *New York Amsterdam News*, December 7, 1963; Herman Ferguson, interview, January 2005; William Booth, interview, May 2005; Paul Gibson, interview, May 2005.

63. On July 23, there were sixty-five protesters and eighty-five police officers. "143 More Seized in Protests Here," *NYT*, July 24, 1963; Hal Shapiro, "Why They Picket at Rochdale," *Long Island Press,* August 8, 1963; Martin Arnold, "Rights Protests Cost City $15,000 a Day in Police Overtime," *NYT*, August 6, 1963; William Booth, "Inside Story of Rochdale Fight," *New York Amsterdam News*, August 10, 1963.

64. Peter Kihss, "143 More Seized in Protests Here," *NYT*, July 24, 1963.

65. "Fifty Years of Service," *Jamaica Branch NAACP Bulletin*, 1977.

66. William Booth would become Mayor Lindsay's first human rights commissioner (the most important civil rights position in the Lindsay administration) and enjoy a stormy tenure. Paul Gibson, under Abraham Beame, would become the first African American deputy mayor in the city's history.

67. August Meier and Elliot Rudwick, *CORE: A Study in the Civil Rights Movement, 1942–1968* (New York: Oxford University Press, 1973), 151; "Long Island CORE Reviews a Year of Crises Met," *New York Amsterdam News*, January 11, 1964.

68. Peter Kihss, "Negroes to Push Picketing in City in Drive for Jobs," *NYT*, July 29, 1963; Herman Ferguson, interview, February 2005; "Rochdale Pickets to Rally Tonight," *Long Island Press*, September 8, 1963; "Everybody's Talkin' 'Bout," *Jamaica Branch NAACP Bulletin*, September 1963.

69. Homer Bigart, "Wagner's Panel on Hiring Negroes Notes Progress," August 3, 1963; Peter Kihss, "Rockefeller Bars Negro Job Quota; Hails Union Plan," *NYT*, July 26, 1963.

70. Peter Kihss, "Pickets Arrested for Blocking Way to Mayor's Office," *NYT*, July 30, 1963; Anita Starr, interview, November 2004; Bill Jones, interview, April 2005.

71. Dave Hepburn and Dera Bush, "Rochdale Village Opens as Community Watches," *New York Amsterdam News*, December 14, 1963.

72. "What's Happening," *Jamaica Branch NAACP Bulletin*, September 1963; Will Lissner, "Pickets Chain Themselves to Cranes," *NYT*, September 6, 1963; "The Man on the Crane," *Jamaica Branch NAACP Bulletin*, October 1963; Herman Ferguson, interview, February 2005.

73. "Small Business Falling in Line with Rochdale," *New York Amsterdam News*, October 19, 1963; "Is Negro Revolution a Kind of Garveyism?" *Pittsburgh Courier*, January 11, 1964; "Rights Fighter Sees Strength, Pride in 'Black

Nationalism,'" *New York Amsterdam News*, April 4, 1964. For a short discussion of the Rochdale movement, see Thomas J. Sugrue, *Sweet Land of Liberty: The Forgotten Struggle for Civil Rights in the North* (New York: Random House, 2008), 313–14.

74. For Malcolm X's two appearances at the Rochdale protests, see *New Pitts-burgh Courier*, December 7, 1963; Herman Ferguson, interview, February 2005; Holly Ho, "Long Island—Inside Out," *New Pittsburgh Courier,* December 7, 1963. Malcolm X mentions the Rochdale movement in his March 1964 interview with A. B. Spellman in *By Any Means Necessary* (New York: Pathfinder Press, 1985), 7.

75. Kenneth B. Clark, *Dark Ghetto* (New York: Harper & Row, 1965), 240.

76. Terence Smith, "New Rights Chief Criticizes Unions," *NYT,* February 2, 1966.

77. Sue Raskin, interview, September 2004.

78. Those who mentioned the school strike as a major factor in the white exodus include Libby Kahane, interview, April 2005; Eddie Abramson, interview, December 2004; Juanita Watkins, interview, January 2005; Harold Ostroff, interview, September 2004; Jack and Sue Raskin, interview, September 2004; Herb and Sylvia Plever, interview, September 2004; Anita Starr, interview, November 2004; Cal Jones, interview, December 2004; Omar Barbour, interview, November 2004. For the teachers' strike, see Jerald E. Podair, *The Strike That Changed New York: Blacks, Whites, and the Ocean Hill–Brownsville Crisis* (New Haven, Conn.: Yale University Press, 2003).

79. Albert Shanker, quoted by Jack and Sue Raskin, interview, September 2004; Cal Jones, interview, December 2004.

80. Jack and Sue Raskin, interview, September 2004; Cal Jones, interview, December 2004.

81. Susan Raskin to Mrs. Helene Lloyd (Board of Education), June 19, 1970, document in possession of the author. For problems at Rochdale's intermediate school, I.S. 72, see Larry Lapka, interview, June 2005; Sue Raskin, interview, September 2004; Anita Starr, interview, November 2004; Ellen Page, interview, November 2004; Nancy Brandon, interview, November 2004; Francesca Spero, interview, November 2004; Kenneth Tewel, interview, March 2005; and George and Beryl Korot, interview, January 2006.

82. Omar Barbour, interview, November 2004.

83. Jonathan Rieder, *Canarsie: The Jews and Italians of Brooklyn against Liberal-ism* (Cambridge, Mass.: Harvard University Press, 1985). For other books with similar themes, see Jim Sleeper, *The Closest of Strangers: Liberalism and the Politics of Race in New York* (New York: Norton, 1990); Samuel G. Freedman, *The Inheri-tance: How Three Families and the American Political Majority Moved from Left to Right* (New York: Simon and Schuster, 1998); Cannato, *The Ungovernable City*; Podair, *The Strike That Changed New York.*

84. Meir Kahane was rabbi of the orthodox synagogue in Rochdale for a year, from the fall of 1968 to 1969, and lived much of the year in Rochdale. His

family moved because his position ended—his congregation was tired of his extra-congregational activities and his penchant for controversy, which led to his growing unease in living in an integrated setting; Libby Kahane, interview, April 2005; Libby Kahane, "Meir Kahane," unpublished ms. in possession of the author.

85. A June 1968 poll in *Inside Rochdale* found 81 percent of Rochdale respondents concluded that victory was not possible in Vietnam; an August 1973 poll in the same publication found a majority declaring the returning POWs were not heroes. Eddie Abramson lost his position as district leader in 1968 because of his support of Johnson's Vietnam policies; a rally for the presidential bid of Robert Kennedy had been planned for Rochdale Village for the Sunday after his assassination, in large part because of his heavy support in Rochdale. Eddie Abramson, interview, December 2004; Cal Jones, interview, December 2004.

86. Technite post, "We Finally Visited Rochdale," post 51, *Rochdale Forum*, March 6, 2002.

87. Hal Levenson, "Channel 13 Responds to Rochdale Complaints," *Inside Rochdale*, May 1973. For reactions to the WNET program by Rochdale, see the issues of *Inside Rochdale* and *Rochdale Village Bulletin*, April 1973.

88. For an argument that economics make a return to the building of middle-income cooperatives impossible, and that as a result New Yorkers "seem reluctantly reconciled to the vertiginous drop in the volume of affordable housing," see Louis Winnick, "When an Apartment Fulfilled an Ideal," *NYT*, July 22, 2000.

89. Sherryl Chasin, *The Failures of Integration: How Race and Class Are Undermining the American Dream* (New York: Public Affairs, 2004.)

90. C. Vann Woodward, *The Strange Career of Jim Crow* (New York: Oxford University Press, 1955).

91. Herb and Sylvia Plever, interview, September 2004.

5. Conservative and Liberal Opposition to the New York City School-Integration Campaign

Clarence Taylor

1. James F. Clarity, "Robert Wagner, 80, Pivotal New York Mayor, Dies," *New York Times*, February 13, 1991.

2. Clarence Taylor, *The Black Churches of Brooklyn* (New York: Columbia University Press, 1994), 142–63.

3. Clarence Taylor, *Knocking at Our Own Door: Milton A. Galamison and the Struggle to Integrate New York City Schools* (Lanham, Md.: Lexington Books, 2001), xxviii–xxix.

4. Joshua B. Freeman, *Working-Class New York: Life and Labor since World War II* (New York: New Press, 2000), 99.

5. Ibid., 101; Jerald Podair, *The Strike That Changed New York: Blacks, Whites and the Ocean Hill–Brownsville Crisis* (New Haven, Conn.: Yale University Press, 2002), 13.

6. Freeman, *Working-Class New York*, 101–03.

7. New York City Commission on Human Rights, "History of the Human Rights Commission," http://www.nyc.gov/html/cchr/html/history.html.

8. Ibid.

9. Wendell Prichett, *Brownsville, Brooklyn: Blacks, Jews and the Changing Face of the Ghetto* (Chicago: University of Chicago Press, 2002), 159–60.

10. Craig Wilder, *A Covenant of Color: Race and Social Power in Brooklyn* (New York: Columbia University Press, 2001), 225.

11. Taylor, *The Black Churches of Brooklyn*, 118.

12. Ibid., 158.

13. Charles R. Morris, *The Cost of Good Intentions: New York City and the Liberal Experiment, 1960–1975* (New York: McGraw-Hill, 1980), 20–23.

14. Gerald Markowitz and David Rosner, *Children, Race, and Power: Kenneth and Mamie Clark's Northside Center* (New York: Routledge, 2000), 92; Taylor, *Knocking at Our Own Door*, 54.

15. Martha Biondi, *To Stand and Fight: The Struggle for Civil Rights in Postwar New York City* (Cambridge, Mass.: Harvard University Press, 2003), 100–101.

16. Wilder, *A Covenant of Color*, 225.

17. Taylor, *The Black Churches of Brooklyn*. 105–6; Morris, *The Cost of Good Intentions*, 23.

18. Markowitz and Rosner, *Children, Race, and Power*, 93.

19. Ibid., 95–96; Taylor, *Knocking at Our Own Door*, 52–53.

20. Taylor, *Knocking at Our Own Door*, 76; Barbara Ransby, *Ella Baker and the Black Freedom Movement: A Radical Democratic Vision* (Chapel Hill: University of North Carolina Press, 2003), 153–54.

21. Taylor, *Knocking at Our Own Door*, 9–31.

22. Lisa Yvette Waller, "Holding Back the Dawn: Milton A. Galamison and the Fight for School Integration," in "New York City: A Northern Civil Rights Struggle, 1948–1968" (PhD diss., Duke University, 1998), 42–43.

23. Taylor, *Knocking at Our Own Door*, 28–29.

24. Ibid., 18–19.

25. Ibid., 60.

26. Ibid., 64–65.

27. Ibid, 65–66.

28. Ibid., 98–99.

29. Morris, *The Cost of Good Intentions*, 20.

30. Vincent J. Cannato, *The Ungovernable City: John Lindsay and His Struggle to Save New York* (New York: Basic Books, 2001), 33.

31. Tamar Jacoby, *Someone Else's House: America's Unfinished Struggle for Integration* (New York: Free Press, 1998), 23–26.

32. Taylor, *Knocking at Our Own Door*, 86–87.

33. Robert H. Tertet, "City School Integration: Dispute Centers on the Way to Improve Negroes' Education," *New York Times*, October 22, 1963.

34. Philip J. Digger, *Negotiator: The Life and Career of James B. Donovan* (Cranbury, N.J.: Associated University Presses, 2006), 181.

35. Clarence Taylor, *Knocking at Our Own Door*, 168.

36. James E. Ryan, "Brown, School Choice, and the Suburban Veto," *Virginia Law Review* 90, no. 6 (2004): 1635–47; *New York Times*, June 9, 1964; John D. Johnson, interview, November 11, 1996, Scholar.lib.vt.edu/faculty_archives/principalship/h/350hodson.html-72K.

37. *New York Times*, September 17, 1964.

38. *New York Times*, September 20, 1964.

39. *New York Times*, September 25, 1964, and October 7, 1964; Taylor, *Black Churches of Brooklyn*.

40. *New York Times*, October 7, 1964.

41. *New York Times*, January 20, 1965; January 28, 1965; and January 30, 1965.

42. *New York Times*, January 31, 1965.

43. *New York Times*, February 18, 1965.

44. *New York Times*, February 18, 1965, and February 19, 1965.

45. "Tragedy for School Integration," *New York Times*, February 19, 1965, 34.

46. *New York Times*, February 23, 1965; February 25, 1965; March 4, 1965; and March 10, 1965.

47. *New York Times*, January 24, 1964.

48. Fred Powledge, "Negroes behind School Plan Risk Loss of White Liberals' Support," *New York Times*, February 3, 1964, 18.

49. Taylor, *Knocking at Our Own Door*, 147.

50. Ibid.

51. "Integration in City Schools," *New York Times*, December 13, 1963, 34.

52. "Civil Wrongs and Civil Rights," *New York Times*, December 19, 1963, 32.

53. "The School Boycott," *New York Times*, February 4, 1964, 32.

54. Earl Brown, letter to the *New York Times*, January 30, 1964, 28.

55. McCandlish Phillips, "Many Clergymen and Educators Say Boycott Dramatized Negroes Aspirations," *New York Times*, February 4, 1964, 21.

56. *New York Times*, February 3, 1964.

57. Taylor, *Knocking at Our Own Door*, 136–37.

58. Markowitz and Rosner, *Children, Race and Power*, 95; *New York Times*, January 1, 29, 1957.

59. *New York Times*, November 11, 1957.

60. *New York Times*, November 18, 1957.

61. Thomas Sugrue, *Origins of the Urban Crisis: Race and Inequality in Postwar Detroit* (Princeton, N.J.: Princeton University Press, 2005), 268.

62. Mathew Countryman, *Up South: Civil Rights and Black Power in Philadelphia* (Philadelphia: University of Pennsylvania Press, 2006).

63. Morris, *The Cost of Good Intentions*, 21.

6. The Dead End of Despair: Bayard Rustin, the 1968 New York School Crisis, and the Struggle for Racial Justice

Daniel Perlstein

An earlier version of this chapter appeared in Daniel Perlstein, *Justice, Justice: School Politics and the Eclipse of Liberalism* (New York: Peter Lang, 2004), 81–96. The book offers an account of the 1968 New York City school conflict and its role in America's evolving racial politics.

1. John D'Emilio, "Homophobia and the Trajectory of Post-war American Radicalism: The Case of Bayard Rustin," *Radical History Review* 62 (1995): 82.

2. Bayard Rustin to Charles Cogen, August 16, 1968, Bayard Rustin Papers, microfilm edition (hereafter BRP), reel 21, 1227; Thomas Brooks, "A Strategist without a Movement," *New York Times Magazine*, February 16, 1969, 24–25; Maurice Carroll, "Giant City Hall Rally Backs Teachers," *New York Times*, September 17, 1968, 1.

3. John D'Emilio, *Lost Prophet: The Life and Times of Bayard Rustin* (Chicago: University of Chicago Press, 2004), 41, 390. See also Devon Carbado and Donald Weise, "The Civil Rights Identity of Bayard Rustin," *Texas Law Review* 82 (2004): 1133–95. For accounts of continuity in white racial attitudes, see Thomas Sugrue, *The Origins of the Urban Crisis: Race and Inequality in Postwar Detroit* (Princeton, N.J.: Princeton University Press, 2005), and Robert Self, *American Babylon: Race and the Struggle for Postwar Oakland* (Princeton, N.J.: Princeton University Press, 2003). On continuity in black school activism, see Jack Dougherty, *More Than One Struggle: The Evolution of Black School Reform in Milwaukee* (Chapel Hill: University of North Carolina Press, 2004).

4. Bayard Rustin, "Integration within Decentralization," speech on receiving the United Federation of Teachers' John Dewey Award, April 6, 1968, in Rustin, *Down the Line: The Collected Writings of Bayard Rustin* (New York: Quadrangle, 1971), 213–14.

5. Rustin, "Integration within Decentralization," 215, 218–20.

6. Ibid., 216.

7. Ibid., 215–16; Bayard Rustin, "Education?" c. 1967, 55, BRP, 17, 862.

8. Bayard Rustin, "The Mind of the Black Militant," speech delivered at the Conference on the Schoolhouse in the City, Stanford University, July 10, 1967, in *Down the Line,* 209.

9. Rustin, "'Black Power' and Coalition Politics," *Commentary*, February 1967, in *Down the Line,* 155; Bayard Rustin, "A Word to Black Students," Tuskegee Institute commencement address, May 31, 1970, in *Dissent*, November–December 1970, 496; Bayard Rustin et al., "Where Is the Negro Movement

Now? A Conversation with Bayard Rustin," *Dissent*, November–December 1968, 491.

10. Bayard Rustin, "The Failure of Black Separatism," *Harper's Magazine*, January 1970, in *Down the Line*, 297–99; Bayard Rustin to Robert Curvin, October 9, 1968, BRP, 6, 193–94; Bayard Rustin, "The Alienated: The Young Rebels of Today . . . and Why They're Different," Speech to the International Labor Press Association, 1967, 1, BRP, 17, 827; Bayard Rustin, "Separatism Repackaged," *New Leader*, June 12, 1972, 11; Rustin, "Integration within Decentralization," 219–20; Brooks, "A Strategist without a Movement," 104.

11. Rustin, "Where Is the Negro Movement Now?" 494–95. Rustin's critique is inaccurate and unfair. While black support of community control did increase with income and educational attainment, blacks of all classes opposed the UFT and supported community control. Advocates of community control included activists such as Sonny Carson and Oliver Leeds, whom Rustin would label lumpen-proletarian and proletarian. Furthermore, non-proletarians have been among the leaders of virtually all social movements, and the presence of black ministers did not preclude Rustin's support of the Montgomery movement. Finally, to charge that black teachers are middle class undermines Rustin's claim that white UFT teachers could lead a civil rights–labor alliance. Louis Harris and Bert Swanson, *Black-Jewish Relations in New York City* (New York: Praeger, 1970), 133.

12. Bayard Rustin, "A Way out of the Exploding Ghetto," *New York Times Magazine*, August 13, 1967, 54, 62; Rustin, " 'Black Power' and Coalition Politics," 155; Bayard Rustin to Robert Curvin.

13. Rustin, "A Word to Black Students," 583; Rustin, "The Mind of the Black Militant," 211; Bayard Rustin to Robert Curvin; Sandra Feldman, "N.Y. City Decentralization," *New America*, March 31, 1968, 5.

14. Bayard Rustin, "The Negroes, the Cops, the Jews," *Dissent*, March–April 1967, 172–73; A. Philip Randolph Institute, "An Appeal to the Community from Black Trade Unionists" (advertisement), *New York Post*, September 19, 1968, 31.

15. Daniel Levine, *Bayard Rustin and the Civil Rights Movement* (New Brunswick, N.J.: Rutgers University Press, 2000), 10–11. Rustin attended a segregated elementary school staffed by a cadre of well-educated, committed, and demanding educators. The excellence of his education was far from unique among segregated schools and might have offered an alternative to the assimilationist politics he pursued in alliance with the UFT. D'Emilio, *Lost Prophet*, 13–14; Vanessa Siddle Walker, *Their Highest Potential: An African American School Community in the Segregated South* (Chapel Hill: University of North Carolina Press, 1996).

16. D'Emilio, *Lost Prophet*, 31. Rustin had also student-taught at the school he had attended as a child in Chester. D'Emilio, *Lost Prophet*, 24.

17. Bayard Rustin, *Strategies for Freedom: The Changing Patterns of Black Protest* (New York: Columbia University Press, 1976), 9–10; Jervis Anderson, *A. Philip*

Randolph: A Biographical Portrait (New York: Harcourt Brace Jovanovich, 1973), 275; Taylor Branch, *Parting the Waters: America in the King Years, 1954–63* (New York: Simon and Schuster, 1988), 168–71.

18. Anderson, *A. Philip Randolph*, 6. D'Emilio argues convincing that although Rustin exaggerated his involvement with the Communist Party, his association with it helped shape his political development. D'Emilio, *Lost Prophet*, 36.

19. Levine, *Bayard Rustin*, 23–33–34, 47.

20. Rustin, *Strategies for Freedom*, 17; D'Emilio, *Lost Prophet*, 127, 158; Paula Pfeffer, *A. Philip Randolph, Pioneer of the Civil Rights Movement* (Baton Rouge: Louisiana State University Press, 1990), 181–88, 228.

21. Pfeffer, *A. Philip Randolph, Pioneer*, 152–55, 187–92; Anderson, *A. Philip Randolph*, 274, 281; August Meier and Elliott Rudwick, *CORE: A Study in the Civil Rights Movement, 1942–1968* (New York: Oxford University Press, 1973), 11–15.

22. Bayard Rustin, "From Protest to Politics: The Future of the Civil Rights Movement," *Commentary*, February 1965, in *Down the Line*, 113; Rustin, "The Negroes, the Cops, the Jews," 172–73; Rustin, "From Protest to Politics," 111. The essay was a revision of a speech urging civil rights activists to end their protests at the 1964 Democratic Party convention. Rustin's argument that the significance of race was declining directly influenced sociologist William Julius Wilson. Bayard Rustin and Norman Hill to William Julius Wilson, September 21, 1982, BRP, 17, 507; William Julius Wilson, *The Bridge over the Racial Divide: Rising Inequality and Coalition Politics* (Berkeley: University of California Press, 2001).

23. Anderson, *A. Philip Randolph*, 324; Meier and Rudwick, *CORE*, 224; Pfeffer, *A. Philip Randolph, Pioneer*, 234, 245–47, 266.

24. Rustin, "The Alienated," 8; Rustin, "From Protest to Politics," 117, 120.

25. Terry Ferrer and Joseph Michalack, "44.8 Per Cent Absent, Pickets Brave Weather," *New York Herald Tribune*, February 4, 1964, 1, 7; "Negroes Mapping School Boycotts in 3 Cities," *New York Times*, February 25, 1964; Marianne Cole, "We Want Respect, Not Love, Declares Dick Gregory Here," *New York World-Telegram*, February 3, 1964, 2.

26. Milton Galamison to Charles Cogen, BRP, 5, 505; Joseph Michalack, "School Plan: A Loud No and Boycott," *New York Herald Tribune*, January 30, 1964, 1; Executive Board minutes, *United Teacher*, January 24, 1964, 7; Oliver Leeds to Bayard Rustin, August 10, 1968, BRP, 23, 1258; Albert Vann, "The Agency Shop" (position paper delivered to the Afro-American Teachers Association, May 6, 1969), in *What Black Educators Are Saying*, ed. Nathan Wright Jr. (New York: Hawthorn, 1970), 235; "Quick and Solid Action by Union Squashes Board of Ed 'Blacklist,'" *United Teacher*, March 5, 1964, 1; AdCom minutes, March 11, 1964, in *United Teacher*, April 23, 1964, 8. One newspaper claimed

that although more than 3,000 teachers participated in the boycott, teacher attendance was actually higher than usual. Alfred Robbins and Donald Flynn, "School Boycott Peaceful: Many Teachers Absent, Most Teachers In," *New York Journal American*, February 3, 1964, 1.

27. Jimmy Breslin, "The Boycotters," *New York Herald Tribune*, January 31, 1964, 1; "A Boycott Solves Nothing," *New York Times*, January 31, 1964, 26; Diane Ravitch, *The Great School Wars, New York City, 1805–1973: A History of the Public Schools as Battlefield of Social Change* (New York: Basic Books, 1974), 275; Leonard Buder, "Split Threatens Boycott Leaders," *New York Times*, February 11, 1964, 1; Leonard Buder, "Galamison Foes Drop Ouster Bid," *New York Times*, February 12, 1964, 25; statement of Frederick Jones, education chairman, New York State Conference of NAACP Chapters, February 17, 1964, BRP, 11, 630; statement of Frederick Richmond, president, New York Urban League, February 9, 1964, BRP, 11, 634; Leonard Buder, "Third CORE Group Will Aid Boycott," *New York Times*, March 5, 1964, 27; James Hicks, "O Ye of Little Faith," *Amsterdam News*, March 21, 1964, 11; Simon Anekwe, "Powell, Galamison Call Boycott Big Victory, Especially in Brooklyn," *Amsterdam News*, March 21, 1964, 27; Levine, *Bayard Rustin*, 275; Milton Galamison, letter to the editor, *New York Times*, May 19, 1964; Peter Obi, "Many Negro Leaders in Thick of March," *Amsterdam News*, March 21, 1964, 27; Meier and Rudwick, *CORE*, 231, 254.

28. Kenneth Gross, "School March Will Support State Report," *New York Post*, May 14, 1964, 3; Woody Klein, "Galamison Promises to Aid School Protest," *New York World Telegram*, May 11, 1964, 12.

29. Bayard Rustin to friend, May 9, 1964, BRP, 12, 279; Gross, "School March," 3; "Our Purpose," n.d., BRP, 12, 273; "Partial List of Sponsors-March for Democratic Schools," n.d., BRP, 12, 218; "Jewish Labor Committee Announces Support for May 18th School Demonstration," press release, BRP, 12, 351. Organizations cool to the boycott included the Anti-Defamation League and the Catholic Interracial Council. Richard Montague and Alfred Hendricks, "The Battle for the Schools," *New York Post*, February 2, 1964, 22.

30. Gross, "School March," 3; Terry Smith, "Pickets, School Boycott, Rally—Rights Protest Falls Short," *New York Herald Tribune*, May 19, 1964, 1.

31. Rustin, "Integration within Decentralization," 218; Bayard Rustin, "Reverberations: Why I Support the UFT," *Amsterdam News*, September 23, 1967, 16.

32. Ben Stahl to Bayard Rustin, January 1, 1965, BRP, 4, 572; Rolland Dewing, "Teacher Organizations and Desegregation," *Phi Delta Kappan* 49 (January 1968): 257–60; "Randolph and Rustin Support UFT Agreement—Breakthrough for Ghetto School," press release, September 28, 1967, BRP, 5, 859.

33. Sandra Feldman to Al Shanker, memorandum, February 9, 1968, BRP, 5, 891–92; "Back UFT Then Rent Office Space," *Amsterdam News*, October 5,

1968, 1; Pfeffer, *A. Philip Randolph, Pioneer*, 281, 293; "A Meeting for Shacht-man," *New America*, December 31, 1972, 8; "APRI, Statement of Income and Expenses," c. August 1965, BRP, 21, 467; Herbert Hill, "Black Protest, Union Democracy & UFT," *New Politics*, Fall 1970, 35; Anderson, *A. Philip Randolph*, 314. Daniel Levine stresses the role of Shachtman and AFL-CIO official Don Slaiman in creating the APRI. Levine, *Bayard Rustin*, 175.

34. Taylor Branch, *At Canaan's Edge: America in the King Years, 1965–68* (New York: Simon and Schuster, 2006), 620; Nat Hentoff, *The New Inequality* (New York: Viking, 1964), 100–105. On the construction job protests, see Perlstein, *Justice, Justice*, 95, 102–3. In a 1969 survey, blacks felt discriminated against in the building trades by a nine-to-one ratio. Harris and Swanson, *Black-Jewish Relations*, 160.

35. Clarence Taylor, *The Black Churches of Brooklyn* (New York: Columbia University Press, 1994), 143–44.

36. Oliver Leeds to Milton Galamison, August 12, 1963, Milton Galamison Papers, State of Wisconsin Historical Society, Madison, Papers, folder 3; Clarence Taylor, "'Whatever the Cost, We Will Set the Nation Straight': The Ministers' Committee and the Downstate Center Campaign," *Long Island Historical Journal* 1 (1989): 136–46; Meier and Rudwick, *CORE*, 231, 237.

37. Meier and Rudwick, *CORE*, 125–26, 182–83; D'Emilio, *Lost Prophet*, 403; Bayard Rustin to Priscilla Berry, July 14, 1964, BRP, 21, 018.

38. Fred Shapiro and James Sullivan, *Race Riots: New York, 1964* (New York: Thomas Crowell, 1964); 80; Levine, *Bayard Rustin*, 163; photograph, *Amsterdam News*, July 25, 1964, 1; George Todd, "James Powell's Funeral," *Amsterdam News*, July 25, 1964, 30; Branch, *At Canaan's Edge*, 383. Rustin's inability to reach protestors in the summer of 1964 in part reflected the distance that had come to separate him from grassroots black New York. In the late 1940s he had moved from Harlem to Manhattan's Lower East Side, after which time his day-to-day contacts with New York civil rights activists diminished even as those with national civil rights leaders grew. See D'Emilio, *Lost Prophet*, 174.

39. Federal Bureau of Investigation, surveillance, July 28–30, 1964, in Kenneth O'Reilly and David Gallen, eds., *Black Americans: The FBI Files* (New York: Carroll & Graf, 1994), 393–95; Bayard Rustin to Whitney Young, July 29, 1964, BRP, 21, 021; Rochelle [Horowitz] to Bayard, July 24, 1964, BRP, 21, 025; Shapiro and Sullivan, *Race Riots*, 80; Jackie Robinson, "Home Plate: Goldwater Ammunition," *Amsterdam News*, August 1, 1964, 19; Levine, *Bayard Rustin*, 164. Ironically, the school at which James Powell was shot was named after Robert Wagner Sr.

40. Bayard Rustin, "Nonviolence on Trial," *Fellowship*, July 1964, 5–7.

41. Peter Drucker, *Max Shachtman and His Left: A Socialist's Odyssey through the "American Century"* (Atlantic Highlands, N.J.: Humanities Press, 1994), 268; "The Leaders Who Would Curb Election Demonstrations," *Amsterdam News*, August 8, 1964, 43; D'Emilio, *Lost Prophet*, 377–78.

42. Branch, *At Canaan's Edge*, 384; "The Leaders Who Would Curb Election Demonstrations," 43; Rustin to A. J. Muste, January 28, 1965, BRP, 21, 265; Rustin to Muste, November 16, 1965, BRP, 21, 454; Staughton Lynd to Rustin, April 19, 1965, BRP, 21, 346; Rustin to Neil Haworth, November 17, 1964, BRP, 21, 455; Norman Thomas to Rustin, August 31, 1966, BRP, 13, 228; Floyd McKissick to Rustin, October 10, 1966, BRP, 13, 617; David McReynolds to Rustin, July 2, 1970, BRP, 14, 613; Eleanor Holmes Norton to Bayard Rustin, January 4, 1968, BRP, 21, 997; Oliver Leeds to Bayard Rustin, June 7, 1968, BRP, 21, 1161.

43. John Lewis, *Walking with the Wind: A Memoir of the Movement* (New York: Simon and Schuster, 1998), 286–88, 291.

44. Federal Bureau of Investigation, August 6–September 29, 1964, in O'Reilly and Gallen, *Black Americans*, 397–402; Levine, *Bayard Rustin*, 122, 168–69.

45. Rustin, "'Black Power' and Coalition Politics," 157; D'Emilio, *Lost Prophet*, 420–21. Black "rioters" did not engage in random violence. They attacked pawnshops and liquor stores but spared schools, libraries, and businesses like gas stations that were not associated with exploitation. The riot, he was forced to concede, "marked the first major rebellion of Negroes against their own masochism." Branch, *At Canaan's Edge*, 398.

46. Federal Bureau of Investigation, December 16, 1966, in O'Reilly and Gallen, *Black Americans*, 414–15; Rustin, "'Black Power' and Coalition Politics."

47. Rustin, "'Black Power' and Coalition Politics."

48. Just before the 1963 March on Washington, segregationist Senator Strom Thurmond denounced Rustin as a homosexual. Branch, *Parting the Waters*, 861–62; Bayard Rustin, "In Answer to Senator Thurmond," in *Down the Line*, 109; "An Interview with Bayard Rustin," 5.

49. John Swomley to Glenn Smily, March 1, 1956, BRP, 4, 237; Branch, *Parting the Waters*, 172, 265, 314–15, 329. Just as African American identity cannot be reduced to the scars created by racist oppression, being gay, as John D'Emilio convincingly demonstrates, not only led to Rustin's marginalization by civil rights leaders. It also contributed profoundly to the creativity and insight he brought to his political work. Still, his most significant activism was within the civil rights movement, and he framed his political analysis in terms of race and class. This chapter addresses that activism and analysis. D'Emilio, *Lost Prophet*, 29–30, 76.

50. D'Emilio, *Lost Prophet*, 210; *Brother Outsider: The Life of Bayard Rustin* (South Burlington, Vt.: California Newsreel, 2002).

51. Anderson, *A. Philip Randolph*, 148–49; John O'Neil, interview, in *Schools against Children: The Case for Community Control*, ed. Annette Rubinstein (New York: Monthly Review Press, 1970), 180; David Selden, *The Teacher Rebellion* (Washington, D.C.: Howard University Press, 1985), 15, 29; Maurice Berube, "'Democratic Socialists' and the Schools," *New Politics*, Summer 1969, 58; Israel

Kugler, "A Life in the Workmen's Circle," *Labor Heritage*, October 1991, 36–49. See Perlstein, *Justice, Justice*, 16–18, 24–25, 57–58, for a fuller discussion of social-democratic notions of race. "As a longtime Socialist," Rustin looked "upon the failure of the Socialist Party to make that special appeal as a tragic error" except for which it "might have changed the whole course of the civil rights movement." Still, Rustin's claim that the elimination of Jim Crow made civil rights protest anachronistic implies that Debs erred in stressing the exclusivity of class relations a half-century too soon. Rustin, *Strategies for Freedom*, 8.

52. Bayard Rustin, "The Case of LeRoi Jones," *Amsterdam News*, January 27, 1968, 14.

53. Bayard Rustin, speech to the Plenary Session of the National Jewish Community Relations Advisory Council, June 30–July 3, 1968, in Robert Browne and Bayard Rustin, *Separatism or Integration: Which Way for America?* (New York: A. Philip Randolph Educational Fund, October 1968), 16.

54. Richard Cloward et al., "Educating the Children of the Welfare Poor: A RECORD Symposium," November 3, 1967, in *Teachers College Record* 69 (1968): 304.

55. Rustin, "The Mind of the Black Militant," 209.

56. Brooks, "A Strategist without a Movement," 104.

57. Cloward et al., "Educating the Children of the Welfare Poor," 305.

58. Bayard Rustin, remarks, World without War Conference, May 3, 1968; BRP, 21, 1184.

59. Frank Karelsen to Bayard Rustin, April 5, 1965, BRP, 21, 341; Lynd to Bayard Rustin, April 19, 1965; Rustin to Irving Howe, November 10, 1966, BRP, 13, 115; Rustin to Robert Paehlke, March 15, 1967, BRP, 13, 278; Thomas to Bayard Rustin, August 31, 1966; McReynolds to Rustin, July 2, 1970; Stokely Carmichael to Bayard Rustin, August 16, 1966, BRP, 13, 226; McKissick to Rustin, October 10, 1966; Thomas to Bayard Rustin, August 31, 1966. For a critique of Rustin's assertion that military spending in Vietnam need not affect the funding of antipoverty programs, see Seymour Melman, "Great Society Priorities," *Commonweal*, August 5, 1966, 494–97. Ironically, McCarthy-era government repression of black radicals did much to weaken interracial labor solidarity. Gerald Horne, "Why N.A.A.C.P. Won't Disown Nation of Islam," *New York Times*, January 19, 1994, 20; Gerald Horne, " 'Myth' and the Making of 'Malcolm X,' " *American Historical Review* 98 (1993): 442–48.

60. Rustin, "Integration within Decentralization," 215.

61. Ralph Poynter to Bayard Rustin, April 2, 1968, BRP, 5, 893; Ad Hoc Committee against Racism, "Join the Freedom Picket Line," n.d., BRP, 5, 894.

62. Pfeffer, *A. Philip Randolph, Pioneer*, 198; Anderson, *A. Philip Randolph*, 259–60; Herbert Hill, "Black Dissent in Organized Labor," in *Seasons of Rebellion: Protest and Radicalism in Recent America*, ed. Joseph Boskin (Washington, D.C.: University Press of America, 1980), 74–75; Richard Parrish, "The New

York City Teacher Strikes: Blow to Education, Boon to Racism," 1, 4, mimeographed leaflet, in *Labor Today*, May 1969.

63. "Spanish-Speaking and Black Unionists Move for School Solution," *Daily World*, October 29, 1968, 5; Statement Adopted at a Meeting of 200 Black and Spanish-Speaking Labor Leaders, October 28, 1968, 1–2, Richard Parrish Papers, Other Organizations file: UFT correspondence and papers, Schomburg Center for Research in Black Culture, New York Public Library, New York City; "Negro Unionists Threaten a City Labor Revolt," *New York Times*, November 14, 1968, 1; "Shanker Is Called 'Racist' by Labor Leaders Here," *New York Times*, November 14, 1968, 39.

64. Naomi Levine, *Ocean Hill–Brownsville: Schools in Crisis* (New York: Popular Library, 1969), 5; Milton Galamison, interview, in *Why Teachers Strike: Teachers' Rights and Community Control*, ed. Melvin Urofsky (Garden City, N.Y.: Doubleday, 1970), 305; *A Summary of the 1969 School Decentralization Law for New York City* (New York: Office of Educational Affairs, n.d.).

65. Melvin Zimet, *Decentralization and School Effectiveness: A Case Study of the 1969 Decentralization Law in New York City* (New York: Teachers College Press, 1973), 46; Jim Gelbman, "Evolution of District 12: The Implementation of Public Policy in a Decentralized New York City School District, 1969–1982" (PhD diss., Fordham University, 1984), 254.

66. Perlstein, *Justice, Justice*, 8–9.

67. Jerald Podair, "Like Strangers: Blacks, Whites, and New York City's Ocean Hill–Brownsville Crisis, 1945–1980" (PhD diss., Princeton University, 1997), 9.

68. Marjorie Murphy, *Blackboard Unions: The AFT and the NEA, 1900–1980* (Ithaca, N.Y.: Cornell University Press, 1990), 236–38.

69. John Hull Mollenkopf, "The Postindustrial Transformation of the Political Order in New York City," in *Power, Culture, and Place: Essays on New York City*, ed. John Mollenkopf (New York: Russell Sage, 1988), 225, 227; Norman Fainstein and Susan Fainstein, "Governing Regimes and the Political Economy of Development in New York City, 1946–1984," in Mollenkopf, *Power*, 161–80; Joshua B. Freeman, *Working-Class New York: Life and Labor since World War II* (New York: New Press, 2000), 17–72.

70. Ira Rosenwanke, *Population History of New York City* (Syracuse, N.Y.: Syracuse University Press, 1972); Susan Fainstein and Norman Fainstein, "Economic Change, National Policy and the System of Cities," in *Restructuring the City: The Political Economy of Urban Redevelopment*, ed. Susan Fainstein et al. (New York; Longman, 1987). On urban renewal, highway construction, and suburbanization, see Robert A. Caro, *The Power Broker: Robert Moses and the Fall of New York* (New York: Vintage, 1975); Kenneth T. Jackson, *Crabgrass Frontier: The Suburbanization of the United States* (New York: Oxford University Press, 1985); Herbert Gans, *The Levittowners* (New York: Pantheon, 1967). The years

of the community control conflict were a time when many teachers moved to the suburbs. Perlstein, *Justice, Justice*, 62.

71. D'Emilio, *Lost Prophet*, 473. On African American debates about the relative role of race and class in black oppression, see, for instance, W. E. B. Du Bois, "Marxism and the Negro Problem," *Crisis*, May 1933, 104.

7. The Young Lords and the Social and Structural Roots of Late Sixties Urban Radicalism

Johanna Fernandez

This review of the history and significance of the Young Lords builds on the arguments I put forth in my doctoral dissertation: Johanna Fernandez, "Radicals in the Late 1960s: A History of the Young Lords Party in New York" (PhD diss., Columbia University, 2005). My work builds upon the following pioneering works on the Young Lords: Frank Browning, "From Rumble to Revolution: The Young Lords," in *The Puerto Rican Experience*, ed. Eugene Cordasco and Eugene Bucchioni (Totowa, N.J.: Littlefield, Adams, 1973), 231–45; Jennifer Lee, "The Young Lords, a New Generation of Puerto Ricans: An Oral History," *Culturefront* 3, no. 3 (Fall 1994): 64–70; Agustin Lao, "Resources of Hope: Imagining the Young Lords and the Politics of Memory," *Centro* 7, no. 1 (1995): 34–49; Suzanne Oboler, "Establishing an Identity in the Sixties: The Mexican-American / Chicano and Puerto Rican Movements," in Susan Oboler, *Ethnic Labels, Latino Lives: Identity and the Politics of (Re)presentation in the United States*, (Minneapolis: University of Minnesota Press, 1995), chap. 4; Carmen Teresa Whalen, "Bridging Homeland and Barrio Politics: The Young Lords in Philadelphia," in *The Puerto Rican Movement: Voices from the Diaspora*, ed. Andres Torres and Jose E. Velazquez (Philadelphia: Temple University Press, 1998), chap. 7. Retrospective accounts by former Young Lord activists have also contributed greatly to my work: Pablo Guzmán, "Puerto Rican Barrio Politics in the United States," in *The Puerto Rican Struggle: Essays on Survival in the U.S.*, ed. Clara Rodriguez, Virginia Sanchez Korrol, and Jose Oscar Alers (Maplewood, N.J.: Waterfront Press, 1984), 121–28; Pablo Guzmán, "Ain't No Party Like the One We Got: The Young Lords Party and *Palante*," in *Voices from the Underground: Insider Histories of the Vietnam Era*, vol. 1, ed. Ken Wachsberger (Tempe, Ariz.: Mica Press, 1993), 293–304; and Pablo Guzmán, "La Vida Pura: A Lord of the Barrio," and Iris Morales, "¡Palante, Siempre Palante! The Young Lords," in Torres and Velazquez, *The Puerto Rican Movement*; Mickey Miguel Melendez, *We Took the Streets: Fighting for Latino Rights and the Young Lords* (New York: St. Martin's Press, 2003).

1. During most of the colonial period, Puerto Rico functioned primarily as a military outpost and had a diverse nonsegregated population consisting of a small number of slaves and Native Americans, a substantial number of freemen of color and poor white tenant farmers, and government officials. In Puerto

Rico, rigid racial demarcations did not form part of the New World colony's social fabric, in part because the slave plantation system was not a central feature of the island's economy. When a plantation economy did develop in the nineteenth century, severe labor shortages led to compulsory labor laws, which forced white land squatters to work alongside slaves and freemen of color in the fields. This development encouraged racial mixing and blurred racial differences as black slaves and white and colored laborers were compelled to intermingle with one another in the fields, an arrangement that eventually led each to find common cause with the other. See Sidney Mintz, *Caribbean Transformations* (New York: Columbia University Press, 1989), 82–94. For a discussion of racial ideology in the United States, see Barbara Jeanne Fields, "Ideology and Race in American History," in *Region, Race and Reconstruction: Essays in Honor of C. Vann Woodward*, ed. J. Morgan Kousser and James M. McPherson (New York: Oxford University Press, 1982), 143–77, and Barbara Jeanne Fields, "Slavery, Race and Ideology in the USA," *New Left Review* 181 (1990): 95–118.

2. Johanna Fernández, "Between Social Service Reform and Revolutionary Politics: The Young Lords, Late Sixties Radicalism, and Community Organizing in New York City," in *Freedom North: Black Freedom Struggles outside of the South, 1940–1980*, ed. Jeanne Theoharis and Komozi Woodard (New York: Palgrave Macmillan, 2003).

3. For a discussion of Chicago gangs, see Andrew Diamond, "Hoodlums, Rebels, and Vice Lords: Street Gangs, Youth Subcultures, and Race in Chicago, 1919–1969" (PhD diss., University of Michigan, 2004), and Frederic Milton Thrasher, *The Gang: A Study of 1,313 Gangs in Chicago* (Chicago: University of Chicago Press, 1963).

4. Henry "Poison" Gaddis, interview by author, January 2007, Chapel Hill, North Carolina.

5. Charles E. Jones, ed., *The Black Panther Party Reconsidered* (New York: Black Classic Press, 1998).

6. Frank Browning, "From Rumble to Revolution: The Young Lords," in *The Puerto Rican Experience*, ed. Eugene Cordasco and Eugene Bucchioni (Totowa, N.J.: Littlefield, Adams, 1973), 232.

7. These included New York State's Educational Opportunity Program and the Search for Education, Elevation, and Knowledge (SEEK) program conducted in public universities and the Higher Educational Opportunity Program in private colleges. For a fuller discussion, see Clara Beatrice Sargeant, "Project Demonstrating Excellence: An Examination of the First Eight Years of the SEEK Program at Bernard M. Baruch College, 1969–1977" (PhD diss., Union Graduate School, 1978).

8. Chapters of the Puerto Rican Student Union at Queens and Herbert Lehman Colleges, in particular, provided resolute leadership to the nascent Puerto Rican student movement in New York by insisting that the political scope of protests be broadened. The most politically conscious elements of this

group linked their particular grievances to the movement for Puerto Rican independence and to the mounting struggles at the University of Puerto Rico against on-campus military recruitment for the Vietnam War. Alfredo Lopez, *The Puerto Rican Papers: Notes on the Re-emergence of a Nation* (New York: Bobbs-Merrill, 1973), 320.

9. Michael Abramson, *Palante: Young Lords Party* (New York: McGraw-Hill, 1971), 8; Lopez, *Puerto Rican Papers*, 324.

10. For a discussion of the Chicago Lords and their activities, see Browning, "From Rumble to Revolution," 231–45.

11. "Interview with Cha Cha Jimenez Chairman of the Young Lords Organization," *Black Panther*, June 7, 1969, 17.

12. Abramson, *Palante: The Young Lords Party*, 9. According to Pablo Guzmán, the Lower East Side chapter of the Young Lords was formed without the consent of the founding Chicago group. Guzmán, "Ain't No Party Like the One We Got," 296.

13. Hiram Maristany, interview by author, summer 2001, New York.

14. Luciano and Maristany, "The Young Lords Party, 1969–1975" (1983), 7; Lao, "Resources of Hope," 36.

15. Morales, "¡Palante, Siempre, Palante!" 214–15.

16. For a fuller discussion, see Ramon Grosfoguel, *Colonial Subjects: Puerto Ricans in a Global Perspective* (Berkeley: University of California Press, 2003), chap. 5.

17. Jack Bloom, *Class, Race, and the Civil Rights Movement: The Changing Political Economy of Southern Racism* (Bloomington: Indiana University Press, 1987), 200; Marable, *Race, Reform, and Rebellion*, 92–93; United States, Kerner Commission, *Report of the National Advisory Commission on Civil Disorders* (Washington, D.C.: Superintendent of Documents, U.S. Government, 1968), 144.

18. Homer Bigart, "Disorders Erupt in East Harlem; Mobs Dispersed," *New York Times*, July 24, 1967, 1, 17.

19. Sylvan Fox, "Police the Target of Ghetto Wrath," *New York Times*, July 24, 1967, 17; "El Barrio Woes Told by Figures," *New York Times*, July 24, 1967, 17.

20. Peter Khiss, "Causes Pondered by Puerto Ricans," *New York Times*, July 25, 1967, 18.

21. Homer Bigart, "2 Killed, 12 Injured," *New York Times*, July 25, 1967, 1, 18; Homer Bigart, "Renewed Violence Erupts in 2 Puerto Rican Areas," *New York Times*, July 26, 1967, 1, 20.

22. "The Puerto Ricans: Behind the Flare-Up," *New York Times*, July 30, 1967, sec. 4, 1; McCandlish Phillips, "Residents of East Harlem Found to Have Ingredients for Violence," *New York Times*, July 27, 1967, 20.

23. Bigart, "2 Killed, 12 Injured," 18.

24. Ibid.; Cannato, 135.

25. "Causes Pondered by Puerto Ricans," *New York Times*, July 25, 1967, 18.

26. Ira Katnelson, *City Trenches: Urban Politics and the Patterning of Class in the United States* (New York: Pantheon Books, 1981), 137; Lindsay, *The City*, 118.

27. Barry Gottehrer, interview by author, January 2005, Washington, D.C.

28. Vincent J. Cannato, *The Ungovernable City: John Lindsay and His Struggle to Save New York* (New York: Basic, 2001), 130.

29. United States Department of Labor, Bureau of Labor Statistics, "Labor Force Experience of the Puerto Rican Worker," *Middle Atlantic Region, Regional Report* no. 9 (June 1968): 13; Joshua Freeman, *Working Class New York: Life and Labor Since World War II* (New York: The New Press, 2000), 183–85.

30. Thomas J. Sugrue, *The Origins of the Urban Crisis: Race and Inequality in Postwar Detroit* (Princeton, N.J.: Princeton University Press, 1996).

31. Bloom, *Class, Race, and the Civil Rights Movement*, chaps. 2 and 3. On the early civil rights movement in New York, see Martha Biondi, *To Stand and Fight: The Struggle for Civil Rights in Postwar New York City* (Cambridge, Mass.: Harvard University Press, 2003).

32. Although service industry jobs replaced blue-collar employment, the process of structural economic conversion failed to absorb large swaths of the urban population into the national economy. As early as the 1960s, the Department of Labor began to track the percentages of displaced workers using a new concept called "subemployment," a statistical index for tracking people who were either unemployed, underemployed, or permanently out of the labor force for lack of success finding employment. USDL, "Labor Force Experience of the Puerto Rican Worker": 21.

33. Arnold R. Hirsch, *Making the Second Ghetto: Race and Housing in Chicago, 1940–1960* (Cambridge: Cambridge University Press, 1983).

34. I am adapting, to the urban environment, an analysis of the general character of 1960s protesters articulated in Michael Denning, *Culture in the Age of Three Worlds* (New York: Verso, 2004), 43.

35. Morales, "¡Palante, Siempre, Palante!" 214–15.

36. Phillip Foner, *The Black Panthers Speak* (New York: Lippincott, 1970), 2–4.

37. Denning, *Culture in the Age of Three Worlds*, 43.

38. "One Year of Struggle," *Palante* 2, no. 8 (July 31, 1970): centerfold. Tamiment Library, New York University.

39. Murray Schumach, "Seas of Garbage Engulf Islands on Broadway," *New York Times*, September 3, 1969, 1; Joseph P. Fried, "East Harlem Youths Explain Garbage-Dumping Demonstrations," *New York Times*, August 19, 1969, 86; Carl Davidson, "Young Lords Organize New York," *Guardian*, October 18, 1969, 6. For a reference to the series of demonstration held by the YLP, see also "Plastic Bags Given East Harlem in War on Garbage Pile Up," *New York Times*, September 13, 1969, 33.

40. Joseph Fried, "Paint-Poisoning Danger to Children Fought," *New York Times*, March 2, 1969, sec. 6, 1, 8; "Lead Poisoning Is Affecting 112,000 Children Annually, Specialists Report," *New York Times*, March 26, 1969, 23. For

more precise figures, see Gary Eidsvold, Anthony Mustalish, and Lloyd F. No-
vick, "The New York City Department of Health: Lesson in Lead Poisoning
Control Program," *American Journal of Public Health* 64, no. 10 (October 1974):
959. The last document was replicated as a pamphlet by the New York City
Department of Health, Vertical File, New York City, Poisoning, Lead (1970s
Folder), Municipal Archives of the City of New York.

41. Juan Gonzalez, quoted in *El Pueblo Se Levanta: The People Are Rising*,
videorecording (New York: Third World Newsreel, 1970); also quoted in "The
Young Lords," recording by Elizabeth Perez-Luna, Pacifica Radio Archives,
1977.

42. For a discussion of the Young Lords' "Lincoln Offensive," see Johanna
Fernandez, "The Young Lords and the Postwar City: Notes on the Geographical
and Structural Reconfigurations of Contemporary Urban Life," in Kenneth
Kusmer and Joe W. Trotter, eds., *African American Urban History Since World War
II* (Chicago: University of Chicago Press, 2009), 60–82.

43. "Bronx Conflict Focused on Community Control," *Hospital Tribune* 3,
no. 9 (n.d.): 1, 20, D. Samuel Gotteson Library, Yeshiva University, Albert Ein-
stein College of Medicine Archives, Lincoln Hospital Papers and Vertical File,
1960–1975; Fitzhugh Mullan, *White Coat, Clenched Fist: The Political Education
of an American Physician* (New York: Macmillan, 1976); Cleo Silvers and Danny
Argote, "Think Lincoln," *Palante,* July 3, 1970, 2, 16; Ellen Frankfort, "The
Community's Role in Healing a Hospital," *Village Voice*, November 26, 1970,
12, 14; "Lords Liberate Hospital," *Old Mole*, August 7, 1970, 5; Alfonzo A.
Narvaez, "Young Lords Seize Lincoln Hospital Building," *New York Times*, July
15 1970, 34.

44. On the popularity of the organization see Juan Gonzalez, interview by
Columbia University Oral History Program, New York, 1988, 61. This is the
most complete publicly accessible oral history of any member of the organization
to date.

8. "Brooklyn College Belongs to Us": Black Students and the Transformation of Public Higher Education in New York City

Martha Biondi

1. "CUNY contains the largest number of black and Latino scholars ever to
attend a single university in the history of the United States. The importance of
CUNY as a source of opportunity for non-white students and their communities
is highlighted by the fact that CUNY traditionally awards the largest number of
master's degrees to black and Latino students of any institution in America. Last
year CUNY conferred 1,011 master's degrees to black and Latino students while
the State University of New York awarded only 233." Ronald B. McGuire,
"The Struggle at CUNY: Open Admissions and Civil Rights," http://leftspot
.com/blog/?q = book/export.html (accessed November 24, 2010).

2. Much has been written about open admissions; see, for example, David
E. Lavin, Richard D. Alba, and. Richard A. Silberstein, *Right versus Privilege: The
Open Admissions Experiment at the City University of New York* (New York: Free

Press, 1981). But scholars of the civil rights and Black Power movements have neglected or ignored it. See for example, Harvard Sitkoff, *The Struggle for Black Equality: 1954–1992* (New York: Hill and Wang, 1993), and, more recently, Peniel E. Joseph, *Waiting 'til the Midnight Hour: A Narrative History of Black Power in America* (New York: Henry Holt, 2006).

3. Conrad M. Dyer, "Protest and the Politics of Open Admissions: The Impact of the Black and Puerto Rican Students' Community (of City College)" (PhD diss., City University of New York, 1990), 193.

4. Bart Meyers, "Radical Struggle for Open Admissions at CUNY," *Kingsman*, February 27, 1976. In 1968, 192 black students entered as part of a new Educational Opportunity Program. Others came through SEEK, which by early 1969 made up of 470 students. Another new 1968 initiative was the One Hundred Scholars program, where the top one hundred graduates of each high school were automatically accepted to college. Forty-five of these students chose Brooklyn College. Still, according to one student who entered that year, black enrollment in the liberal arts college was only 1 percent. *New York Times,* May 21, 1968; Duncan Pardue to Franklin Williams, February 5, 1969, Institute of the Black World Papers, box: Survey of Black Studies Programs, folder: Brooklyn College, Schomburg Center for Research in Black Culture, New York Public Library; Orlando Pile, telephone interview by author, June 30, 2005.

5. United States Congress, Senate Committee on Government Operations, Permanent Subcommittee on Investigations, *Riots, Civil and Criminal Disorders,* 91st Cong., 1st sess. (Washington, D.C.: Government Printing Office, 1969), 5193.

6. Students at City College advocated admitting black and Puerto Rican students in proportion to their presence in local high schools. They also called for access for poor whites as well and said they should constitute 20 percent of the freshmen class, reflecting their presence in the local high school population. Students at Brooklyn College called for the admission of all black and Puerto Rican applicants, regardless of their scholastic record.

7. Duncan Pardue to Franklin Williams, February 5, 1969.

8. Askia Davis, interview by author, July 19, 2005, New York City.

9. Pile interview; Davis interview. The president said he "deplored racism but procedures of academic freedom must be maintained." Only the Board of Higher Education, he said, could take action on specific evidence of racism. Bart Meyers, "Radical Struggle for Open Admissions at CUNY," *Kingsman,* February 27, 1976.

10. At City College, SEEK professor Fran Geteles said that the students there "were very sensitive to the issues of under-preparedness and were not asking for indiscriminate entrance." Conrad Dyer found that many former student activists reiterated this point in interviews. See Dyer, "Protest and the Politics of Open Admissions," 103.

11. *Riots, Civil and Criminal Disorders,* 5197–99.

12. Pile interview.

13. *Kingsman,* April 23, 1969.

14. Meyers, "Radical Struggle."
15. Davis interview.
16. Ibid.; *New York Times*, May 1, 1969.
17. *Riots, Civil and Criminal Disorders*, 5203.
18. *New York Times*, May 14, 1969; *Kingsman* (special edition), May 12, 1969; Davis interview; Pile interview.
19. Davis interview.
20. *New York Post*, May 13, 1969, Five Demands Conflict Collection, box 2, University Archives and Special Collections, City College of New York (hereafter CCNY).
21. *New York Daily News*, May 14, 1969.
22. Ibid.; *Kingsman*, May 16, 1969; Davis interview. Ironically, Dr. Matthews also went to jail in 1969—for refusing to pay federal income tax. An outspoken advocate of self-help and black capitalism, Matthews, the first black neurosurgeon in the United States, said he gave his taxes to his organization, NEGRO, rather than to pay for welfare programs. President Nixon commuted the six-month sentence after sixty-nine days. *New York Times*, April 2, 1973.
23. *Kingsman*, February 27, 1970, and March 6, 1970; Judge Rinaldi said the indictments would be dismissed after six months "if they behaved." Things didn't turn out as well for the prosecutor or the judge. In 1983 Eugene Gold, who was Brooklyn district attorney from 1968 to 1981, admitted to "unlawful sexual fondling" of a ten-year-old girl—the daughter of an Alabama prosecutor—in a Nashville hotel room during a convention of district attorneys. And Judge Dominic Rinaldi was suspended from the bench after being indicted for perjury in 1973, although a jury later acquitted him. See "Gold Gets Probation in Fondling of Child; Agrees to Treatment," *New York Times*, October 21, 1983, and "Dominic Rinaldi Dies: A Retired Justice," *New York Times*, November 27, 1983.
24. "STRIKE!" editorial, *Kingsman*, May 12, 1969.
25. *Riots, Civil and Criminal Disorders*, 5191.
26. Sekou Sundiata (formerly Robert Feaster), interview transcript, n.d., Legacy of Struggle Collection, box 1, CCNY.
27. "Chronology of a Crisis," n.d., Legacy of Struggle Collection, box 1, CCNY; Sundiata interview.
28. These statistics describe 1967. Dyer, "Protest and the Politics of Open Admissions," 64. This was the first official ethnic census conducted at CUNY schools.
29. Barbara Christian, "City College Saga Part 2: Dual Admissions," *Inside and Outside the Plaza*, n.d., reprinted from *Harlem News,* June 1969, Legacy of Struggle Collection, box 2, CCNY.
30. The Black and Puerto Rican Student Community to the faculty and students of City College, press release, April 26, 1969, Five Demands Conflict Collection, box 4, CCNY. Conrad's spouse, the writer Adrienne Rich, also taught at CCNY and was a supporter of the student activists. Frances Geteles, telephone interview by author, August 29, 2007.

31. Barbara Christian, "City College Saga Part 2: Dual Admissions," *Inside and Outside the Plaza*, n.d., reprinted from *Harlem News*, June 1969, Legacy of Struggle Collection, box 2, CCNY.

32. Dyer, "Protest and the Politics of Open Admissions," 98; Toni Cade, "Realizing the Dream of the Black University," *Observation Post*, February 14, 1969, Martha Weisman Papers, Open Admissions folder, CCNY. In 1970 Toni Cade became Toni Cade Bambara.

33. See, for example, Steve Estes, *I Am a Man! Race, Manhood and the Civil Rights Movement* (Chapel Hill: University of North Carolina Press, 2005).

34. Miss Cade to "Dear Bloods," n.d., Five Demands Conflict Collection, Public Relations folder, CCNY.

35. Toni Cade, "Realizing the Dream of the Black University," *Observation Post*, February 14, 1969, Martha Weisman Papers, Open Admissions folder, CCNY.

36. Barbara Christian, "City College Saga: Lesson in Democracy," *Inside and Outside the Plaza*, August–September 1969, Legacy of Struggle Collection, box 2, CCNY.

37. Alecia Edwards-Sibley, "The Five Demands," *Paper*, April 2002, Martha Weisman Papers, Strike of 1969 folder, CCNY.

38. Black and Puerto Rican Student Community, "Queries and Answers on Demands #1 and #4," May 28, 1969, Five Demands Conflict Collection, box 7, CCNY.

39. There was some overlap—Betty Rawls and Barbara Christian were in both groups. Geteles interview.

40. See Clayborne Carson, *In Struggle: SNCC and the Black Awakening of the 1960s* (Cambridge, Mass.: Harvard University Press, 1981).

41. Carlos Russell, interview by author, June 11, 2005, New York City.

42. Bart Meyers, "Radical Struggle for Open Admissions at CUNY"; "Talk of the Town," *New Yorker*, May 3, 1969, in Legacy of Struggle Collection, box 1, CCNY; Davis interview.

43. WCBS Transcript, "Campus Disruption—II," April 23, 1969, Five Demands Conflict Collection, Public Relations folder, CCNY.

44. *New York Post*, April 30, 1969, Five Demands Conflict Collection, box 1, CCNY.

45. *New York Times*, May 1, 1969.

46. Transcript of film (unfinished), Legacy of Struggle Collection, box 2, CCNY.

47. Bart Meyers, "Radical Struggle for Open Admissions at CUNY," *Kingsman*, February 27, 1976.

48. *New York Post*, May 10, 1969, Five Demands Conflict Collection, box 1, CCNY.

49. Editorial, *Daily News*, May 10, 1969, Five Demands Conflict Collection, box 1, CCNY; *New York Post*, June 13, 1969, Five Conflict Collection, box 1, CCNY.

50. *New York Times*, May 18, 1969.

51. *New York Times*, May 5, 6, and 25, 1969; Davis interview.

52. Allen B. Ballard, *The Education of Black Folk: The Afro-American Struggle for Knowledge in White America* (New York: Harper and Row, 1973), 127, 141.

53. Dyer, "Protest and the Politics of Open Admissions," 176.

54. "Urban and Ethnic Studies Dept. Created," *Campus*, September 2, 1969, Martha Weisman Papers, CCNY.

55. "A Negro Professor at C.C.N.Y. Charges Slander," *New York Times*, September 20, 1969.

56. Dr. Pile graduated in 1972, attended medical school at Rutgers University, and did his internship and residency at MLK/Drew Medical Center in Los Angeles. Askia Davis is an administrator for the New York Public School system. He has served as special assistant to three chancellors.

57. Davis interview; Pile interview.

58. Russell interview; Memorandum, n.d., and "Report of the Committee to Evaluate the School for Contemporary Studies at Brooklyn College," March 1976, Information Files, #91–021; folder: BC—Schools—School for Contemporary Studies, Brooklyn College Special Collections and University Archive.

59. "Dean Quitting CCNY Post Tells Why," *New York Post,* May 28, 1969.

60. Ed Quinn and Leonard Kriegal, "How the Dream Was Deferred," *Nation,* April 7, 1984, 412–14.

61. Albert H. Bowker, oral history by Harriet Niathon, September 6, 1991, Bancroft Library, University of California, Berkeley.

62. Martha Weisman, "Legacy of Student Activism at the City College," April 21, 1989, Legacy of Struggle Collection, CCNY.

63. Geteles interview.

64. Frank Rich, quoted in Quinn and Kriegal, "How the Dream Was Deferred," 412.

65. Dyer, "Protest and the Politics of Open Admissions," 184.

66. *Closing the Door: The Fight for a College Education,* a film by Ellie Bernstein, c. 1999, CCNY; Kelechi Onwuchekwa, "The Truth behind Open Admissions," *The Paper,* April 2002, Martha Weisman Papers, CCNY.

67. Barbara Christian, "City College Saga Part 2: Dual Admissions," *Inside and Outside the Plaza*, reprinted from *Harlem News,* June 1969, Legacy of Struggle Collection, box 2, CCNY.

68. See Martha Biondi, *To Stand and Fight: The Struggle for Civil Rights in Postwar New York City* (Cambridge, Mass.: Harvard University Press, 2003).

9. Racial Events, Diplomacy, and Dinkins's Image

Wilbur C. Rich

1. See M. A. Farber, "Black-Korean Who-Pushed-Whom Festers," *New York Times*, May 7, 1990, B1.

2. See Claire Jean Kim, *Bitter Fruit* (Chicago: University of Chicago Press, 2000).

3. Howard Kurtz, "Bonfire of Inanities: How News Fuel Racial Tension," *Washington Post*, May 10, 1990, B1.

4. See Don Terry, "Diplomacy Falls to End Store Boycott in Flatbush," *New York Times*, July 16, 1990, B1

5. Farber, "Black-Korean Who-Pushed-Whom Festers."

6. See Kim, *Bitter Fruit*, 2.

7. Russell W. Baker, "New York's Korean Grocery Turmoil Rooted in Cultural and Economic Conditions" *Christian Science Monitor*, May 31, 1990, 7.

8. Kim, *Bitter Fruit*, 11.

9. "All for the Price of a Lime," *Economist*, May 19, 1990, 31

10. "Sonny Carson, Koreans and Racism," *New York Times*, May 8, 1990, A28.

11. Ibid.

12. Cited in David Seifman and Rita Delfiner, "Ed: I'd Personally Bust Boycott of Korean," *New York Post*, May 10 1990, 3.

13. Sam Roberts, "Metro Matters: Which Mayor Knows Best on the Boycott?" *New York Times*, July 30, 1990, B1.

14. Todd Purdum, "Dinkins Steps up Criticism of Brooklyn Protesters," *New York Times*, May 10, 1990, B3.

15. Sam Roberts, "From an Unlikely Source, Praise for Koch," *New York Times*, February 2, 1990, 61.

16. Todd Purdum, "Judge Critical of Dinkins over Boycott," *New York Times*, May 11, 1990, B1.

17. Ibid.

18. Rita Delfiner, "Dave 'Diplomat' on Korean Boycott," *New York Post*, May 9, 1990, 7.

19. Ari L. Goldman, "Racial Unity and Dissent in Brooklyn," *New York Times*, May 18, 1990.

20. William W. Sales Jr. and Rod Bush, "The Political Awakening of Blacks and Latinos in New York City: Competition or Cooperation?" *Social Justice* 27, no. 1 (2000): 28.

21. Ibid.

22. Ibid.

23. Ibid.

24. "Talking Like a Leader," *New York Times*, May 13, 1990, 18.

25. Reported in Rita Delfiner, David Seifman, and Karen Phillip, "Raves and Raspberries for Dinkins Speech," *New York Post*, May 12, 1990, 5.

26. Todd Purdum, "Dinkins Asks for Racial Unity and Offers to Mediate Boycott," *New York Times*, May 12, 1990, 1.

27. "This City Is Sick of Violence: Dinkins's Address," *New York Times*, May 12, 1990, A1.

28. The comment got coverage in several out-of-town media outlets. See "Korean Store at Center of Racial Strife," *St. Petersburg Times*, May 17, 1990, 1A.

29. Jim Sleeper, *The Closest of Strangers* (New York: Norton, 1990), 301.

30. David Gonzalez, "Koreans See a Gain from Boycott: Unity," *New York Times*, September 25, 1990, 3.

31. Don Terry, "Dinkins to Ask State Inquiry on 2d Boycott," *New York Times*, August 29, 1990, B1.

32. Lee Daniels, "U.S. Report Faults Mayor on Boycott," *New York Times*, February 28, 1992 B1.

33. Gonzalez, "Koreans See a Gain from Boycott."

34. Larry Simonberg, "For Mayor Dinkins: A Few Don'ts," *Daily News*, October 7, 1990, 47.

35. Miguel Garalazo, Rocco Parascandola, David Seifman, Anne E. Murray, and Don Broderick, "Race Riot in Brooklyn," *New York Post*, August 22, 1991, 19.

36. Ibid.

37. Dean Chang, "Fatal Crash Inflamed Old Feelings," *Daily News*, August 21, 1991, 6.

38. Mike McAlary, "Hate Lines Both Sides of Eastern Parkway Gantlet," *New York Post*, August 21, 1991, 191.

39. David Dinkins, interview, October 14, 2002.

40. David Seufnab, "Unmarked Cop Car Led Rabbi Convoy," *New York Post*, August 22, 1991, 3.

41. Ibid.

42. Miguel Garalazo et al., "Anarchy Grips Crown Heights," *New York Post*, August 22, 1991, 2.

43. Ibid.

44. Dinkins, interview.

45. Bill Lynch, telephone interview, January 21, 2005.

46. Ellen Tumposky, "Dinkins Watches, Waits: No Tour of Areas for Now," *New York Daily News*, August 21, 1991, 32.

47. Ibid.

48. Joel Sigel and Ruth Landa, "Insults, Bottles Fly," *New York Daily News*, August 22, 1991, 27.

49. Don Singleton, "In the Melting Pot, It's Hot Ethnic Stew," *New York Daily News*, August 21, 1991, 6.

50. "Streets of Rage," *New York Daily News*, August 22, 1991, 1.

51. Bob Herbert, "Blood Feud in Crown Heights," *New York Daily News*, August 22, 1991, 2.

52. "Cooling Crown Heights Is a Long Term Job," *New York Daily News*, August 22, 1991, 3.

53. Earl Caldwell, "The Fire Next Time Is Alarmingly Near," *New York Daily News*, August 13, 1991, 32.

54. Charles Sennott, "Dinkins Mourns Mosaic's Tiles," *New York Daily News*, August 26, 1991, 21.

55. Ellen Tumposky, "After Week of Tension, Dinkins Left City Hall to Watch US Open," *New York Daily News*, August 27, 1991, 15.

56. "Crown Heights: Crisis Not Over Yet," *New York Daily News*, August 27, 1991, 32.

57. Eric Breindel, "Race and Riot in New York," *Wall Street Journal*, November 18, 1992, A16.

58. David Remnick, "Waiting for the Apocalypse in Crown Heights," *New Yorker,* December 21, 1992, 52–57.

59. Joel Sigel, "For Me, It's a Lose-Lose," *New York Daily News*, August 28, 1991, 5.

60. Ibid.

61. Wayne Barrett, "Dinkins Dilemma," *Village Voice*, December 1, 1992, 1.

62. Ibid.

63. Martin Gottlieb, "Report for Cuomo Cited a Chain of Failures in 1991 Disturbances," *New York Times*, July 21, 1993, 1.

64. Leland Jones, interview.

65. Herb Boyd, "Crown Heights Report Exonerates Mayor Dinkins from Any Blame," *New York Amsterdam News*, July 3, 1993, 3.

66. Wilbert Tatum, "Governor's Report on Crown Heights: A Redundancy at Best," *New York Amsterdam News*, July 24, 1993, 1.

67. Martin Gottlieb, "The Crown Heights Report: The Overview; Crown Heights Study Finds Dinkins and Police at Fault in Letting Unrest Escalate," *New York Times*, July 21, 1993, A1.

68. Bob Herbert, "Blood Feud in Crown Heights."

69. David Dinkins, "Reason, Respect and Reconciliation in New York City," *New York Amsterdam News*, November 28, 1992, 12.

70. Michael Tomasky, "How Dave Botched Crown Heights," *Village Voice*, November 24, 1992, 13.

71. Sam Roberts, interview, March 15, 2001.

72. Carol Conaway, "Framing Identity: The Press in Crown Heights" (John F. Kennedy School of Government Research Paper R-16, Cambridge, Mass., December 1996).

73. *CBS Morning News,* November 26, 1992.

74. Ibid.

75. Albert Scardino, telephone interview, June 25, 2004.

76. "Race Relations," *The MacNeil/Lehrer NewsHour*, Transcript 3735 (May 18, 1990).

77. Ibid.

78. David Dinkins maintained this position in our interview.

79. Ibid.

80. Kim, *Bitter Fruit*.

81. Ibid.

82. "Summer in the City: Boiling Point: Korean Grocers Meet with Attorney in Attempt to Crush Boycott," *48 Hours,* July 12, 1990.

83. Todd Purdum, "Maze of Troubles Posing Challenges to Power and Popularity of Dinkins," *New York Times,* January 16, 1991, B3.

84. "New York Mayor Dinkins Faulted," *News India-Times,* November 20, 1992, 55.

85. James Besser, "Crown Heights and Beyond: Is the Tension between Blacks and Jews in Brooklyn the Harbinger of a National Crisis?" *Baltimore Jewish Times,* December 25, 1992, 36.

86. David Dinkins, interview.

87. Ibid.

88. Gottlieb, "The Crown Heights Report."

89. Wayne Barrett, "Girgenti's Ghostwriter: How Cuomo Shaped the Report," *Village Voice,* August 2, 1993, 1.

90. Paul Delaney, interview, February 1, 2001.

91. David Dinkins, interview.

92. Debra Cohen, "Dinkins Asks G. A. Leaders for Help in Healing Rift with Black Community," Jewish Telegraphic Agency, November 13, 1992, 12.

93. "Mayor Dinkins, Blacks, Jews: A Turning Point?" *New York Amsterdam News,* November 21, 1992, 12.

94. David Saperstein, "The Paradox of Crown Heights: Situation Unique, Lessons Universal," Jewish Telegraphic Agency, December 18, 1992. 12.

95. Herbert Daughtry, *No Monopoly on Suffering: Blacks and Jews in Crown Heights* (Trenton, N.J.: Africa World, 1997), 263.

96. Mike McAlary, "Dave Lets City Wound Fester," *New York Post,* August 23, 1991, 7.

10. "One City, One Standard": The Struggle for Equality in Rudolph Giuliani's New York

Jerald Podair

1. See Martha Biondi, "How New York Changes the Story of the Civil Rights Movement," *Afro-Americans in New York Life and History* 31 (July 2007): 15–31.

2. Ibid.

3. Quoted in Vincent J. Cannato, *The Ungovernable City: John Lindsay and His Struggle to Save New York* (New York: Basic Books, 2001), 403.

4. Eric Foner, *Free Soil, Free Labor, Free Men: The Ideology of the Republican Party before the Civil War* (New York: Oxford University Press, 1970), 30.

5. See Jerald E. Podair, *The Strike That Changed New York: Blacks, Whites, and the Ocean Hill–Brownsville Crisis* (New Haven, Conn.: Yale University Press, 2002), 203.

6. Fred Siegel, *The Prince of the City: Giuliani, New York and the Genius of American Life* (San Francisco: Encounter Books, 2005), 156.

7. See Henry Hampton and Steve Fayer, *Voices of Freedom: An Oral History of the Civil Rights Movement from the 1950s through the 1980s* (New York: Bantam Books, 1990), 244, 254–55.

8. Rudolph Giuliani, *Leadership* (New York: Hyperion, 2002), xi.

9. Ibid., 360, 86.

10. See Jacob Laksin, "The *Times* vs. Rudy," July 31, 2007, FrontPage Magazine.com.

11. Giuliani's autobiography, *Leadership*, does not contain a single reference to Sharpton in its 380 pages.

12. Quoted in Andrew Kirtzman, *Rudy Giuliani: Emperor of the City* (New York: William Morrow, 2000), 73.

13. Giuliani, *Leadership*, 77.

14. Ibid., 381.

15. Ibid., 178, 78.

16. Ibid., 381; Siegel, *The Prince of the City*, 187.

17. Quoted in Kirtzman, *Rudy Giuliani: Emperor of the City*, 186.

18. Giuliani, *Leadership*, xi.

19. Wayne Barrett, *Rudy! An Investigative Biography of Rudolph Giuliani* (New York: Basic Books, 2000), 334. See also *Giuliani Time*, DVD, directed by Kevin Keating (Los Angeles: Cinema Libre Studio, 2005).

20. Kirtzman, *Rudy Giuliani: Emperor of the City*, 246.

21. Ibid., 249–50, 247.

22. Barrett, *Rudy!* 332.

23. Quinnipiac College Polling Institute, Quinnipiac College New York City Poll, April 19, 2000, http://www.quinnipiac.edu/x1302.xml.

24. Quinnipiac College Polling Institute, Quinnipiac College New York City Poll, April 8, 1999, http://www.quinnipiac.edu/x1302.xml.

25. The officers involved in the Diallo shooting were tried on criminal charges and acquitted in February 2000 by an upstate New York jury that included four blacks.

26. Quinnipiac College Polling Institute, Quinnipiac College New York City Poll, April 8, 1999, http://www.quinnipiac.edu/x1302.xml.

27. Black and white reactions to police behaviors were virtually mirror opposites. In 1999, 71 percent of whites and 20 percent of blacks in a Quinnipiac College New York City Poll approved of the way the city's police were doing their jobs, with 23 percent of whites and 71 percent of blacks disapproving. The next year, whites approved of Giuliani's anticrime policies by 67 to 27 percent; blacks disapproved by 27 to 67 percent. See Quinnipiac College Polling Institute, Quinnipiac College New York City Poll, June 17, 1999, and April 19, 2000, http://www.quinnipiac.edu/x1302.xml.

28. Quinnipiac College Polling Institute, Quinnipiac College New York City Poll, June 17, 1999, http://www.quinnipiac.edu/x1302.xml.

29. Maurice Carroll, quoted in Quinnipiac College Polling Institute, Quinnipiac College New York City Poll, March 15, 2000, http://www.quinnipiac.edu/x1302.xml.

30. Siegel, *The Prince of the City*, xii.

31. See Robert Polner, *America's Mayor, America's President? The Strange Career of Rudy Giuliani* (New York: Soft Skull Press, 2007), 42.

32. Jonathan P. Hicks, "Giuliani Tells Blacks His Budget Won't Cut into the Gains They Have Made," *New York Times*, March 22, 1994, B2.

33. Siegel, *The Prince of the City*, 99.

34. Ibid., 158.

35. Quinnipiac College Polling Institute, Quinnipiac College New York City Poll, August 5, 1997, and November 18, 1998, http://www.quinnipiac.edu/x1302.xml.

36. Giuliani, *Leadership*, 383.

37. Quoted in Kirtzman, *Rudy Giuliani: Emperor of the City*, 173.

38. Quinnipiac College Polling Institute, Quinnipiac College New York City Poll, November 18, 1998, and June 14, 2000, http://www.quinnipiac.edu/x1302.xml.

39. Giuliani, *Leadership*, 383.

40. Siegel, *The Prince of the City*, 285–90.

41. Barrett, *Rudy!* 324.

42. Melissa Levitt, "Circling the Wagons: Middle Class Whites and the Election of Rudolph Giuliani" (PhD diss., City University of New York, 2001), 188; Kirtzman, *Rudy Giuliani: Emperor of the City*, 219; Siegel, *The Prince of the City*, 210.

43. In 2000, 91 percent of African Americans polled said they disapproved of the way Giuliani was handling his job; 36 percent of whites disapproved. Quinnipiac College Polling Institute, Quinnipiac College New York City Poll, April 19, 2000, http://www.quinnipiac.edu/x1302.xml.

Contributors

Martha Biondi is an associate professor of African American studies at Northwestern University and the author of *To Stand and Fight: The Struggle for Civil Rights in Postwar New York City* (Harvard University Press, 2006).

Peter Eisenstadt, an independent professional historian living in Rochester, New York, was editor-in-chief of *The Encyclopedia of New York State*.

Johanna Fernandez is assistant professor of history and black and Hispanic studies at Baruch College, CUNY. Her book on the Young Lords Party is forthcoming from Princeton University Press.

Daniel Perlstein is a professor in the School of Education, University of California at Berkeley. Professor Perlstein's scholarship promotes the creation of more equitable and humane schools. He is the author of *Justice, Justice: School Politics and the Eclipse of Liberalism* (Peter Lang, 2004).

Jerald Podair is a professor of history and Robert S. French Professor of American Studies at Lawrence University, Appleton, Wisconsin. He is the author of *The Strike That Changed New York: Blacks, Whites, and the Ocean Hill–Brownsville Crisis* (Princeton University Press, 2004).

Brian Purnell is an assistant professor of Africana Studies at Bowdoin College. His book *A Movement Grows in Brooklyn: Civil Rights and Black Power in Brooklyn* is forthcoming from the University Press of Kentucky.

Barbara Ransby is a professor of history and African American studies at the University of Illinois at Chicago. She is the author of *Ella Baker and the Black Freedom Movement: A Radical Democratic Vision* (University of North Carolina Press, 2003).

Wilbur C. Rich is a professor of political science at Wellesley College and the author of *David Dinkins and New York City Politics: Race, Images, and the Media* (SUNY Press, 2006).

Clarence Taylor is a professor of history and black and Hispanic studies at Baruch College and a professor of history at the Graduate Center, CUNY. His book *Reds at the Blackboard: Communism, Academic Freedom, Civil Rights, and the New York City Teachers Union* is forthcoming from Columbia University Press.

Index